CW00568571

THE OXFORD HISTORY OF PHILOSOPHY

Thinking the Impossible

THE OXFORD HISTORY OF PHILOSOPHY

The Lost Age of Reason: Philosophy in Early Modern India 1450–1700
Jonardon Ganeri

Thinking the Impossible: French Philosophy since 1960
Gary Gutting

Thinking the Impossible

French Philosophy Since 1960

Gary Gutting

OXFORD
UNIVERSITY PRESS

OXFORD
UNIVERSITY PRESS

Great Clarendon Street, Oxford OX2 6DP

Oxford University Press is a department of the University of Oxford.
It furthers the University's objective of excellence in research, scholarship,
and education by publishing worldwide in

Oxford New York

Auckland Cape Town Dar es Salaam Hong Kong Karachi
Kuala Lumpur Madrid Melbourne Mexico City Nairobi
New Delhi Shanghai Taipei Toronto

With offices in

Argentina Austria Brazil Chile Czech Republic France Greece
Guatemala Hungary Italy Japan Poland Portugal Singapore
South Korea Switzerland Thailand Turkey Ukraine Vietnam

Published in the United States
by Oxford University Press Inc., New York

First published 2011

British Library Cataloguing in Publication Data
Data available

Library of Congress Cataloging in Publication Data
Data available

Typeset by SPI Publisher Services, Pondicherry, India
Printed in Great Britain
on acid-free paper by
MPG Books Group, Bodmin and King's Lynn

ISBN 978-0-19-922703-7

5 7 9 10 8 6 4

For Anastasia
one, true, good, and beautiful

Acknowledgments

My thanks first of all to Peter Momtchiloff for suggesting this project and for his assistance as it developed. Thanks also to Jennifer Lunsford, my production editor, and to Hilary Walford for careful copy-editing.

I am grateful to the patient and probing graduate students in my seminars, who helped me grapple with this material: Natalia Baenza, Michael Bocchino, Joseph Christianson, Jordan Corwin, James De La Torre, Patrick Gamez, Stacy Greiner, Daniel Immerman, Erik Larsen, Thomas Mulherin, Jason Miller, Marianne Peracchio, Anna Rafalski, Daniel Richter, Jordan Rodgers, Jennifer Rosato, Solomon Schneider, and Joshua Tepley.

I am grateful to Len Lawlor, Todd May, Diane Perpich, and Dan Smith, who read and commented on various sections and chapters. They have saved me from many errors, and I apologize for those that remain because I did not follow their advice. Two anonymous readers for Oxford University Press made numerous helpful corrections and suggestions. Discussions with Anastasia Friel Gutting showed the way through numerous conceptual problems.

As so often, I owe a special debt to Karl Ameriks, both for a continual flow of engaging and enlightening conversation on philosophical and other topics, and for a careful reading of and response to the entire manuscript. He has saved me from many mistakes in my treatment of Hegel, and the entire book is better for the perceptive and sensible Kantian eye he cast on these French shenanigans.

When I wrote my first book, in the early 1980s, my children, Tasha, Edward, and Tom, were really children. Now they are admirable adults, not just relatives but friends, and continuing sources of pride, joy, and inspiration.

I am most of all grateful to my wife, Anastasia, whose loving support, intellectual and emotional, always makes all the difference.

Contents

Introduction: *Philosophes* vs Philosophers

"The *philosophes* were not philosophers." Whitehead's bilingual paradox makes a salient point about eighteenth-century Enlightenment thought, but the words also express a (rather different) truth about American and French thinkers of the twentieth century. Consider, for example, W. V. Quine and Jean-Paul Sartre. At our starting date of 1960, it would be hard to find two philosophers more important in their respective countries. Both are rightly described as "philosophers", since they are both concerned with fundamental ontological issues of what there is and what it means to be. But beyond this generic similarity, there are vast differences. Quine was a specialist in philosophical logic, philosophy of language, and philosophy of science. He had few professional interests in other areas, including ethics, aesthetics, political philosophy, and even much of epistemology and philosophy of mind; nor did he have any serious interest in the history of philosophy, either for its own sake or as a propaedeutic to contemporary issues. Sartre, by contrast, was philosophically omnivorous (except for technical issues in logic and philosophy of science) and approached most topics with an eye on at least some part of philosophical history. Moreover, he wrote extensively on issues outside philosophy, particularly literature and politics, was himself a major novelist and playwright, and prominently active in French politics. Quine had no significant public presence beyond his specialized philosophical work.

A similar comparison could be made between almost any pair of the leading French and American philosophers of the last half of the twentieth century. The work of French philosophers is wide ranging, historically informed, often beyond the boundaries of philosophy, and they are public intellectuals, taken seriously as contributors to debates outside the academy. With a few exceptions such as Richard Rorty, American philosophers are specialists even within their own discipline, deal with its history only if their specialty is history of philosophy, and play little role in political and general cultural debates.[1]

The above contrast, of course, is merely the external accompaniment of much deeper metaphilosophical differences. Talk of the old analytic/continental divide is

[1] Including Anglophone philosophers born outside the USA provides more exceptions (e.g., Alasdair MacIntyre, Charles Taylor, and Bernard Williams) but does not alter the overall picture.

no longer fashionable. The language was always less than perspicuous, and there are younger philosophers who fruitfully work both sides of the street. But you can still be a successful metaphysician in the United States and have never read a word of Heidegger, Deleuze, or Badiou; or be a prominent French philosopher of religion and know nothing about Plantinga. Even those of us who move with some ease across the divide are well aware of how different things look from the two perspectives, and we can easily separate new philosophy books into "analytic" and "continental" stacks.

The distinction has, however, misled us into grouping so many disparate approaches to philosophy under the "continental" heading. Despite the huge variety of topics covered and positions held, analytic philosophers basically agree on the sort of evidence (roughly, the "obvious truths" of ordinary experience) that is decisive for philosophically evaluating their claims. It is their emphasis on this sort of evidence that results in what they see as the superior clarity and rigor of their philosophizing and in what others see as the relative triviality of their approach to profound questions. So-called continental philosophers work with quite different standards of evaluation: rigor of phenomenological description, perceptiveness of hermeneutical insight, originality of conceptual innovation, even soundness of political instincts. There can be fruitful comparisons and contrasts of, say, phenomenology, hermeneutics, or critical theory with analytic philosophy in general. But the differences among varieties of continental philosophy are so great that generic comparisons yield only the vaguest generalities.

This book is a history of one very specific—and important—manifestation of "continental" philosophy: the distinctive body of work in France from the 1960s through the 1990s.[2] Such a specific focus will, among other things, offer an opportunity for more fruitful metaphilosophical reflections. Overall, my project is to examine key episodes in the recent history of French philosophy in order to arrive at an account of what it was to "do philosophy" in France during this period, what this sort of philosophizing was able to achieve, and how it differs from the analytic philosophy dominant in anglophone countries.

My initial focus will be on the three most important philosophers who came to prominence in the 1960s: Michel Foucault, Gilles Deleuze, and Jacques Derrida. Part I begins with a discussion of the educational system and cultural milieu that produced them (Chapter 1), and then moves to a detailed treatment of how they formulated and began to carry out their philosophical projects in the 1960s and 1970s. This treatment will first of all require (in Chapter 2) an understanding of their reaction to Hegel's philosophy, particularly in the extremely influential interpretation provided by their teacher, Jean Hyppolite. I will argue that their desire to appropriate what was valuable and avoid what was dangerous in Hegelian thought (as presented by Hyppolite) was a

[2] For a stimulating French treatment of roughly the same period (but not including Badiou and Marion), see the concluding section of Fréderic Worms, *La Philosophie en France au xxe siècle: Moments* (Paris: Gallimard, 2009). Worms's discussion has the advantage of situating recent French thinkers in the context of the whole of French philosophy since 1900, but his treatment of these thinkers is highly selective and schematic.

primary motivation of their philosophizing. In Chapter 3, I take up the influence of Heidegger on these philosophers, arguing that it is significant but far from the overwhelming force it is often made out to be. Chapter 4 discusses the role of Sartre, so strong an influence on the students of the 1950s and so abused or ignored by the philosophers they became a few years later. I argue that the new generation never coherently formulated the grounds for its animosity toward its father-figure and was closer to Sartre than it was willing to admit. But I resist the suggestions that Sartre's views essentially anticipate or converge with later critiques of the subject. In Chapter 5, I show in detail how Foucault, Derrida, and Deleuze can all be seen as developing their fundamental philosophical stances out of distinctive readings of Nietzsche, so that their work is properly regarded as "Nietzschean".

In Part II, I expand the discussion to topics and philosophers that became prominent in the 1980s and 1990s. Chapter 6 treats the revival of ethics, associated above all with the (long-delayed) rise of general interest in Emmanuel Levinas, and includes a comparison of Levinas's and Deleuze's accounts of the Other. Chapter 7 turns to the relation of Derrida's interest in ethics to Levinas and also discusses the ethical turn of the "final Foucault". Chapter 8 looks at the return to phenomenology and its use to revive religious experience as a philosophical topic. The chapter will focus on Jean-Luc Marion and his debate with Derrida on religion and phenomenology. Chapter 9 treats Alain Badiou's new ontology of the event and also includes a discussion of his ethics.

Finally, Chapter 10 puts to the fore the meta-philosophical theme of the book, developing my thesis that French philosophy since the 1960s has been primarily concerned with *thinking the impossible*. I explain the various forms this project takes and evaluate its significance and success in comparison with anglophone analytic philosophy, making a particular effort to formulate effectively the complaint that the achievement of recent French philosophy is limited by its obscurity.

Throughout, I have made no effort to repeat the systematic survey of major figures and themes covered in the third part of my *French Philosophy in the Twentieth Century*, to which I refer those seeking a comprehensive account. I entirely appreciate the importance of figures such as Lyotard, Irigaray, Nancy, and Rancière, who play no role here; and I similarly realize that I have looked at only a few of the major writings of the figures I do discuss. Here I am after a deeper penetration into the nature and significance of a certain style of philosophizing, rather than a broader but inevitably more superficial coverage of the *doxa* of the period. To this end, I have selected the thinkers I judge most important and, rather than trying to cover all aspects of their work, have offered detailed analyses of some central texts.

This book in certain ways parallels my earlier book, *What Philosophers Know*,[3] where I used case studies in recent analytic philosophy to reflect on just what this mode of philosophizing has achieved. The very different style of the French required

[3] Gary Gutting, *What Philosophers Know: Case Studies in Recent Analytic Philosophy* (Cambridge: Cambridge University Press, 2009).

considerable differences in approach, but here too I have used detailed accounts of particular examples to ground conclusions about what an important group of philosophers has accomplished. Although the two volumes are entirely independent, together they offer complementary perspectives on two very different modes of contemporary philosophizing.

PART I

1

Philosophical Educations

The French system

The distinctive character of French philosophy derives, first of all, from the educational system that produces French philosophers. The first point to keep in mind is the privileged status philosophy has in France. All high-school (*lycée*) students must take, in their final year, a course in philosophy, which means almost everyone in France has a basic acquaintance with the discipline. It also means that there is a cadre of about 8,000 philosophers especially trained to teach this course. As a result, there is a considerable public for philosophical discussion—for example, French radio's weekly series *Vendredis de la philosophie* (Philosophical Fridays)—and considerable interest in the views of philosophers on issues of the day. The recent publication of Alain Badiou's book on Nicholas Sarkozy and his interviews about it on national television were nothing unusual.[1] From 1951 to 2001, there were over 3,500 programs on philosophy shown on French television.[2] For example, between 1969 and 1971, Jean-Paul Sartre's political views were discussed on television news over a dozen times, and in 1966 Michel Foucault spent fifteen minutes explaining the main theses of his recently published *Les Mots et les choses* (pp. 79–83). Of the 714 segments of Bernard Pivot's *Apostrophes* show aired from 1975 to 1990, 90 were about philosophy. (On average, *Apostrophes* was watched by 12–20 per cent of the television audience (pp. 132–3).) In 1994, there was a television broadcast on the topic "Why is philosophy so popular?" (p. 11).

In France, then, philosophy is not an esoteric pursuit with little or no public profile. Philosophy is part of the general culture, and philosophers, precisely as philosophers, are accepted and respected figures in the public world. The deaths of major figures such as Foucault and Derrida were leading stories in the French media, accompanied by official statements from the government and extensive appreciations from commentators. French philosophers expect the attention of the general public

[1] Alain Badiou, *The Meaning of Sarkozy* (London: Verso, 2009).

[2] Tamara Chaplin, *Turning on the Mind: French Philosophers on Television* (Chicago: University of Chicago Press, 2007), 82. Further references will be given in the text.

and move easily between philosophical reflection and political activism—from Sartre's street-corner distribution of a forbidden newspaper to Luc Ferry's serving as Jean-Pierre Raffarin's Minister of Education.

The French privileging of philosophy combined with their penchant for centralized education has led to a high degree of homogeneity in philosophical training. Almost all the major French philosophers of the twentieth century were graduates of the super-elite École Normale Supérieure (ENS) in Paris. The entrance exam for the ENS was and is brutally competitive. During the 1950s, when Foucault, Deleuze, and Derrida were students, only about thirty-five students were accepted a year in the entire humanities division (*lettres*). Deleuze failed the exam and instead went to the Sorbonne; Foucault failed on the first try but succeeded on the second; Derrida succeeded only on his third attempt. Further, students who prepare at two elite Parisian schools, Lycée Louis-le-Grand and Lycée Henri IV, have by far the greater chance of entrance. (Foucault failed after preparing at a lycée in his home town, Poitiers, but passed after further preparation at Henri IV; Deleuze and Derrida both prepared at Louis-le-Grand.) Of the major French philosophers of the second half of the twentieth century, only Ricoeur, Deleuze, and Lyotard were not *normaliens*.

After three years of intense work at the ENS (or other institutions), those who want a position teaching philosophy present themselves for the *agrégation*, a rigorous written and oral exam with a strong historical component. (Despite new, alternative routes, the exam remains essential for anyone wanting to be a university professor.) The historical emphasis is assured by the reading list for the exam, which until recently consisted entirely of classic texts from the Greeks up through Kant. During the period when Foucault, Deleuze, and Derrida took the *agrégation* (1948–56), the written test required three essays (each composed in a period of seven hours), two on general philosophical topics and one on the history of philosophy. (In recent years, the writing requirement has been reduced to two essays.) For each year, the jury overseeing the test publishes a year before a *Programme* that provides the general reading list and specifies certain authors as a focus for some of the written questions and particular texts for the oral presentations. Students passing the written part go on to the oral section, designed to test their teaching abilities. In the 1940s and 1950s, this required explications of three assigned classic texts (with one hour of preparation for each), followed by a lecture on an assigned topic (with six hours of preparation, including access to library materials).

Foucault's *agrégation* experience gives a sense of the sorts of questions asked.[3] When he sat for the exam in 1950, one of his general essay topics was "Is man part of nature?" and the historical essay was on Auguste Comte. His oral lecture was on the topic "Hypotheses". Foucault failed the exam, in part because he spent most of his oral lecture on the hypotheses of Plato's *Parmenides* and did not discuss the more obvious topic of scientific hypotheses. Retaking the exam in 1951, his general essays were on "Experiment and Theory" and "Perception and Activity", while his historical topic

[3] Didier Eribon, *Michel Foucault*, tr. Betsy Wing (Cambridge, MA: Harvard University Press, 1991), 36–8.

required writing a dialogue between Spinoza and Bergson on time and eternity. His oral lecture was on the topic of sexuality. This time he passed the exam, finishing third in a field of several hundred.[4]

There is no doubt that the *agrégation* plays an important role in the formation of French philosophers. As students they spend a great deal of time studying for the exam, and many of their courses are designed to cover material specified in the *Programme* for the upcoming exam. Alan Schrift has shown some suggestive strong correlations between the content of the *Programmes* and the later publications of both the students taking the test and the teachers preparing them for it.[5] He notes, in particular, that there were hardly any serious philosophical treatments of Nietzsche until after his works began (in the later 1950s and in the 1960s) to appear on the *Programmes*. In particular, Deleuze wrote his ground-breaking book on Nietzsche after teaching a course on his *Genealogy of Morality* to prepare students for the 1958 *agrégation*.[6]

At a minimum, the demands of the *agrégation* reinforced the strong focus of French philosophy on classic texts from Plato through Kant. In contrast to Anglophone philosophers of the same time, Foucault, Derrida, and Deleuze (and all their contemporaries) had a good, textually grounded training in the major ancient and early modern philosophers. At the same time, they had hardly any knowledge of Russell, Moore, Wittgenstein, and their followers in the analytic tradition. More importantly, they were trained in the hermeneutic skills of textual explication based on historical erudition, not in the logical skills of argumentative acuity and imaginative counter-examples. As a result, they saw philosophical thinking as an intense engagement with rich philosophical vocabularies of the past, for the purpose of taking them to even higher levels of subtlety and nuance. Analytic philosophers, by contrast, saw their

[4] In 1951 (not an untypical year), only 21 of the 343 who signed up for the test passed. Sartre had also failed on his first attempt, and there was frequent concern about the difficulty star *normaliens* had with the exam. These thoroughbred intellectuals may have had some problem conforming to the bit and reins of conventional academic expectations.

[5] Alan Schrift, "The Effects of the *Agrégation de Philosophie* on Twentieth-Century French Philosophy", *Journal of the History of Philosophy*, 46 (2008), 449–74.

[6] Such correlations are, of course, not always decisive in establishing a causal connection between the exam and subsequent publishing. At a minimum, we would need to know whether—as was the case for Deleuze and Nietzsche—the subsequent publications on given figures were authored by philosophers who had studied or taught them in preparation for the exam. Schrift shows striking correlations between Plotinus' appearance on the *Programme* and subsequent publications about him, but does not discuss whether the authors of these books had taken or taught exam-preparation courses on Plotinus. If they did not, their interest in Plotinus and his appearance on the *Programme* may have been the product of a third factor (e.g., an influential professor might have developed an interest in Plotinus, without publishing on him, and, in passing this interest on to other professors and students, led both to the publications on Plotinus and his appearance on the *Programme*). It is also necessary to pay careful attention to chronology. Schrift suggests that Deleuze published his book on Hume after Hume had appeared on the *Programme* in 1958 and 1959, but Deleuze's book appeared in 1953. Even knowing that someone taught a philosopher to prepare students for the *agrégation* is not decisive. Deleuze, for example, may have already been interested in Nietzsche (perhaps, like Foucault, because of the attention paid to Nietzsche by literary figures such as Bataille and Blanchot) and volunteered to teach the test-preparation course because of this antecedent interest. Nonetheless, Schrift's correlations are an excellent starting point for further studies.

thinking as a way of drilling through the obscurities of such vocabularies with the clarity of "innocent" pre-philosophical insight and the rigor of logical analysis and argument.

It is entirely possible to make a successful career in the French (or any other) philosophical world merely by continuing to mine the classic themes and texts of the set syllabi and reading lists. One can simply continue teaching what one had been taught, adding minor improvements and extensions, without ever really venturing beyond the established boundaries. The homogeneity of the French training, with a national exam certifying one generation of students to prepare other students for the same exam, might seem incapable of producing anything better than intelligent conformity. This would seem to be especially so because of the restriction of elite education to the École Normale and the Sorbonne. As we have seen, almost all prominent philosophers are *normaliens*, and the few exceptions studied at the Sorbonne. (*Normaliens* also can take courses at the Sorbonne, from which they had, in any case, to receive their official degrees.) Further, even within this limited institutional framework, there was further homogeneity because of the small number of teachers who worked closely with most of the best students.

This latter sort of homogeneity was, however, interestingly limited by the very institutional system that led to it. There is always a temptation to turn brilliant students into disciples, but, as we have seen, the French system gives high priority to students' success in competitive examinations. Even charismatic teachers with an agenda requiring disciples need to put rigorous preparation for examinations above all. One striking example is Jean Beaufret, a passionate Heideggerian, who cultivated a "chapel" (as the French say) of devotees to support his vigorous propagation of the German philosopher's cause. But his teaching was primarily in the crucial years (*hypokhâgne* and *khâgne*) of preparation for the ENS entrance exam, and his students, such as Jean-Luc Marion and Jean-Franois Courtine, recall that his courses rarely mentioned Heidegger and provided a highly perceptive and effective survey of the history of philosophy needed for the test. As Marion put it: "It was quite amazing, since [Beaufret] never talked about Heidegger. He offered an excellent course, very clear [*précis*]; I learned an enormous amount, but he never referred to Heidegger."[7] In retrospect, they realized that the course had been based on a Heideggerian reading of history—"without knowing it," Marion says, "I had imbibed, much more deeply than I believed, a Heideggerian vision of the history of metaphysics"[8]—and found the fruitfulness of the reading a good reason for studying Heidegger directly. But they carried out this study independently of Beaufret and developed their own quite independent Heideggerianism. There is no

[7] Jean-Luc Marion, "Entretien du 3 décembre 1999", in Dominique Janicaud, *Heidegger en France* (2 vols; Paris: Albin Michel, 2001), ii. 210. My translation. For Courtine's parallel comments, see p. 48. (Courtine mentions that Beaufret did refer to Heidegger in discussions with students after class.)

[8] Marion, "Entretien du 3 décembre 1999", 211.

doubt that Beaufret recruited members of his super-orthodox group from those he taught, but his teaching had a strong positive effect far beyond this sectarian purpose.

Similarly, Louis Althusser was a deeply committed Marxist and the leading intellectual voice of the French Communist Party. His anti-humanist (structuralist) reading of Marx, which marginalized the early "existentialist" texts that French thinkers from Wahl to Sartre had made canonical in favor of the later "scientific" texts, attracted many students and played an important role in the 1960s move away from subject-centered philosophy. But Althusser was also from 1948 to 1980 a dominant influence at the ENS as the *agrégé-répétiteur*, the teacher who gave *normaliens* their intensive preparation for the *agrégation*.[9] It was primarily in this role, rather than as Marxist partisan, that he had a decisive effect on Foucault, Derrida, and Badiou, just to cite the most prominent of his many students. This is not to deny that, especially among the leftist-inclined *normaliens*, Althusser attracted a circle of students strongly influenced by his interpretation of Marx. Indeed, a group of students, including such subsequently well-known figures as Étienne Balibar, Jacques Rancière, and Pierre Macherey, collaborated with Althusser on *Lire le capital*, a collection of articles developing his anti-humantist approach to Marx. But none of these turned into mere epigones. Balibar and Rancière both developed political philosophies that move well beyond Althusser's Marxism, and Macherey, while drawing more sustained inspiration from Althusser, transformed his teacher's intimations about literary theory and about Spinoza into a magisterial *Theory of Literary Production* and a five-volume work on the *Ethics*. Althusser also led quite a few students (including Michel Foucault) into the Communist Party, though here many students moved in radical Maoist directions that Althusser never contemplated.

The force of discipleship was also diminished by the fact that by far the most powerful figure in the mid-twentieth century, Jean-Paul Sartre, never developed a base in the academic system. He held a few starting positions at lycées, but soon had enough literary success to need no employment as a professor and so operated as a free-standing intellectual, known through his books and other public interventions but with no students. This was a major reason why, for all the interest in his work, there never was much of a Sartrean school. An enduring school of existential phenomenology might have formed around Merleau-Ponty, who was an important influence at the Sorbonne. But in 1952 he was elected to the Collège de France, an institution (rather like the Princeton Institute for Advanced Study) where he was required merely to give a series of public lectures and lead a seminar each year on his research, but had no responsibility for teaching and directing students seeking degrees. This (along with his early death in 1961) cut off what might have been a much stronger academic presence for existential phenomenology.

[9] This instructor was called the "caïman" (literally "alligator") in the arcane slang of the *normaliens*.

In any case, there were, as we shall see, other factors that cut short the reign of existential phenomenology in France, and the most influential teachers, such as Jean Wahl and Jean Hyppolite, presented themselves as guides to the great thinkers of the past, master-teachers rather than master-thinkers worthy of disciples. Similarly, students were seldom encouraged to become mere disciples of the great thinkers but rather to regard them, collectively, as resources for developing their own philosophical abilities and critical judgment. One does not do well on comprehensive national examinations by having committed to one great system at the expense of others. The idea is rather that each student—selected over so many in intense competitive trials—is a candidate to be a master-thinker, one day to be required reading for the *agrégation*. In this way, the elitism of the closed French system came round to encouraging, at least in its most brilliant products, philosophical creativity.

Another way the system encouraged a wider view and greater creativity was by exposing students to figures and approaches that were far from popular but maintained a presence primarily through the pedagogical force of a great teacher. In these cases, the limited range of influential teachers actually had the effect of broadening many students who might otherwise never have encountered a forceful presentation of marginal views. For example, there were at the Sorbonne Georges Canguilhem and Vladimir Jankélévich, experts respectively in the history and philosophy of science and in the thought of Bergson. Even through the heyday of existential phenomenology, Canguilhem (along with his predecessor at the Sorbonne, Gaston Bachelard) championed a position that gave priority to the rational development of scientific concepts, rather than the philosophies of experience that Sartre and Merleau-Ponty made so popular. Foucault found this alternative to phenomenology (and Marxism) particularly important, and the influence of Canguilhem is essential for understanding Foucault's project for an archaeology of knowledge in *The Order of Things*. Canguilhem (along with Althusser) was also crucial for the group of advanced students who formed the Cercle d'Épistémologie at the ENS and published the remarkable journal, *Cahiers pour l'analyse* from 1966 to 1969. In its ten issues, the *Cahiers* presented important discussions of psychoanalysis, political philosophy, and the philosophy of logic and mathematics, combining texts by long-established figures such as Canguilhem, Althusser, Lacan, and Dumézil, by emerging stars such as Foucault and Derrida, and by later-famous members of the *Cercle* such as Alain Badiou and Jacques Bouveresse.

Jankélévich (1903–83) held the Sorbonne's chair in moral philosophy from 1952 until he retired in 1978. His traditional approach to ethics (his major work was a *Treatise on the Virtues*) and the strong influence of Bergson on his work put him far outside the mainstream. But Jankélévich, descended from Russian Jews, was a powerful spokesman on the Holocaust and related moral issues, such as the question of how to forgive the "unforgiveable". His moral standing, powerful personality, and superb teaching attracted numerous students to his course on Morality and Metaphysics, and he directed many theses, including (with Jean Hyppolite) Louis Althusser's work on

"Politics and Philosophy in the Eighteenth Century". He also had significant influence on Sara Kofman and Michelle Le Doeuff.[10]

The French system also encouraged philosophy students to engage with various intellectual enterprises outside philosophy. This was, first, done directly through a requirement that all candidates for a philosophy degree obtain a certificate (roughly, a minor) in some scientific area. Most chose psychology or one of the social sciences, but some, such as Michel Serres, did considerable work in physics and mathematics. As we shall see, it was this provision that opened the door to Foucault's background in psychology and psychiatry. More generally, their work in psychology gave many philosophy students an introduction to the work of Freud and, especially, Lacan, whose psychoanalytic writings had strong affinities to philosophy. A second factor, not tied to any official requirement, was that the general French intellectual culture, and especially the atmosphere at the ENS, where top students in all humanistic areas were educated, encouraged interests in history and, especially, literature. Not surprisingly, many students were attracted to the avant-garde work of writers such as Roussel, Bataille, and Blanchot, and Klossowski. These factors, along with the insistence on their mastering a broad range of history of philosophy, gave French philosophers a much broader cultural perspective than their anglophone counterparts.

The education of three philosophers

To get a more specific sense of just how the French system of philosophical education functioned (and to provide some background for later discussions), we will look briefly at the academic careers of the three most important philosophers who first made their mark in the 1960s: Michel Foucault, Jacques Derrida, and Gilles Deleuze. Their stories will illustrate what I have been saying about the small circle drawn by the French educational system, but it will also show how it could open up opportunities, at least for the best students, to move beyond the system's constraints.

Michel Foucault

Foucault first came to full philosophical life when he encountered Jean Hyppolite, who taught the second-year philosophy class at Lycée Henri IV, where Foucault was preparing for his second try for entrance to the ENS. This initial encounter lasted for only two months, after which Hyppolite left for an appointment at the University of Strasbourg. Nonetheless, he had a startling impact on Foucault. In his eulogy for Hyppolite in 1968, Foucault recalled "M. Hyppolite's course on *Phenomenology of Spirit*: in this voice that kept on stopping, as if meditating was part of its rhythm, were heard not just the voice of a teacher, but also something of Hegel's voice and, perhaps

[10] I postpone to the next chapter a discussion of the two most influential professors of philosophy, Jean Wahl and Jean Hyppolite.

even, the voice of philosophy itself".[11] Inspired by Hyppolite, "Foucault was now caught up in philosophy and devoted himself to it passionately" (p. 22), ending up first in his class in philosophy as well as in history. In his second try in the ENS entrance exam, Foucault readily passed the written exam and, after an oral exam before a board including Georges Canguilhem, finished fourth among the thirty-eight students admitted for Fall 1946 to the humanities program of the ENS.

At the ENS, Foucault threw himself into the study of philosophy. He took a course from Jean Beaufret on Kant and Heidegger and one from Jean Wahl on Parmenides. He was particularly impressed by the lectures Merleau-Ponty gave at the ENS from 1947 to 1949 (where he discussed the mind–body problem in classic French philosophy—Malebranche, Maine de Biran, and Bergson—and introduced students to Saussure's structuralist linguistics). Foucault also followed Merleau-Ponty's lectures from 1949 onward at the Sorbonne; these covered the relations between consciousness and language and between the human sciences and phenomenology. Also at the Sorbonne, Foucault had access to the lectures of Hyppolite, who had been appointed a professor there in 1949, the same year that Foucault wrote a thesis under his direction on "The Constitution of an Historical Transcendental in Hegel's *Phenomenology of Spirit*".

Foucault also did a great deal of work in psychology, including a fair amount of clinical experience.[12] He followed the courses of Daniel Lagache, a prominent psychiatrist, at the Sorbonne, as well as other courses required for a psychology degree from the faculty of sciences. He received this degree in 1949 and followed it up with another degree in psychopathology from the Institut de Psychologie in 1952. On his own, he read Freud with great enthusiasm and followed the newly emerging work of Jacques Lacan.

Perhaps the strongest influence on Foucault at the ENS was Althusser, who prepared students for the *agrégation* exam (the all-important bureaucratic *telos* of the ENS training) and, despite frequent bouts with depression, got to know them quite well personally. Althusser had moved from a socially activist Catholicism to the Communist Party in 1948, the same year he passed his *agrégation* and began teaching at the ENS. He was soon at the center of a strong presence of the Party at the school (along with Jean-Toussaint Desanti, from whom Foucault took a course and who was particularly interested in connecting Marxism and phenomenology). Under Althusser's influence, Foucault, despite his difficulty with accepting the intellectual conformity and practical discipline of the Party, became a member in 1950, but he soon became disillusioned and withdrew from party activities, although he did not officially quit until 1953.

After passing the *agrégation* on his second attempt, Foucault avoided the standard post-*agrégation* requirement of teaching in a lycée by obtaining a research fellowship

[11] Eribon, *Michel Foucault*, 17. Eribon is my main source for information about Foucault's eduation and academic career. Further references will be given in the text.

[12] Eribon (*Michel Foucault*, 25–30) ties this interest to Foucault's own intense psychological problems—apparently connected to the difficulty of coming to terms with his homosexuality in the intolerant 1940s and 1950s.

from the Thiers Foundation beginning in 1951, with proposed projects for a primary doctoral thesis on contemporary psychological analyses of culture, with a secondary thesis on Malebranche (neither thesis was ever written). At the same time, he accepted Althusser's invitation to lecture on psychology at the ENS. He gave up the fellowship the next year (uncomfortable with the communal living it required at the Foundation's headquarters), but continued to teach at the ENS until 1955. Among his students was Jacques Derrida, who found his "eloquence, authority, and brilliance . . . impressive" (p. 50). In 1952 Foucault accepted an offer for an assistant professorship in psychology at the University of Lille, where he commuted once a week to teach his classes, an arrangement that continued until 1955. In these first three years of teaching, in Paris and Lille, Foucault also wrote a considerable amount, all on psychological topics, including his long introduction to the French translation of Ludwig Binswanger's Heideggerian *Traum und Existenz* and his first, short, book, *Mental Illness and Personality*.

At this point Foucault broke off what was becoming a path to a fairly standard university career. In 1955, he took a surprising offer to go to Uppsala, Sweden, to teach in the University's French department and also run the Maison de France, a center (like many others in Europe) supported by the French government to promote French culture through language classes, musical events, and occasional visits from prominent French intellectuals. Foucault was very active and very successful with both aspects of his job, and managed to keep up some important contacts by bringing in visitors such as Jean Hyppolite, Roland Barthes, and Georges Dumézil. Most importantly, he found that the University of Uppsala had a world-class collection of materials on the history of medicine. These materials formed the basis of the book that eventually became his doctoral thesis, *Madness and Unreason: The History of Madness in the Age of Reason*, much of which he wrote during his three years in Sweden. In 1958 he left to take a post in Warsaw similar to the one he had held in Uppsala; the next year he moved to a similar position in Hamburg. By 1960 he was able to return to Paris with his massive thesis completed.

Since he had written his thesis without a director, it was necessary to find one to present it for his doctoral degree (at that time, the *doctorat d'etat*). He first showed it to Hyppolite, who said that it was not in an area of his expertise, although he would happily take the role of director for Foucault's secondary thesis, a translation and commentary on Kant's *Anthropology*. For the primary thesis, Hyppolite suggested that Foucault ask Georges Canguilhem. Foucault knew Canguilhem personally only through the latter's role on his examining boards for entrance to the ENS and for the oral part of the *agrégation*. He had, however, studied with profit Canguilhem's writings, on the history and philosophy of the biological sciences, and had reason to think that the author of a major book on the medical distinction between the normal and the pathological would be interested in his history of perceptions of madness from the sixteenth through the nineteenth centuries. Canguilhem agreed to sign on as director of a thesis he had known nothing about until it was finished. He suggested some essentially stylistic changes, but Foucault insisted on submitting the book as he had written it. After this somewhat awkward beginning to their relationship, Canguilhem came to join Hyppolite as Foucault's academic mentor. (His influence was especially strong on Foucault's next two historical studies, *The Birth of the Clinic* and *The Order of Things*.) The two theses were successfully defended on May 20, 1960, and the new Dr Foucault was soon offered a position as professor of philosophy at the University of Clermont-Ferrand beginning in Fall 1962.

From this point on, Foucault moved rapidly up—and soon beyond—the French academic ladder. After a few years at Clermont-Ferrand and two years visiting in Tunisia at the University of Tunis, the immense success of *The Order of Things* (published 1966) led to his return in 1968 to Paris as chair of the philosophy department at the new experimental branch of the University of Paris in the suburb of Vincennes. The next year, Foucault was elevated to the Collège de France (succeeding Hyppolite). The prestige and minimal academic duties of the Collège provided the perfect base for Foucault's last fifteen years as a world-traveling celebrity intellectual.

Jacques Derrida

Derrida began at a much greater distance from the Parisian center than Foucault, both geographically and intellectually.[13] Born and raised in El-Briar, Algeria (a suburb of Algiers), in a (not especially observant) Jewish family, he felt the weight of Pétainist anti-Semitism as a schoolboy. This culminated in his expulsion from his Lycée in 1942 to maintain a newly lowered quota of Jewish students. Even after the Allied invasion and a relative return to "normality" by Fall 1943, Derrida was an "uneven" student, combining serious intellectual interests (Rousseau, Nietzsche, Valéry, Camus) with a preference for sports (especially soccer) over classroom work. As a result, he failed the exam for his high school diploma (*baccalauréat*) in June 1947. After a final year, where he was impressed by Bergson and Sartre in his *classe de philo*, he passed the *baccalauréat* and decided that he wanted to be a literary writer and that teaching literature would be his only viable way of earning a living.

The young Derrida and his family knew little about the system of French advanced education, but he heard a radio broadcast in which a literature teacher, who had had Camus as a pupil, explained the value of studying for two years in *hypokhâge* and *khâghe* before moving on to more specialized academic work. "'Without knowing anything more about it, without ever having heard of the École Normale Supérieure, J.D. goes to see this teacher the next morning and enrolls" in his lycée (p. 328). Over the next year (1948/9), Derrida developed a strong interest in philosophy, sprung (for example) from his "'awed'" reading of Kierkegaard and Heidegger. Now presumably well aware of the ENS and the ways into it, he left Algeria for the first time to take his *khâgne* year of preparation at the Lycée Louis-le-Grand in Paris. Here he struggled "except perhaps in philosophy" and at the end of the year failed the ENS entrance exam. The next year

[13] My account of Derrida's academic career is mostly based on the "Curriculum Vitae" by Geoffrey Bennington in the book he wrote with Derrida, *Jacques Derrida*, tr. Geoffrey Bennington (Chicago: University of Chicago Press, 1993). References will be given in the text.

he continued at Louis-le-Grand, but his health was fragile, he suffered a "nervous collapse" (p. 328) that sent him back home for three months, and he again failed the entrance exam. Not giving up, he took a third year at Louis-le-Grand and this time gained entrance to the École Normale in 1952.

At the ENS Derrida followed courses from Althusser and Foucault, and soon turned to intensive work on Husserl. During the 1953/4 academic year, he visited the Husserl Archives at the University of Louvain in Belgium to work on a preliminary thesis (for his Diplôme d'études supérieures, roughly a master's degree), "The Problem of Genesis in Husserl's Philosophy", which was directed by Jean Hyppolite and Maurice de Gandillac. In 1955, he failed the oral section of the *agrégation* but passed the exam the next year. During the 1957/8 academic year, he had a grant for work at Harvard ("on the somewhat fictitious pretext of consulting microfilms of unpublished work by Husserl" (p. 329)), where he worked on his translation of and long introduction to Husserl's *Origin of Geometry*. From 1957 to 1959, he fulfilled his obligatory military service (Foucault had been excused because of bad health) by teaching at a school for the children of soldiers outside Algiers. In 1959, he returned to France and took a teaching assignment at a lycée in Le Man, where he taught *hypokhâgne*.

In 1960, he took a position at the Sorbonne, where at different times he assisted Wahl, Canguilhem, Ricoeur, and Suzanne Bachelard (daughter of the philosopher of science Gaston Bachelard). Here he remained until 1964, when Hyppolite and Althusser offered him a job at the ENS as a *maître-assistant* (assistant or associate professor), a position he held for the next twenty years.

Whether by his own choice or not, Derrida never held a professorship in the French university system. But his publications established him first as a leading Husserl scholar and, after his *annus mirabilis*, 1967, when three major books, *Speech and Phenomena, Of Grammatology*, and *Writing and Difference*, all appeared, he became famous in France and abroad as the master of the exciting new literary–philosophical technique of "deconstruction". The popularity of his work in the United States (where he frequently visited and held various regular part-time positions) and in literature departments worked to separate him from French philosophical institutions. But he remained a constant strong presence on the French intellectual scene.

Gilles Deleuze

Unlike Foucault and Derrida, Deleuze was born and educated in Paris, and, except for a few early years teaching in lycées outside Paris, lived there for the rest of his life, with little of the international travel that made the other two philosophers familiar figures around the world. Deleuze took to philosophy as soon as he encountered it in the last year of high school: "From my first philo courses I knew that was what I would do".[14]

[14] François Dosse, *Deleuze/Guattari: Biographie croisée* (Paris: La Découverte, 2007), 115. This is the main source for my account of Deleuze's academic career. Further references will be given in the text.

His friend, the future novelist Michel Tournier, had two years before taken his *classe de philo* with Maurice de Gandillac (soon to be a professor of the history of philosophy at the Sorbonne). Through Gandillac, Deleuze and his friend were invited to attend various intellectual gatherings, where they met and talked with major cultural figures, including the philosophers Gaston Bachelard, Jean Wahl, and Jean Hyppolite. Although still a high-school student, just beginning his philosophical studies, Deleuze was brilliantly impressive. Gandillac recalls people remarking, as the young student engaged in a lively exchange with Pierre Klossowski on Nietzsche, "This fellow will be a new Sartre" (p. 116).

Sartre, who had just published *Being and Nothingness* (1943), was Deleuze's philosophical hero. Tournier says: "Gilles called me up every day to tell me what he had read that day. He knew it by heart" (cited p. 118). But Sartre's defense of an existentialist humanism at his famous1945 lecture (attended by Deleuze and Tournier, apparently along with most of the rest of Paris) was a huge disappointment. "We were stunned," Tournier reports. "Here was our master rummaging around in the garbage can where we had thrown this worn out idiocy, stinking with the sweat of the interior life—humanism" (cited p. 120). Nonetheless, Sartre remained a strong influence on articles Deleuze published as a student in the mid-1940s, and, unlike Foucault and Derrida, and despite deep disagreements, he always spoke of Sartre with warm appreciation.

Intent on a philosophical career, Deleuze prepared for the ENS entrance exam at Lycée Louis-le-Grand in Paris, where he worked closely with Ferdinand Alquié (later Professor of the History of Modern Philosophy at the Sorbonne) and Jean Hyppolite. He also took some courses at Lycée Henri IV with Jean Beaufret. Despite brilliant work in *hypokhâge* and *khâge*, Deleuze failed the entrance exam. But he was well regarded by, among others, Georges Canguilhem, and he was awarded a scholarship to study philosophy at the Sorbonne.

At the Sorbonne Deleuze worked particularly with Bachelard, Wahl, and Martial Guéroult (a leading historian of philosophy), as well as Hyppolite and Canguilhem, who jointly directed his Diplôme thesis on Hume. He was reluctant to take the *agrégation*, perhaps because of his bad experience with the ENS entry exam, and his friend Franois Châtelet virtually had to force him to show up. In the end, however, he was placed second in the competition.

Unlike Foucault and Derrida, Deleuze followed the normal path of philosophy *agrégés*, teaching at provincial lycées for several years (1948–55) and then moving back to Paris for a prestigious position at Louis-le-Grand. After three years at Louis-le-Grand he went to the Sorbonne as a *maître-assistant* (in history of philosophy) from 1957 to 1960. Although he published his thesis on Hume in 1953, he did not publish another book until his study of Nietzsche in 1962. This was a product of a research position he held at the Centre National de Recherche Scientifique from 1960 to 1964. During the eight relatively unproductive years, Deleuze did a large amount of teaching in the history of philosophy, and at the same time, moved away from two of his main mentors, Hyppolite and Alquié. In 1959, Hyppolite vetoed (with a brusque "I don't want to") a request by several students to invite Deleuze to lecture at the ENS. In 1967, contrary to custom, Deleuze did not ask Hyppolite, the director of his DES thesis, to direct his thesis for the Doctorat d'état, but instead worked with Gandillac. Whereas the reasons for this break remain obscure, a similar break with Alquié seems to have been due to Alquié's strong public expression of his deep reservations about Deleuze's approach to the history of philosophy. These breaks no doubt explain why Deleuze did not contribute to the memorial volume for Hyppolite or the *Festschrift* for Alquié.

From 1964 to 1969 Deleuze taught at the University of Lyons. Then, after receiving his Doctorat d'état (with *Difference and Repetition*, published in 1968, as his thesis), he was appointed professor of philosophy at the new branch of the University of Paris at Vincennes. This appointment was due to Foucault, who was the department head, charged with recruiting a founding faculty. Deleuze had first met Foucault in 1962, and the two became very close friends, sharing both philosophical and political interests, until they gradually drifted apart in the mid-1970s because of political disagreements. After Foucault's death, however, Deleuze published an impressive analysis and appreciation of his work.[15]

Mainly because of continuing ill-health—he suffered from respiratory diseases throughout his life—Deleuze traveled little and had a much lower public profile than Foucault and Derrida. Eventually, his health problems led to his relatively early retirement from teaching in 1987 and to his suicide in 1995.

Philosophy and politics

We need to take account of one further feature of French philosophical life: its political activism. I commented earlier about the natural move to politics, given the integration of philosophers into French culture and society. It is as natural for French philosophers to take political stands as it is for American actors and entertainers. But political involvement is also an integral part of French philosophizing. From the time of Sartre on, philosophy itself has been seen as a means of political engagement. The leading French philosophers think for the sake of acting, of transforming a society they find intolerable. This is not to say that there are no other motives for philosophical thought or that it is always or even usually subordinated to concrete political goals. But it is to say that the ultimate point and test of philosophical thought is seen in its relevance to political goals. As Vincent Descombes, writing in the late 1970s put it:

> In France the development of a political position remains the decisive test, disclosing as it does the definitive meaning of a mode of thought. It is as if the heart of the matter has not been reached until, from suppositions about the One and the Many, or about the nature of knowledge, the subject shifted to the issue of the next elections or the attitude of the Communist Party.[16]

[15] Gilles Deleuze, *Foucault*, tr. Seán Hand (Minneapolis, MN: University of Minnesota Press, 1988).

[16] Vincent Descombes, *Modern French Philosophy*, tr. L. Scott-Fox and J. M. Harding, (Cambridge: Cambridge University Press, 1980), 7.

As Descombes notes, this ultimate political orientation is entirely understandable, given the role of philosophy in French society. Society supports and privileges philosophical activity and institutions precisely because the French see philosophical thought as relevant to the basic goals of those institutions. During the Third Republic (from the end of the Franco-Prussian War until the beginning of the Second World War, 1870–1940), these goals were those of the Revolution, as expressed, for example, in the Declaration of the Rights of Man. These goals, to cite Descombes again, were based on the idea that "mankind, from its distant origins onwards, has not ceased to progress towards the agreement of all human beings upon certain reasonable principles—precisely those on which Republican institutions are based" (p. 6).

Of course, throughout the twentieth century, both political events and philosophical ideas have severely challenged this Enlightenment conception of social and political good. But, as such challenges (for example, from fascism, from Marxism, from the ideologies of the 1968 student revolts) permeated both the political and the philosophical worlds, the conviction remained that philosophy had an essential role in discussions of how the French should shape their society. And, in this spirit, major philosophers, from Sartre to Derrida, saw connections between their thought and political action.

Foucault and Deleuze were, for example, both active in the Groupe d'Information sur les Prisons, of which Foucault was one of the founders. This was an organization devoted to creating situations in which prisoners themselves could take the lead in opposing the intolerable conditions of French prisons. In a 1972 discussion about this work, Foucault and Deleuze explicate what they see as the close relationship between their "theoretical work" and this political activism. In particular, Deleuze puts forward the view (elsewhere endorsed by Foucault) that "a theory [e.g., of social power] is exactly like a box of tools" for the use of those challenging power and notes that "I fully agree" with Foucault's position that "theory is by nature opposed to power".[17] The tool-box model rejects the idea that philosophical theories can be directly applied to derive logically plans of political action. Rather, philosophical ideas can be instruments of such action, chosen and adapted to particular situations, not (to use a distinction of Foucault's) by the "universal intellectuals" who create theoretical viewpoints, but by the "specific intellectuals" who are concretely involved in struggles with particular systems of power. Here we find a typically French combination of political engagement with philosophical thinking about the relation of that engagement to philosophical thought.

Jacques Derrida showed an uncommon ambivalence toward both political engagement and philosophical reflection with explicit political significance. For example, in

[17] "Intellectuals and Power: A Conversation between Michel Foucault and Gilles Deleuze", in Michel Foucault, *Language, Counter-Memory, Practice: Selected Essays and Interviews*, ed. Donald F. Bouchard (Ithaca, NY: Cornell University Press, 2008).

contrast to most other French philosophers, including Foucault and Deleuze, he maintained a certain discrete distance from the student revolt of May 1968. For example, in "The Ends of Man", originally presented in October 1968, in a talk at an international meeting in New York, he did evoke *les evénéments de mai* (along with "the opening of the Vietnam peace talks and the assassination of Martin Luther King"). He had been asked to talk about the status of humanism (man) in France today, and says that he felt the need to note the connection of this topic to recent political events. He seems to imply some sympathy for the students: "the universities were invaded by the forces of order—and for the first time at the demand of a rector—and then reoccupied in the upheaval you are familiar with." But then he concludes by merely saying: "This historical and political horizon would call for a long analysis. I have simply found it necessary to mark, date, and make known to you the historical circumstances in which I prepared this communication."[18] This sort of sympathetic distance to leftist causes was typical of Derrida.

But beginning in the 1990s, Derrida did publish a good number of philosophical discussions of political questions, including works on politics and friendship, on Marx, and on the relation of his method of deconstructive analysis to justice. In a 1993 symposium, he directly asserted his political allegiance and what he hoped would be the political significance of his philosophical work:

> My hope, as a man of the left, is that certain elements of deconstruction will have served or... *will* serve to politicize or repoliticize the left with regard to positions which are not simply academic. I hope—and if I can continue to contribute a little to this I will be very content—that the political left in universities in the United States, France and elsewhere, will gain politically by employing deconstruction.[19]

So, although Derrida never had the same sorts of radical commitments that Deleuze and Foucault often did, he did see his philosophizing as having significant political import.

The project of 1960s philosophy

This connection with politics allows us to understand better the specific philosophical standpoint from which the philosophers of the 1960s begin. With few exceptions, the political orientation of twentieth-century French philosophy was in solid accord with the secularism of the Third Republic in rejecting traditional theistic philosophies that made sense of the evils of human existence and offered hope for a better future. Prior to the First World War, this sense and hope were grounded in the anticipated progress of

[18] Jacques Derrida, "The Ends of Man", in his *Margins of Philosophy*, tr. Alan Bass (Chicago: University of Chicago Press, 1982), 114.

[19] Jacques Derrida, "Remarks on Deconstruction and Pragmatism", in Chantal Mouffe (ed.), *Deconstruction and Pragmatism* (London: Routledge, 1996), 85. Derrida is replying to comments Richard Rorty had made about the "weakening of the political left in the United States". He later makes a point of saying, "I would not be in agreement when Rorty speaks of philosophy as depoliticizing" (p. 87).

science. Comte had put forward a similar secular Gospel of Science in the mid-nineteenth century. But, during the early decades of the twentieth century, the philosophical engine of secularism was not empiricism but a historicized neo-Kantian idealism (most thoroughly worked out by Léon Brunschvicg) that presented the evolution of mathematical physics as the sun enlightening and sustaining the progress of "man". This accorded with those philosophers' "center-left" political orientation, supporting reforms such as workers' rights and the emancipation of women, but opposing revolutionary movements such as Marxism.

The young philosophers of the 1930s such as Sartre and Merleau-Ponty found this optimistic scientific humanism wholly inadequate to make sense of the brutalities of two world wars. They turned instead to existentialist versions of Hegelianism and its materialist offshoot, Marxism, which saw human existence not as a continuous ascent to the good but as a violent struggle in which meaning emerges as a final resolution of tragic conflicts. But the philosophical generation that emerged in the 1960s in turn found such tragic but ultimately redeeming visions inconsistent with the world they saw as unredeemable. They rejected all forms of humanism—religious, scientific, and existentialist. They did not, however, abandon the hope that there might be modes of philosophical thought that could provide some sort of guidance adequate to human needs. French philosophy from 1960 on has been defined by the search for such modes of thought.

So understood, these philosophers, for all their iconoclasm and even "anti-philosophy", have maintained, in their own distinctive ways, the perennial philosophical goal of finding some sort of guiding vision. Here their view differs from that of many analytic philosophers (and of Richard Rorty) who reject the classical view of philosophy as somehow a primary instrument of whatever salvation we can hope for.

The French philosophers of the 1960s reject from the start both the supernaturalist visions of traditional religions and reductions of human existence to its description by natural science. Instead, like the existentialists of the previous generation, they seek meaning in history, but without the existentialist (and earlier secular humanist) view of history as culminating in or constituted by human consciousness. The goal is a livable vision that neither eliminates the distinctively human nor makes human beings the center of the universe.

For those seeking such a vision—particularly those who, like these French philosophers, also want that vision to be rooted in an engagement with past philosophical thought and to connect with science, art, and literature—the philosophy of Hegel will almost inevitably be of great interest. As Hyppolite put it in a 1952 lecture on the recent resurgence of Hegelianism in France: "We . . . direct our interest toward Hegelianism because there is in his thought a philosophy of history, an effort to reveal the ultimate meaning [*sens*] of history."[20] Initially, this interest came from existentialists (including Sartre himself) looking for a way to situate their radically individual account

[20] Jean Hyppolite, "Humanisme et Hégélianisme", in his *Figures de la pensée philosophique* (2 vols; Paris: Presses Universitaires de France, 1971), i. 147.

of freedom in a more realistic social and historical context. The full fruition of this interest was Sartre's *Critique of Dialectical Reason*, where he tried to synthesize existentialist freedom with a left-Hegelian Marxist social theory.

But Sartre's existential Marxism remained a humanism because, for all its contextualization, free human consciousness was still the source of all meaning. The Sartrean world was still one of pre-Copernican anthropomorphism, unable to accept the fact that our world (our language, our unconscious) is not of our making. This was possible because the reading of Hegel (and of Marx) from which he began was itself an existentialist interpretation that reduced dialectic to the level of human consciousness. If this were the only possible reading, the philosophers of the 1960s would have rejected Hegel as readily as they rejected Sartre himself. But, as we shall see, Jean Hyppolite himself suggested a non-existentialist interpretation of Hegel that accorded with their anti-humanism. However, this anti-humanism did not go so far as to countenance the total absorption of human beings in absolute spirit. French philosophers' commitment to leftist political goals of individual liberation was inconsistent with this sort of Hegelianism. But perhaps there was a path between the existentialist and the absolutist Hegel? Hyppolite at least suggested that this might be possible. If so, Hegel's system would be just what the young philosophers were looking for: a secular philosophical vision of history that made sense of human existence (and thereby provided guidance for political action) without making it the center of the world. In any case, it seemed clear that their philosophical project required coming to terms with Hegel. Our next task is to see how Foucault, Deleuze, and Derrida each tried to do this.

2

The Hegelian Challenge

The main access to Hegel for students who came of philosophical age in the 1960s was provided by Jean Wahl and, especially, Jean Hyppolite. The French had warmed to Hegel very slowly, despite a number of attempts from the early nineteenth century on to import his thought. In particular, the neo-Kantianism that dominated the French university from the Franco-Prussian War until just before the Second World War had a strong antipathy to absolute idealism. The founder of the neo-Kantian school, Jules Lachelier, is said to have told his students: "There'll be no Hegel here as long as I'm around."[1] The neo-Kantians had persistently rejected Hegel's philosophy on the grounds that its ultimate telos in Absolute Spirit's all-encompassing self-knowledge was incompatible with the irreducible reality of finite human freedom. A genuine move toward Hegel began with the publication in 1929 of *Le Malheur de conscience dans la philosophie de Hegel* by Jean Wahl, who taught history of philosophy at the Sorbonne from 1927 to 1967. Wahl's books on Hegel and Kierkegaard were an important influence on the development of existentialism. Later, Wahl worked closely with Foucault, Derrida, and Deleuze and was a good friend of Levinas.

Jean Wahl's Hegel

Wahl approached Hegel through the famous chapter of the *Phenomenology of Spirit* on the "unhappy consciousness".[2] In Hegel's presentation, this chapter corresponds to just one stage in the dialectical development of spirit, the stage that Hegel characterized as "the Unhappy Consciousness [which] is the consciousness of self as a divided nature, a

[1] Sartre reports hearing this story as part of the lore of the ENS (J.-P. Sartre, *Sartre by Himself*, tr. Richard Seaver (New York: Urizen Books, 1980), 25).

[2] Jean Wahl, *Le Malheur de la conscience dans la philosophie de Hegel* (1929; 2nd edn, Paris: Presses Universitaires de France, 1951). For an excellent discussion of Wahl's role in the French reception of Hegel, see Bruce Baugh, *French Hegel* (London: Routledge, 2003).

dual-natured, merely contradictory being".[3] The division is that between the contingent, multiple, and changeable self of my experience and the essential, simple, and unchanging self that I know I must be. On the one hand, this unhappy consciousness is the higher truth implicit in the preceding stage of skepticism, in which the doubting self unreflectively accepts the contradiction between its explicit effort to question everything and its implicit acceptance of truths essential for its life in the world. The "doubling" of the unhappy consciousness is its reflective awareness of both the explicit, contingent doubting self and the implicit, essential self that escaped genuine doubt. On the other hand, at the stage of unhappy consciousness, spirit continues to see the essential self as outside its own contingent being in the world, thinking of it as an unattainable—though deeply desired—end (for example, the transcendent God of Christianity). At the next stage, that of Reason, spirit realizes that the unhappy separation of its contingency from essential reality is an illusion: spirit itself *is* the essential nature from which it seemed to be separated. This, for Hegel, is the first stage of idealism, where the spirit begins to realize its identity with the essential, absolute truth.

Wahl, however, suggests that the unhappy consciousness, which Hegel presents as just one stage of spirit's development, can in fact be taken as the condition of consciousness at every stage of the dialectic short of the final synthesis in the Absolute's self-knowledge. At each point, there is a lived division between what spirit experiences itself as being and an apparently unattainable other that it aspires to be. From this standpoint, unhappy consciousness becomes a basis for interpreting the whole of the *Phenomenology*. Given such an interpretation, Wahl is led to what came to be called an "anthropological reading" of Hegel. Hegel's description of the unhappy consciousness is taken as corresponding to the quintessential human experience, as, for example, embodied in the great Greek and Shakespearean tragedies that we see as the fullest expression of our lived reality. Human experience, then, becomes the privileged model for the life of Hegel's spirit. The result, as Wahl puts it, is a "pantragicist" interpretation of Hegel, which extends the tragic vision of human life to Being itself.

Apart from its (debatable) merits as Hegel interpretation, the beauty of Wahl's book was that it showed how even philosophers who had no sympathy with Hegel's general approach or final conclusions could extract an attractive core from his system. Whether or not you accepted the general adequacy of the dialectical method or the absolute idealism to which Hegel thought it led, you could appreciate the power of applying the method to the special case of human consciousness. Even if relentless dialectical self-negation is vapid as an account of nature or implausible as an account of history, it rings true of the endlessly self-reflective and self-questing of our lived experience. Whatever else Hegel achieved, he honed a language well suited—precisely because of its continual self-conflict—to describe the complex torsions of consciousness.

[3] G. W. F. Hegel, *Phenomenology of Spirit*, tr. A. V. Miller (Oxford: Oxford University Press, 1977), sect. 206, 126.c.

Wahl's approach also had the advantage of allowing French philosophers to assimilate Hegel's phenomenology—construed as the careful description of concrete experience—to that practiced by Husserl and by Heidegger in *Being and Time*. (The last two were closely connected, because the Husserl imported into France—for example, by Koyré and Levinas—was read through Heideggerian lenses.) Add the vocabulary of Hegelian unhappy consciousness to a Heideggerized Husserlian phenomenology and you have the means to carry out Sartre's ontology of freedom. For example, the key formulation that *human consciousness is not what it is and is what it is not* came to Sartre from Hegel through Wahl.

Even more importantly, Wahl's reading of Hegel suggested ways of finding an overall meaning in history that was consistent with existentialist freedom and excluded the facile optimism of the French neo-Kantians. On this view, tragic conflict and suffering were inevitable, but the logic of the dialectic grounded the hope that earlier losses would, to some extent, be redeemed in future syntheses—even if, contrary to Hegel, we would never reach an absolute end to our struggles. Beginning in 1929, the very year in which Wahl's book appeared, Marx's 1844 manuscripts were published. These early works, strongly influenced by Hegel's notion of alienation, provided a basis for a parallel existential reading of Marx. The culmination of such readings was Sartre's effort at a synthesis of existentialism and Marxism in his *Critique of Dialectical Reason* (1960), which, however, came well after the days of existentialist dominance.

Four years after Wahl's book on unhappy consciousness, Alexandre Kojève began teaching his famous seminar at the École Practique des Hautes Études. This seminar, which ran from 1933 to 1939, was at various points attended by Bataille, Lacan, and Merleau-Ponty,[4] and, although notes on his lectures were not published until 1947, from the beginning they exerted considerable influence through informal dissemination.[5] Whereas Wahl took Hegel's section on unhappy consciousness as the key to understanding his system, Kojève's reading was based on the chapter of the *Phenomenology* on the master–slave dialectic. But, like Wahl, Kojève provided ways of toning down Hegel's absolutism, reading the dialectic in terms of a purely human struggle. Wahl and Kojève also bridged the apparent distance of Hegel from Marx and Heidegger by offering humanist readings of the latter two thinkers. The result was a Hegel of extreme interest to the rising generation of existentialist thought at mid-century.

The next generation's rejection of humanism made these interpretations of Hegel far less attractive, although Wahl's influence remained stronger than Kojève's because of his close university contacts with students. Moreover, Wahl's approach was an important starting point for Jean Hyppolite, who nonetheless moved beyond it to a more balanced reading of Hegel that made him a key reference point for the next

[4] For a list of participants, see the appendix to Michael S. Roth, *Knowing and History: Appropriations of Hegel in Twentieth-Century France* (Ithaca, NY: Cornell University Press, 1988).

[5] For a partial English translation, see Alexandre Kojève, *Introduction to the Reading of Hegel*, tr. James Nichols Jr (New York: Basic Books, 1969).

generation's efforts to find meaning beyond humanism. Older accounts[6] of twentieth-century French philosophy present Kojève as the center of interest in Hegel, and Bruce Baugh has rightly emphasized the at least equally important role of Wahl.[7] But an understanding of the confrontation of the philosophers of the 1960s with Hegel needs to give pride of place to Hyppolite.[8]

Jean Hyppolite's Hegel

Hyppolite became professor in history of philosophy at the Sorbonne in 1949 and was also, from 1954, director of the ENS. He held both positions until 1963 (when he was elected to the Collège de France), teaching influential courses on the history of philosophy (especially Hegel) and directing, as we have seen, many theses.

Hyppolite became the dominant figure in French Hegel studies with his translation of Hegel's *Phenomenology* (1939, 1941) and his massive commentary *The Genesis and Structure of Hegel's Phenomenology of Spirit* (1946). In the very beginning of his commentary's chapter on "The Unhappy Consciousness", Hyppolite acknowledges the validity of Wahl's interpretation, saying that "unhappy consciousness is the fundamental theme of the *Phenomenology*" and noting that "we constantly find the theme of the unhappy consciousness in the *Phenomenology* presented in different ways". But he goes on to point out that "nonetheless unhappy consciousness—in the strict sense of the term—is the result of the development of self-consciousness",[9] thus implicitly distinguishing Wahl's broad sense of "unhappy consciousness" from the narrow sense Hegel has in mind in his chapter explicitly on the topic. This chapter treats unhappy consciousness as due simply to reflection on the specific form of self-consciousness that makes explicit the contradiction of skepticism by bringing the conflict between finite and infinite mind into the individual's own self-image. Wahl, he implies, is right because "this reflection implies a break with life, a separation so radical that consciousness of this separation is the unhappy consciousness of all reflection". But Hyppolite restricts his own detailed discussion to Hegel's narrow sense.

Later in his chapter, Hyppolite alludes to the use made of Wahl's interpretation by the existentialists. He points out that in Hegel's idealism there is eventually a synthesis whereby the division of the unhappy consciousness is overcome and spirit achieves "an objectivity ... that ... is no longer the pure and simple in-itself but has become the

[6] For a prominent example, see Vincent Descombes, *Modern French Philosophy* (Cambridge: Cambridge University Press, 1980).

[7] Baugh, *French Hegel*.

[8] Roth, *Knowing and History*, offers an excellent overview of Hyppolite's work and its influence. Earlier, Mark Poster had noted Hyppolite's importance in his *Existential Marxism in Postwar France* (Princeton: Princeton University Press, 1975), 18–32. But Poster overemphasizes the role of the unhappy consciousness in Hyppolite's interpretation of Hegel.

[9] Jean Hyppolite, *Genesis and Structure of Hegel's* Phenomenology of Spirit, tr. Samuel Cherniak and John Heckman (Evanston, IL: Northwestern University Press, 1974), 184. Further references will be given in the text.

in-itself for-itself or the for-itself in-itself". The result is "a substance that is at the same time subject, a substance that [in contrast to the self-division of unhappy consciousness] poses itself as what it is". Hyppolite then notes that "most contemporary thinkers deny the possibility of such a synthesis of the in-itself and the for-itself, and it is precisely on this ground that they criticize Hegel's system as a system" (p. 204). Instead, "they generally prefer what Hegel calls 'unhappy consciousness' to what he calls 'spirit'. They willingly take up Hegel's description of self-certitude which fails to be in-itself... but they abandon Hegel when, according to him, specific self-consciousness—subjectivity—becomes universal self-consciousness—'thingness'—a movement through which being is posed as subject and subject is posed as being". In other words, "they accept Hegel's phenomenology but reject his ontology" (p. 205). Hyppolite diplomatically says that his brief here is not to debate this issue, but simply to "elucidate as clearly as possible the endeavor of the *Phenomenology*". In this regard, he concludes, there "can be no doubt about the meaning [*sens*] of the dialectic of unhappy consciousness. As Hegel put it explicitly: 'Self-consciousness which reaches its fulfillment in the figure of unhappy consciousness is only the torment of the spirit struggling to rise again to an objective state but failing to reach it'" (p. 205). Hyppolite at least makes it clear that the existentialist reading is not Hegel's own.

Hyppolite's later book on Hegel, *Logic and Existence* (1953),[10] moves more decisively away from the existentialists' anthropological reading and gives central place to language rather than human consciousness. He begins with the idea that there are aspects of being that are ineffable and so accessible not to knowledge but only to some sort of non-cognitive apprehension. The ineffable might take the form of an immediate sensation "beneath" knowledge, which Hegel discusses at the beginning of the *Phenomenology*, or, at the other extreme, a faith in an absolute that transcends knowledge, which Hegel discusses in his early critique of Jacobi (in *Faith and Knowledge*). As Hyppolite emphasizes, the existence of an ineffable contradicts Hegel's fundamental assertion that knowledge is absolute; that is, complete and all-encompassing.

To appreciate this point, Hyppolite briefly recalls some basic features of Hegel's project in the *Phenomenology*. In that book, Hegel tries to demonstrate through a detailed analysis of various sorts (stages) of experience that all being is pervaded by conceptual structures that make it exhaustively knowable. Of course, the subject that has this knowledge is not the finite human consciousness as we experience it in everyday life but rather the subject that the *Phenomenology* ultimately reveals as identical with being itself, which thus turns out to be its own self-knowledge. But the project of the *Phenomenology* is to examine successive forms of finite human experience, starting with the immediate certainty of our sensations and moving through perception of physical objects, the understanding achieved by experimental and theoretical science, and so on, to the highest cultural forms of experience (art, religion). For each stage of

[10] Jean Hyppolite, *Logic and Existence*, tr. Leonard Lawlor and Amit Sen (Albany, NY: SUNY Press, 1997). References will be given in the text.

experience, Hegel develops arguments purporting to show that the stage contains contradictions, resulting from the fact that the knowledge it achieves leaves out something that appears to be essentially unknowable. The process of working through these contradictions is what Hegel calls "dialectic".

For example, the certainty of sensation derives from what seems to be the sheer immediacy of the sensory experience; that is, the experience is apparently not "mediated" by interpretative concepts, which would open up the possibility of our misunderstanding the experience's content. We are, we think, certain because we are in direct contact with a unique object (a "this") in its full concrete singularity. But, Hegel argues, the exclusion (in the name of certainty) of conceptual content is inconsistent with the singularity and determinateness of the "this" we are experiencing. For, if there is no conceptual content in our experience, there is nothing to distinguish the "this" from any other concrete "this" of which we might have a sensation. As a result, the "this", which seemed to apply to a unique singularity, applies universally to all possible sensations. But this result contradicts the claim that we are in direct contact with a specific object and thereby undermines the certainty of the experience. Later stages of consciousness can be analyzed in a parallel way. One that Hyppolite discusses (§§ 360–3) is illustrated by an episode from Goethe's *Faust*, in which "consciousness, weary of the universality of knowledge and of the burden of mediation, . . . claims to turn back completely to ineffable pleasure" (p. 16). Another is that corresponding to the development of philosophical empiricism (§ 558).

After working through many successive stages of experience in this way, Hegel eventually reaches the stage of "absolute knowledge"; that is, an experience that encompasses unlimited knowledge of all being. Each successive stage resolves the contradictions of the preceding stage by reconciling ("sublating") them under a higher, synthesizing concept. For example, the stage of unhappy consciousness, discussed above, resolves the contradiction between the doubt and the certainty of skeptical consciousness by ascribing the doubts to a finite self and the certainty to an infinite self from which the finite self is separated. The final stage, the experience of absolute knowledge, effects a total synthesis, a total reconciliation, of the contradictions of all the preceding stages. The subject of this experience is, as we noted above, not our ordinary human consciousness but "absolute spirit", the grasp of the totality of all being, existing as the historical process of its knowledge of itself. Since absolute spirit contains literally everything in its total self-knowledge, there is no ineffable that would escape its final conceptual synthesis.

So far, we have spoken of knowledge as knowledge of being. Such knowledge is universal, which means that, in particular, "it sublates and absorbs all the consciousnesses of singular selves" (p. 10). On Hyppolite's reading of Hegel, this implies "the possibility of a universal recognition, of an intelligible *discourse* which is simultaneously this 'I' and all 'I's'" (p. 11, emphasis added). In other words, "language . . . is the universal instrument of mutual recognition" (p. 10). It follows that "knowledge . . . is not only knowledge of being, it is also what makes the instituted community of consciousnesses possible", which means that knowledge is essentially linguistic, since language is the instrument of communication. Nor is language present only in the final synthesis that is absolute spirit. Each stage of Hegel's dialectic can be understood as a process of dialogue. As Hyppolite says, "originally, what does the word dialectic mean, if not the art of discussion and dialogue? . . . Human life is always language, sense, without which human life loses its character and returns to animal life". At any stage, "dialectical discourse could be interrupted, and skepticism [about the conceptual synthesis that moves the dialectic forward] is in effect always possible". This happens when consciousness "rejects language and discourse and claims to reach an ineffable absolute". But such a claim either "says the opposite of what it intends [by trying to say anything at all], and [then] it is language which is right"; or else, if a consciousness "stubbornly renounces language, this consciousness can only get lost, dissolved". What is supposed to be the ineffable is merely "the abstraction of nothingness" (p. 11).

Granted that Hegel has established that language is the engine of his dialectic, the "Dasein [*l'être-là*] of spirit" (p. 19), the next question is just how to understand language in this sense. Hyppolite rejects the "humanistic" interpretation (which is just a variation on the anthropological interpretation in terms of lived experience). Even "in the *Phenomenology*, Hegel does not say man, but self-consciousness. The modern interpreters who have immediately translated this term by man have somewhat falsified Hegel's thought." Hyppolite agrees that, for Hegel, "the Logos appears in the human knowledge that interprets and says itself". But he emphasizes that, nonetheless, "man is only the intersection of this knowledge and this sense. Man is consciousness and self-consciousness, but consciousness and self-consciousness are not man." We need to understand "that Hegel's philosophy results at least as much in a speculative logic as in a philosophy of history" (p. 20).[11] Correspondingly, the language that drives the dialectic is not that of ordinary "natural" human speech; it is, rather, "the authentic language of being" (p. 26). Nonetheless, natural human language is not separate from the "language of being", any more than finite human consciousness is separate from absolute spirit. By Hegel's definition, spirit is not a transcendent reality, existing outside human history; on the contrary, it is ultimately identical with that history. Accordingly, as Hyppolite puts it, the language of being exists "within natural language", even though it is not the same as the merely human language spoken in any particular stage, short of absolute knowledge, of Hegel's phenomenology of consciousness. What we need to understand, however, is "how is this language, which is no longer that of anyone, which is being's universal self-consciousness, to be distinguished from human, all-too-human language? In other words how does the passage from Phenomenology to absolute Knowledge work?" (pp. 26–7). This, Hyppolite tells us, "is the Hegelian question par excellence" (p. 27).

[11] "Speculative" not in the sense of "improbable" or "unwarranted" but rather "operating at a level of reason, above ordinary human consciousness".

Even at the end of Hyppolite's detailed reflection on this question, the answer is not entirely clear. What is clear is that "Hegel believed himself able to comprehend human reflection in the light of absolute knowledge", and Hyppolite allows that "the principle of this comprehension is contained in the meaning of Hegelian ontology". In other words, given Hegelian dialectic, we are able to understand how finite human existence is included (sublated) into the final synthesis of spirit's absolute knowledge. But Hegel also believed that he could "exhibit human consciousness's becoming-absolute-knowledge, as if this becoming were a history"; that is, an occurrence within the temporal framework of human history. If this were not the case, how could we, who exist in human history, move to the level of absolute knowledge? Hyppolite agrees that human history "is the place of this passage" of human consciousness to absolute knowledge. But he notes that "this passage is not itself a *historical fact*" (p. 189). This is because, for Hegel, although absolute knowledge does not exist outside the historical world (the historical world is the only world), there is still a priority of the absolute over history: "The Logos [absolute knowledge] is absolute genesis, and time is the image of this mediation, not the reverse" (p. 188). But how can the genesis of absolute knowledge occur unless human consciousness makes the passage to absolute knowledge? And how can this happen unless this passage is an event of human history, so that, contrary to Hegel's claim about the priority of the absolute, time would be the ultimate expression of absolute knowledge? Hegel seems to have no answer to this final question about how we reach absolute knowledge.

Hyppolite's students, Foucault, Deleuze, and Derrida, had no stake in saving the self-consistency of the Hegelian system. Like their existentialist predecessors, they found no plausibility or even charm in the idea of absolute knowledge and, indeed, insisted on giving priority to the finite world of human existence. Again like the existentialists, they emphasized the need to explore the differences that remain irreducible given the failure of absolute knowledge. On the other hand, they rejected the existentialists' prioritization of human consciousness and accordingly found attractive Hegel's emphasis (at least in Hyppolite's interpretation) on language, which they could use to decenter lived experience. Indeed, they thought they could use Hegelian arguments to refute existentialist claims about the absolute position of human consciousness. Such arguments could, moreover, show that consciousness existed only in an ontological field of linguistic structures, which themselves had to be understood in terms of differences. The result was a domain of philosophical investigation that occupied, to adapt a phrase of Leonard Lawler's, the Hyppolitean middle: a turbulent space delimited by the two unacceptable resting points of existential phenomenology and Hegelian absolute knowledge.[12] It is in this domain that we must place the philosophical work of Foucault, Deleuze, and Derrida.

[12] Leonard Lawler, *Thinking through French Philosophy: The Being of the Question* (Bloomington, IN: Indiana University Press, 2003), 12.

Their focus on the Hyppolitean middle reflects a long-standing concern of French philosophy with the tension between the concrete experience of the life-world and the universal concepts of rational thought. Alain Badiou has recently emphasized the role of this tension in French thought at least from the days of Bergson and Brunschvicg (with roots as far back as Descartes) and, in particular, has proposed reading the story of French philosophy since 1940 as an effort to combine a philosophy of concrete life with a philosophy of the abstract concept.[13] After about 1960, younger philosophers who had found existentialist reductions of Hegel to the endless dialectic of unhappy consciousness philosophically inadequate (and likewise, as the French always had, rejected a culmination of dialectic in absolute knowledge) were naturally drawn to a rethinking of the role of the concept (rational structure) in Hegelian terms.

Foucault and Hegel

In his eulogy for Hyppolite at the École Normale, Michel Foucault formulates the problem in terms of the fundamental question Hyppolite posed for Hegel: how to unite the standpoint of the *Phenomenology* and that of the *Logic*. "M. Hyppolite has always, from the beginning," focused his work on "the point where the tragedy of life finds its meaning in a Logic, where the genesis of a thought becomes the structure of a system, where existence itself is articulated in a Logic".[14] This, indeed, was the theme of Hyppolite's *Logic and Existence*, which Foucault calls "one of the great books of our time" (p. 136).

About two years later, in his inaugural lecture at the Collège de France, where he succeeded Hyppolite, Foucault, in a warm and informative concluding tribute to his teacher, put the matter in more personal terms.[15] Hyppolite, he said, was crucial for his own effort to "truly escape Hegel", an enterprise requiring "an exact appreciation of the price we have to pay to detach ourselves from him" and of "the extent to which our anti-Hegelianism is possibly one of his tricks directed against us, at the end of which he stands, motionless, waiting for us" (p. 235). The price of escaping Hegel (and the risk of failure), Foucault suggests, arises from what he sees as the central concern of Hyppolite's study of Hegel: "Can one still philosophize where Hegel is no longer

[13] See Alain Badiou, "The Adventure of French Philosophy", *New Left Review*, 35 (Sept.–Oct. 2005), 67–77. This recalls Foucault's similar distinction between the philosophy of experience and the philosophy of the concept, although, speaking of his student days, he presented this as a choice between existential phenomenology and philosophy of science (as developed by Bachelard and Canguilhem), not a project of reconciliation. From a broader perspective, however, the choice between, say, Merleau-Ponty and Canguilhem was between two ways of resolving Badiou's tension, the first giving priority to experience and the second to concepts. See Michel Foucault, "Life: Experience and Science", in *Essential Works of Foucault 1954–1984*, ed. Paul Rabinow, vol. ii, ed. James D. Faubion (New York: New Press, 1998), 466.

[14] Michel Foucault, "Jean Hyppolite (1907–1968)", *Revue de métaphysique et de morale*, 74 (1969), 134. My translation. Further references will be given in the text.

[15] Michel Foucault, "The Discourse on Language", in *The Archaeology of Knowledge*, tr. Alan Sheridan (New York: Pantheon, 1972). References will be given in the text.

possible? Can any philosophy continue to exist that is no longer Hegelian? Are the non-Hegelian elements in our thought necessarily non-philosophical? Is that which is antiphilosophical necessarily non-Hegelian?" (pp. 236–7). In short, is being a Hegelian a necessary and sufficient condition of being a philosopher?

We may well wonder why Foucault thinks there's a serious question of whether there can be a non-Hegelian philosophy. As a first step in answering this question, we need to recall how Foucault saw the range of choices confronting him as a young philosophy student. In a 1978 interview with Duccio Trombadori,[16] Foucault describes the "intellectual panorama" presented to him in the early 1950s as he tried to choose his own approach. The two extremes of the panorama were "Hegel's theory of systems" and "the philosophy of the subject . . . in the form of phenomenology and existentialism". Outside the university, "it was Sartre", with his particular version of the philosophy of the subject, "who was in fashion". Within the university, Hegelianism was dominant, although "it was a Hegelianism permeated with phenomenology and existentialism, centered on the theme of the unhappy consciousness". A third alternative, "establishing a meeting point between the academic philosophical tradition and phenomenology", was the work of Merleau-Ponty (friend of Sartre but also a Sorbonne professor), "who extended existential discourse into specific domains" (p. 247).

In assessing these alternatives, the young Foucault sought an approach that offered "the broadest possible mode of understanding the contemporary world" (p. 246). Nor was this just a vague matter of wanting a philosophy that was "up-to-date". Foucault saw an urgent need to escape from the mistakes that had led to the horrors of the Second World War. "The experience of the war had shown us the urgent need of a society radically different from the one in which we were living, this society that had permitted Nazism, that had lain down in front of it, and that had gone over en masse to de Gaulle". Foucault shared the "total disgust toward all that" with "a large sector of French youth" (p. 247). As a result, "we wanted a world and a society that were not only different but that would be an alternative version of ourselves: we wanted to be completely other in a completely different world" (pp. 247–8).

This desire for a complete break with the past excluded "the Hegelianism offered to us at the university", since Hegel's dialectic, "with its model of history's unbroken intelligibility" (p. 248), required the continual inclusion of the past in the future. But, at the same time, Foucault was firmly opposed to existential phenomenology, whether formulated by Sartre or Merleau-Ponty, because he questioned "the category of the subject, its supremacy, its foundational function" (p. 247). *The Order of Things* deploys philosophical critiques of the subject, but, apart from such critiques, Foucault found a philosophy of the subject incapable of taking him beyond the self that the society he rejected wanted to mold for him.

[16] "Interview with Michel Foucault", in *Essential Works of Foucault 1954–1984*, ed. Paul Rabinow, vol. iii, ed. James D. Faubion (New York: New Press, 2000), 239–97. References will be given in the text.

> The phenomenologist's experience is basically a way of bringing a reflective gaze to bear on some object of 'lived experience', on the everyday in its transitory form, in order to grasp its meanings.... Moreover, phenomenology attempts to recapture the meaning of everyday experience in order to rediscover the sense in which the subject that I am is indeed responsible, in its transcendental functions, for founding that experience together with its meanings. (p. 241)

Foucault did not deny that there is a subject in this phenomenological sense. No doubt, "the subject dispenses significations"; "that point was not called back in question". Rather, he says, "the question was: Can it be said that the subject is the only possible form of experience? Can't there be experiences in the course of which the subject is no longer posited, in its constitutive relations, as what makes it identical with itself?" (p. 248).

Foucault saw postwar society as turning its youth into subjects who would continue the sordid history that had produced the war. Mere descriptions of the essential characteristics of all subjects, à la phenomenology, would do nothing to stop this process. What was needed, rather, were "experiences in which the subject might be able to dissociate from itself, sever the relation with itself, lose its identity" (p. 248). Put this way, it might seem that all Foucault needed was an existentialist Hegel of the unhappy consciousness. His rejection of the phenomenological subject seems to extend only to a Husserlian transcendental subject, secure in its essential identity delineated by eidetic descriptions. It might seem that a move to the Sartrean–Hegelian subjectivity of a for-itself that "is not what it is" would have been just what Foucault was looking for.

But Foucault also opted for what he called "a philosophy of the concept" over a "philosophy of experience".[17] "Philosophy of the concept" refers, in the first instance, to Canguilhem's view to the history of science as an account of how concepts have emerged and developed, rather than an account of the conflicting opinions of individual scientists. But Foucault also took it more broadly as an effort to understand history in general not in terms of the experiences and choices of individual subjects but in terms of the unconscious conceptual structures that underlie subjective life. For all his interest in radically transformative experiences, he still insisted that even such experiences did not take us outside the domain of conceptual intelligibility. They would require new concepts but could not escape to an ineffable world of non-conceptual experience. In short, Foucault required a philosophy that did justice both to existence (experience) and to logic (concepts)—precisely, on Hyppolite's reading, the Hegelian project. It is in this sense that Foucault saw the need for a philosophy that was essentially Hegelian.

Hegelian but, at the same time, not Hegelian. That is, not the Hegel of the complete system, of absolute knowledge, of total synthesis, of final necessity, but the Hegel of Hyppolite, who "never saw the Hegelian system as a reassuring universe" but as "the field in which philosophy took the ultimate risk" (p. 236). The project, then, is to

[17] A. Foucault, *Dits et écrits*, iv, 764.

avoid this "bad Hegel" while preserving the "good Hegel" for whom experience is given its undeniable place as a historical reality, but is nonetheless subordinated to a more fundamental objective structure, which, however, allows for new forms of experience whereby we can break out of the pattern set for us by the past. According to Foucault, Hyppolite set the parameters for this project by proposing five "alterations... not within Hegelian philosophy, but upon it", each injecting into the Hegelian vision an element from some other major modern philosopher.

First, Hyppolite gave up Hegel's claim that philosophy could culminate in a "totality" that synthesized and reconciled all oppositions, and instead presented philosophy, as, Foucault says, Husserl did, as "an endless task, against the background of an infinite horizon". Second, Hyppolite replaced the finality of absolute knowledge with the idea of "continuous recommencement", thereby transferring "the Hegelian theme of the end of self-consciousness into one of repeated interrogation" (recalling Kierkegaard's category of repetition). Third, rather than absorbing all non-philosophical experience and knowledge into the Absolute's final philosophical synthesis, Hyppolite, in the manner of Bergson, "reestablish[ed] the contact with the non-philosophical" in a non-reductive manner. Fourth, the irreducibilty of the non-philosophical led Hyppolite to look back, like Fichte rather than Hegel, to the question of how philosophy might find its beginning in the non-philosophical. Specifically (and this is the last alteration), Hyppolite invoked the challenge of Marx, and asked, "if philosophy must begin as absolute discourse, then what of history and what is this beginning which starts out with a singular individual, within a society and a social class, and in the midst of struggle?"[18] This invocation of the "singular individual" also refers to the fixed point of French philosophy throughout the twentieth century, the irreducibility of the free individual, which had always stood as the fundamental obstacle to a French appropriation of Hegel's thought.

These five alternations are interrelated, and each of the philosophers we are discussing implements them all in one way or another. But it is also illuminating to connect each philosopher to one of the alternations. We shall see, for example, that Derrida has a particular concern with understanding philosophy as an endless task and Deleuze a particular interest in the category of repetition. Foucault's focus, however, is on the non-reductive "contact with the non-philosophical", specifically with the history of what he calls "the human sciences".[19]

Because Foucault aims to write genuine histories, based on his own archival research, his projects have to be judged by criteria of factual accuracy that, in principle at least, guard against the Hegelian temptation of fitting everything too neatly into an independently posited philosophical system. On the other hand, within the discipline of history, his work is much closer to an "idealist history" that deploys broad interpreta-

[18] Foucault, "The Discourse on Language", 236.

[19] We can even, without straining things too much, see Levinas and Marion as particularly concerned with seeking a non-philosophical (ethical, religious) beginning for philosophy and Badiou as posing the "Marxist" question of how the "absolute discourse" of ontology relates to the historical reality of the event.

tive schemes, more illustrated than proven by data, than to an "empiricist history" that fears to venture much beyond the bare catalogue of facts.[20] This sort of high-flying history can readily find itself taking on, for better or worse, Hegelian features.

Foucault's first historical work, *History of Madness in the Age of Reason*, is an instructive example. On the one hand, the history makes effective use of Hegelian concepts—for example, alienation, recognition, unhappy consciousness, master–slave relation—to describe various aspects of the existence of the mad and of society's perception of them.[21] But finding Hegel's concepts appropriate to describe a specific region of historical realities implies no commitment to his overall metaphysical view.

On the other hand, the *History of Madness* is framed in terms of what Foucault presents as Reason's effort, beginning in the mid-seventeenth century, to exclude madness as its simple denial, rather than (as, Foucault claims, in the Middle Ages and Renaissance) treating madness as the essential complement of Reason, in continuing dialogue with it. Moreover, Foucault describes these historical developments as changes in the *experience* of madness. If we ask who or what has this experience, the only answer would seem to be Reason itself, which, even if it avoids a progressive teleology, seems to posit something like Hegelian spirit as the subject of the historical experience of madness.[22] Foucault himself seems to recognize this in the self-critique of *The Archaeology of Knowledge*, when he says that his *History of Madness* "accorded far too great a place, and a very enigmatic one too, to what I called an 'experience', thus showing to what extent one was still close to admitting an anonymous and general subject of history".[23]

Foucault's next two histories, *The Birth of the Clinic* and, especially, *The Order of Things*, have distinctive features that might be seen as avoiding Hegelian pitfalls. First, they claim to uncover an "archeological" level of unconscious rules that constrained the thought of individual conscious minds in a given era. Beyond the consciously accessible rules of grammar and logic, there were, Foucault showed, a set of unconscious material (nonformal) rules that made certain grammatically and logically coherent ways of thinking nonetheless impossible. (Such rules corresponded to what Foucault called the *episteme* of a given period.) This explained why, for example, thinkers of the Classical age (for example, Lamarck) were unable to conceive of the possibility of the kind of evolution Darwin later discovered. The existence of such unconscious structures seemed to show that even the most striking achievements of conscious thought were, contrary to Hegel, based on and restricted by outside factors. Second, Foucault's histories avoided any hint of Hegelian dialectical development by

[20] For the idealist–empiricist distinction and its application to Foucault's *History of Madness*, see my "Foucault and the History of Madness", in Gary Gutting (ed.), *The Cambridge Companion to Foucault* (2nd edn, Cambridge: Cambridge University Press, 2005), 49–73.

[21] For a good overview of these Hegelian elements in Foucault's account of madness, see Baugh, *French Hegel*, 162–4.

[22] Derrida's critique of the *History of Madness* is a complex development of this sort of reading. See "Cogito and the History of Madness", in *Writing and Difference* (Chicago: University of Chicago Press, 1978), 31–63.

[23] Foucault, *The Archaeology of Knowledge*, 16 (translation modified).

renouncing any attempt to explain changes in episteme, since he limited himself to archaeological descriptions of the deep structure of thought in discrete periods. Foucault could demonstrate that Renaissance thought took place within an episteme quite different from that of the Classical age, and that the episteme of the Classical age was likewise quite different from that of modernity. But he made no effort to account for the processes whereby one episteme was replaced by another, but rather presented isolated snapshots of different periods.

But neither of these features was a sure protection against Hegelian totalization. Structures that are unconscious for individual human minds at a given time may still be part of the conscious life of absolute spirit. (Even if we require that absolute consciousness be manifested in human consciousness, Foucault's subsequent discovery of these structures can be taken as precisely this manifestation.) And, as Foucault realized, full-blooded history requires explanations of why changes in thinking occurred. Unless he was able to find a satisfactory explanatory alternative to Hegelian dialectic, he had no reason to think that he had avoided Hegelian history. Moreover, even the avowedly explanation-free history of *The Order of Things* turned, at its most crucial point, to something very like Hegelian dialectic. This occurs when Foucault is trying to show how the modern episteme, centered on the concept of man as simultaneously empirical (an object in the world) and transcendental (constituting the world), is on the verge of collapse. In his section on "The Analytic of Finitude", Foucault deploys a series of philosophical analyses that seem designed to show, in classic Hegelian fashion, how successive attempts at thinking man as both empirical and transcendental make some progress in reconciling the two aspects but eventually fall into contradiction.

The lesson of Foucault's archaeological histories was the need to develop an effective alternative to the dialectical method of explaining historical change. Only in this way could Foucault carry out Hyppolite's "alternation" by confronting philosophical thought with a historical reality that thought could not reduce to itself. We shall see in Chapter 5 how Foucault eventually found such a method in Nietzsche's genealogy.

Foucault's historical "alteration" of Hegel took him quite a distance away from traditional philosophical projects. Not only is there no effort to construct a comprehensive account of reality; there is also no engagement with general questions about freedom, consciousness, values, religion, and so on. Since Foucault is dealing with the history of sciences (or would-be sciences), questions about knowledge often arise, but these are about how a given age (or, better, particular disciplines in a given age) understood knowledge. Foucault's historical methods and concerns no doubt imply some assumptions about knowledge (for example, rejections of foundationalism and naive empiricism), but he never develops full-fledged philosophical accounts of such assumptions. The efforts of enthusiastic admirers to extrapolate such accounts typically lead to self-refuting versions of skepticism or relativism that have no real tie to Foucault's thought beyond the fact that he sees knowledge as having a history and always existing in a socio-political context. Foucault did have an excellent philosophical ear and could, when it proved useful, deploy Kantian, Hegelian, Heideggerian, or other appropriate vocabularies. But he readily abandons such vocabularies when they are no longer useful, and never pursues any of them for their own sake.

The closest Foucault comes to a philosophical credo is his endorsement in "What Is Enlightenment?" of the "philosophical ethos", which he associates with Kant, "consisting in a critique of what we are saying, thinking, and doing, through a historical ontology of ourselves".[24] He agrees with Kant's idea that "criticism . . . consists of analyzing and reflecting upon limits". But he characteristically inverts Kant's own project:

> If the Kantian question was that of knowing [*savoir*] what limits knowledge [*connaissance*] must renounce exceeding, it seems to me that the critical question today must be turned back into a positive one: in what is given to us as universal, necessary, obligatory, what place is occupied by what is singular, contingent, and the product of arbitrary constraints? The point, in brief, is to transform the critique conducted in the form of necessary limitation into a practical critique that takes the form of a possible crossing-over [*franchissement*]. (p. 315)

In principle, the possible "crossing-over" might take the form of a philosophical project of creating new metaphysical vocabularies. As we shall see, Foucault is very supportive of Deleuze's work in this direction. But he makes it clear that his own inverse Kantianism does not share such philosophical ambitions. His criticism "is no longer to be practiced in the search for formal structures with universal value but, rather, as a historical investigation into the events that have led us to constitute ourselves". Accordingly, "this criticism is not transcendental, and its goal is not that of making a metaphysics possible", and "it will not seek to identify the universal structures of all knowledge [*connaissance*] or of all possible moral action, but will seek to treat the instances of discourse that articulate what we think, say, and do as so many historical events" (p. 315). Finally, emphasizing the stated *practical* nature of his critique, Foucault says that he "is not seeking to make possible a metaphysics that has finally become a science" but "to give new impetus, as far and wide as possible, to the undefined work of freedom" (p. 316).

We will see in Chapter 6 how Foucault eventually came to see this practical project as philosophical in the ancients' sense of a reflective way of life. But his alteration of Hegel took him far away from the sorts of analyses and theories that define the modern philosophical journey. Deleuze and Derrida, however, alter Hegel in ways that open up new directions for this journey.

Deleuze and Hegel

Gilles Deleuze takes up Hyppolite's idea of replacing the finality of absolute knowledge with a "continuous recommencement", achieved through the endless creation of new

[24] Michel Foucault, "What Is Enlightenment?" in *Essential Works of Foucault 1954–1984*, ed. Paul Rabinow, vol. i, ed. Paul Rabinow (New York: New Press, 1997), 315. Further references will be given in the text.

philosophical concepts. This led him, in contrast to Foucault, to challenge Hegel directly by constructing a non-Hegelian metaphysics of difference. Deleuze, like Foucault, had first studied Hegel with Hyppolite and, very early in his career (1954), published a review of *Logic and Existence* in which he explained how he saw his own work in relation to Hegel's.[25]

Like Hyppolite's Hegel, Deleuze begins with the idea that "philosophy must be ontology, it cannot be anything else". Also like Hyppolite's Hegel, he maintains that to say "that philosophy must be ontology means first of all that it is not anthropology" (p. 191). Here "anthropology" is understood as any view of knowledge that sharply separates the knowing subject from the known object. In its "empiricist" form, anthropology treats the subject as simply one of many distinct things in the world (along with its objects) and presents itself "as the science of this fact". (Reductionist views in analytic philosophy of mind fit this understanding of "anthropology".) But Deleuze also includes Kant's position as an example of anthropology: "Kant goes beyond the psychological and the empirical, but remains within the anthropological" (p. 192). His critical philosophy unites subject and object in that he sees the known object as constituted by the subject. But this union has no ontological significance—does not occur at the level of metaphysical reality—because Kant still insists on a distinction between the object and the thing in itself, which remains entirely separate from (and unknown by) the subject. As Deleuze puts it, "in Kant, thought and the thing [known] are identical, but what is identical to thought is only a relative thing, not the thing as being, in itself'" (p. 192).

On Hyppolite's interpretation, Deleuze notes, Hegel's *Phenomenology of Spirit* refutes all versions of anthropology by showing that any distinction between being as an object and a subject's reflection on being leads to contradictions. Eliminating these contradictions requires, at each stage, unifying what seem to be distinct subjects and objects into a single self-knowing subject. Hegel's phenomenology is a matter of "'eliminating the hypothesis' of a knowledge whose source is alien" (p. 192, citing *Logic and Existence*, 158).

In the *Phenomenology*, we are shown that the general difference of being and reflection, of the in-itself and the for-itself... is developed in the concrete moments of a dialectic whose very movement is to sublate this difference.... In this sense, the *Phenomenology* starts from human reflection [anthropology] in order to show that human reflection and what follows from it lead to the absolute knowledge that they presuppose.

What anthropology viewed as "the external difference between reflection and being" thus becomes "the internal difference of being itself" (p. 192). The final result is that knowledge is always Absolute knowledge; that is, the self-knowledge of a single subject (the Absolute), the life of which includes all reality (including all the things—subjects and objects—that earlier stages of thought take as independent realities). Hegel's

[25] "Appendix. Review of Jean Hyppolite, *Logique et existence*, by Gilles Deleuze", in Hyppolite, *Logic and Existence*, tr. Leonard Lawlor and Amit Sen, 191–5. References will be given in the text.

idealism is the assertion that this all-inclusive Absolute subject is literally all there is. Here Hyppolite and Deleuze are using Hegel against the existentialist humanism that would make individual subjectivity the source of historical meaning. They maintain that, although this subjectivity has an essential place, it should not be the center of our understanding of reality. In fact, according to the Hegelian analysis, it cannot, since making it the center requires a subject–object dualism (man as simultaneously transcendental subject and empirical object) that, as Hegel shows, leads to a series of contradictions. (Foucault later developed a similar point at length in his discussion of "the analytic of finitude" in *The Order of Things*—although there he suggests that even Hegel does not escape from the fatal dualism.) To avoid the contradictions, we must realize that the subject–object division is not ontologically ultimate and begin instead from a single entity, "Being itself" (the Absolute), that contains within its own identity the root of subsequent distinctions between subject and object.

Hyppolite insists, however, that, for Hegel, there is only one world: "'There is nothing to see behind the curtain' . . . or, as Hyppolite says, 'the secret is that there is no secret'" (p. 193, citing *Logic and Existence*, 60, 90). Being is the sense (intelligible meaning) of the only world there is, not a world of reality beyond the world of appearances. Nor, for Hegel, is there a separation within Being of thought from its object (which would lead back to the contradictions of anthropology) "because being thinks itself in thought".

So far, Deleuze has no quarrel with Hyppolite's Hegel. He agrees that a coherent ontology must be based on a unity of Being, not a dualism, that this unity must itself be the principle of all the diversity we find in the world, and that this diversity is one with the reality of Being itself, not a mere "appearance" of that reality. We have, then, an ontology that rejects both the dualism of subject–object and the dualism of reality–appearance.

Now, Deleuze says, we can see the difficulty for Hegel "that Hyppolite emphasizes forcefully: if ontology is an ontology of sense and not of essence [in the sense of a hidden ground], if there is no second world, how can absolute knowledge still be distinguished from empirical knowledge?" If there is only one world, "absolute knowledge must simultaneously comprehend all empirical knowledge and comprehend nothing else, since [given that there is only one world], there is nothing else to comprehend". It would seem, then, that "we . . . fall back into the simple anthropology" that we earlier rejected (p. 193).

We can read this objection as challenging the temptation to "naturalize" Hegel's idealism by reducing *Deus* to *Natura* in Spinoza's famous disjunction. We might, for example, try to tame Hegel by saying that he really asserts the existence of just the ordinary natural world (of subjects and objects) but sees that world as having an overall structure or significance because of the way that its temporal parts relate to one another. But such a move, Hyppolite points out, simply brings back all the contradictions of the subject–object distinction.

To avoid this regression, we must, Hyppolite says, realize that Hegel replaces the *external difference* between subject and object (found in empiricism, Kantianism, and even idealisms of essence) with *internal difference*: "in the empirical and in the absolute, it is the same being and the same thought; but the external, empirical difference of thought and being has given way to the difference identical with Being, to the difference internal to the Being which thinks itself". This response in effect insists on maintaining the priority of *Deus* over *Natura* by, as Deleuze puts it, asserting that "Absolute knowledge is not a human reflection, but a reflection of the Absolute in man" (p. 194). The existence of the Absolute cannot be reduced to human existence, although it is always expressed through human existence. In the end, Hegel's Logic takes precedence over his Phenomenology.

But, Deleuze points out, giving priority to the Absolute over man raises the question of how the Absolute relates to history—to the time of the human struggle we are hoping for Hegelian philosophy to illuminate. The Absolute is a process of becoming (from one synthesis to another), but, precisely because the Absolute is not reducible to man, "this becoming is not a historical becoming". Indeed, we saw above that Hyppolite himself makes this very point: "the passage [from human consciousness to absolute knowledge] is not itself a *historical fact*" (*Logic and Existance*, p. 189). From this there arises what for Deleuze is the fundamental question posed by Hegelianism: What is "the relation between ontology and historical man"? (p. 194).

Deleuze reviews the terms in which Hegel has to answer this question. As we have seen, "philosophy, if it is to have a meaning, must be an ontology", giving priority to being rather than to man. Moreover, the ontology must be one of sense rather than essence; that is, being (absolute reality) must not be distinguished from appearance but must rather include everything, even the empirical realm of appearances: "the same being and the same thought are in the empirical and in the absolute" (p. 194). As a result, the difference that empiricism and Kantianism view as an external relation between being (sensible things, the thing in itself) and thought becomes for Hegel an internal relation of absolute being to itself. "The difference between thought and being is sublated in the absolute by the positing of Being identical to difference which, as such, thinks itself and reflects itself in man" (pp. 194–5).

At this point, the very end of his review, Deleuze briefly and cryptically introduces his fundamental criticism of Hyppolite's Hegel—and, as it turns out, the key to his own anti-Hegelian ontology. Here, Deleuze says, "Hyppolite shows himself to be altogether Hegelian, understanding the internal difference of Being as contradiction. Speculative difference [the internal difference of the Absolute] is the Being which contradicts itself." Why, he asks, must we understand the difference that is identical with being in terms of contradiction? "Can we not construct an ontology of difference which would not have to go up to contradiction, because contradiction would be less than difference and not more?" (p. 195). Deleuze points out that, in insisting on understanding difference in terms of contradiction, Hegel must distinguish two quite different sorts of contradiction: on the level of Phenomenology, between a thing and other things that it is not; on the level of Logic, within the Being that is other than itself. But, Deleuze argues, this approach requires Hyppolite (and Hegel) to assume two sorts of self-contradiction. On the phenomenological level, "the thing contradicts itself because, in being distinguished from *all* it is not, it finds its being in this difference itself; it reflects itself only by reflecting itself into the other, since the other is *its* other". What the thing is, is entirely a matter of what it is not—its other. (This is what leads to a higher level of synthesis in which the thing is reconciled with its other and the contradiction is removed.) But this sort of contradiction cannot apply to the Absolute, which includes everything and has literally *nothing* that could be its other. Since Being has no other, we cannot understand its internal difference as a contradiction between it and its other. If we did, we would have to remove the contradiction by finding a higher synthesis in which Being and its other were reconciled. But there could be no such synthesis: since there is nothing besides Being, it has no other, and there is nothing else that could synthesize it.

Deleuze suggests that Hegel's mistake is to understand the internal difference of absolute being in terms of contradiction, which is in fact appropriate only for external differences between things. "Is not contradiction itself only the phenomenal and anthropological aspect of difference?" (p. 195). The problem with contradiction, as Deleuze's later work makes clear, is that it brings into the heart of being the structures of conceptual rationality that make it impossible to supply a viable answer to the great Hyppolitean question about the relation between ontology and "historical man". Hegel's prioritization of the conceptual forces him to exclude the radical historicity that is needed to make ontological room for the freedom and creativity that are the hallmarks of human history. Deleuze's counter-ontology, barely hinted at here, will fly the banner of a "higher empiricism" based on contingent causal relations, not ideal rational connections. This will be an "ontology of pure difference"; that is, of difference understood not in terms of contradiction and negation but in terms of a fundamental affirmation. This is the ontology that Deleuze will eventually develop much later in *Difference and Repetition* and *The Logic of Sense*.

Deleuze notes that Hyppolite (like Hegel) would say that such an ontology of pure difference "would prove in the final analysis to be an ontology of essence" (that is, of a hidden ground) and so "would return us to a purely external and formal reflection" (p. 195). Here the idea is presumably that pure difference, being free of contradiction, could not contain the contraries it is supposed to synthesize and so could only be a matter of thought taking the contraries as objects of its reflection from the standpoint of a higher level of reality. But this objection assumes precisely the view that Deleuze is challenging: that the ultimate structure of being must be understood in terms of the negations that distinguish the terms of a conceptual system. Deleuze does not deny the contention of Hyppolite's Hegel that the self-expression of being is linguistic. But he suggests that the language of being is an expression of pure affirmation. His final suggestion is that Hyppolite's discussion of language in Part I of *Logic and Existence* (particularly the chapter on "Philosophical Dialectic, Poetry and Mathematics") could ground "a theory of expression where difference is expression itself"; that is, where the internal difference of Being is understood as its purely affirmative self-expression. In Chapter 5 we will see how Deleuze locates the resources for developing such a theory through his reading of Nietzsche.

Derrida and Hegel

Derrida pursues Hyppolite's first manner of "altering" Hegel: the rejection of final synthesis in favor of undertaking philosophy as "an endless task, against the background of an infinite horizon". His most detailed discussion of Hyppolite's Hegel is in "The Pit and the Pyramid: Introduction to Hegel's Semiology", first presented as a paper in Hyppolite's seminar at the Collège de France in January 1968. The theme of this paper is Hegel's theory of signs. Here, as in his earlier study of Husserl on signs (*Speech and Phenomena*), Derrida uses the apparently marginal question of how Hegel understands signs, particularly language, to point out fundamental tensions in his philosophical project, tensions that permit and require an infinite task of complicating engagement.

Hegel develops his theory of signs (semiology) in his "Philosophy of Spirit", the third and last part of the *Encyclopedia of Philosophical Sciences*. His treatment is a psychological account in terms of memory and, especially, imagination. Although Derrida gives no detailed references to Hyppolite's commentaries on Hegel, he notes at the beginning that he "will be making an implicit and permanent reference" to Hyppolite's chapter "Sense and Sensible" in *Logic and Existence*.[26] A survey of some key passages in this chapter provides a helpful entrée to Derrida's treatment of Hegel on signs.

The great project of Hegel's philosophy is to show that (and how) what "common sense"—and even much philosophical reflection—sees as an unbridgeable distinction between the subject and the object of knowledge needs to be rejected in favor of an idealist identity of subject and object. Hyppolite points out that, in terms of the Kantian context from which Hegel's thought arises, the subject–object distinction can be formulated in terms of a distinction between sensibility (immediate sense experience), which "seems to come from a 'beyond' of knowledge or from a thing in itself", and understanding, which seems, on the contrary, to come from the subject itself and to order the "given" of sensibility through its concepts (p. 23). Hegel, however, maintains that the two apparently opposing poles of sensibility and understanding each contain the seeds of the other: implicit in the exteriority of sensibility is the interiority of the understanding, and implicit in the interiority of the understanding is the exteriority of sensibility. There is between the two apparent opposites a "dialectic" in which "the sensible becomes the Logos, meaningful language, and the thought of the sensible [understanding] does not remain interior and mute" but expresses its sense in language (pp. 23–4). As a result, "language is not only a system of signs alien to the signified, it is

[26] Hyppolite, *Logic and Existence*. References will be given in the text.

also the existing universe of sense, and this universe is the interiorization of the world as well as the exteriorization of the 'I'" (p. 24).

Hegel sees this overcoming of the subject–object gap implicit in "this wonderful word [*Sinn*], which is used in two opposite meanings". It means both "the organ of immediate apprehension [immediate sense experience = sensibility] and "the sense, the significance, the thought, the universal underlying the thing" (p. 24). The principle of mediation, which overcomes the distinction, is language: "Object and subject finally transcend themselves as such in the authentic language of being, in the Hegelian ontology" (p. 26). Specifically, "the sensible itself interiorizes itself into thought, and thought exteriorizes itself into language" (p. 27).

This, however, raises the prior question of how language in the fundamental ontological sense is related to the language of human beings. "How is this language, which is no longer that of anyone, which is being's universal self-consciousness, to be distinguished from human, all-too-human language?" (pp. 26–7). This question amounts to what, as we have seen, Hyppolite regards as "the Hegelian question par excellence": how does Hegel understand "the passage from the Phenomenology to absolute Knowledge"? (p. 27). Hyppolite thus underwrites Derrida's strategy of approaching the heart of Hegel's philosophy through his theory of linguistic signs.

This theory revolves around the faculties of memory and of imagination. Let us start first from immediate sense experience (sensibility). Here we seem to have a direct intuition of something external. But intuition is not simply external because it can be remembered; that is, preserved internally ("in the mind", we say) as an image that remains even after the intuition itself has vanished with the flow of time. To emphasize the point, Hegel here uses the German word *Erinnerung*, which means memory with a connotation of interiority (*er-innerung*) (that is, a process of interiorizing). The interiorizing of a sense intuition transforms ("sublates") the exteriority of the intuition into the interiority of the experiencing "I". As Hyppolite puts its, "Pure memory is the interiorization (*Erinnerung*) of the world" (p. 28). But, corresponding to the internalization of the intuition, there is an externalization of the intuiting "I". The image itself exists as an object over against (and to this extent "outside of") the "I". Here Hegel employs *Gedächtnis*, another German term for "memory", with connotations of thought (*Denken*). Since the image exists in itself only in virtue of the "I"'s thinking itself, "*Erinnerung* exists only through *Gedächtnis*" (p. 29). Hyppolite points out that "the intimate connection of these two memories and their inseparability" allows us to understand "the concrete identity of the immediate and the universal". Moreover, this understanding provides "a glimpse already of the reason why the Logic will be able to treat immediate being, the structure of the sensible, while remaining in the universe of significations" (p. 29).

An image is, initially, a symbol, representing the intuition in virtue of a certain similarity (resemblance) of content (for example, an image of a lion *looks like* a lion). Symbols are the result of the merely *reproductive imagination*, and in using them "intelligence is still the prisoner of the external datum" (p. 30), the content of which it can merely repeat, although it is free to do so independently of the actual occurrence of the intuition. Full freedom, however, comes to the intelligence when the symbol is replaced by a sign, understood as an image that does not represent in virtue of resemblance. A sign in this sense is a word, a linguistic expression that signifies without resembling what it signifies. "Lion" does not resemble a lion. Hyppolite cites Hegel: "Given the name lion, we neither need the actual vision of the animal, nor its image even: the name alone, if we understand it, is the simple and unimagined representation. We think in names."[27]

Signs are produced by the *productive imagination*—productive because the sign is not limited to the sensible experience from which the image was derived. It is arbitrary in that any sign can name any object, so long as it is formed so as to fit in with our overall system of signs. As a result, the nature of the sign (name) as a thing is in no way determined by the intuition in which its referent is given. The significance (meaning) of the sign comes not from "a sense which would be behind language" but from "other significations, themselves expressed and expressible" (p. 33). Here Hegel anticipates the fundamental premise of Saussure's structuralist linguistics: that meaning is entirely a function of the relations among a system of signs. Accordingly, through the production of language, "intelligence finds itself in an exteriority which is completely its own, a being which, while remaining entirely being, is nevertheless its creation, an alienation of itself into itself" (p. 31). Put otherwise, language is thought made (by thought itself) a reality external to thought. Moreover, language is the whole of the reality of the thinking I: "This 'I', the one who speaks, finds itself only in and through language. It does not exist elsewhere as a true or universal singularity" (p. 33).

Hegel's discussion of language occurs in the first section of his "Philosophy of Spirit" and so directly applies only to the first stage of spirit's development ("subjective spirit"), corresponding to the psychology of individual human beings. But Hyppolite emphasizes that language maintains an essential role in the further stages of objective spirit and absolute spirit. Words "can be more or less contingent or necessary, according to the nature of... language" at a given stage of spirit's development. "But in philosophical dialectic this language tends towards the unity of intuitive understanding and discursive understanding, towards the unity that is the soul of Hegelian logic" (p. 33). On the individual psychological level of subjective spirit, "this identity of thought and reflection... is still only a formal identity" and the full content of thought is assigned an "alien source" (p. 34). But "Hegelian logic as ontology will be concerned with sublating" this distinction between thought and content. When, in the *Logic*, we reach the final stage of synthesis, we reach "the discourse which says universal being in itself and for itself. It is the Absolute itself which says itself as universal self-consciousness" (p. 35).

For about the first half of his essay (that is, until the concluding section, "*Relever*—What Talking Means"), Derrida mostly operates within the context of Hyppolite's

[27] *Hegel's Philosophy of Mind: Being Part Three of the Encyclopedia of Philosophical Sciences* (1830), tr. William Wallace (Oxford: Oxford University Press, 1971), sect. 462. Cited in Hyppolite, *Logic and Existence*, 32.

exposition, providing considerably more textual detail and introducing some distinctive emphases. In particular, he pays considerable attention to Hegel's figures of the pit as a symbol of the unconscious storage of images derived from sense intuition, and of the Egyptian pyramid as a symbol of the sign. The last section, however, moves well beyond Hyppolite by turning to a distinctively Derridean analysis of the priority of speech over writing in Hegel's view of language.

Derrida immediately states "the heart of [his] thesis": that Hegel's System privileges "speech over writing and . . . phonetic writing over every other system of inscription, particularly over hieroglyphic [e.g., Egyptian] or ideographic [e.g., Chinese] writing, but equally over mathematical writing, over all formal symbols . . . and other projects of the Leibnizian sort".[28] The priority of speech derives from the role of *Aufhebung* ("sublation") in Hegel's theory of signs. Derrida translates *Aufhebung* with the French "relever", which combines "the senses in which one can be both raised in one's functions and relieved of them, replaced in a kind of promotion, by that which follows and relays or relieves one" (p. 88)). As we have seen, intelligence produces a sign by negating a sensible intuition. Specifically, Derrida points out, this is "the *relève* of spatial intuition", an intuition of what is spatially located. He further notes, referring to Hegel's discussion in his "Philosophy of Nature" (*Encyclopedia*, sects. 254–60), that "the *relève* . . . of space is time" (p. 89): space is an externalized form that, when negated, is internalized as the form of time. As a particular negation of spatial intuition, the sign therefore is "ein Dasein in der Zeit" (presence or existence in time) (p. 89). Since time sublates space, it is, "in Hegelian terms, the truth, the essence [*Wesen*] as Being-past [*Gewesenheit*] . . . of space"; that is, "time is the true, essential, past space, space as it will have been thought" (p. 89).

But for the sign to exist in time it must exist as a sound: "animated sound, phonic sound, the voice [*Ton*]" (p. 89). The alternative would be a written sign, but Derrida finds in Hegel (as in all the great metaphysicians from Plato on) a telling insistence on the priority of speech. A primary reason for this insistence is the connection of sound with metaphysical presence: "The language of sound, speech, which carries the inside to the outside, does not simply abandon it there, as writing does. . . . Speech is par excellence that which confers existence, presence [*Dasein*], upon the interior representation, making the concept (the signified) exist". Or, as Hegel himself says: "The vocal note [the phonic sound: *der Ton*] . . . gives to sensations, intuitions, conceptions, a second and higher existence than they naturally possess—invests them with the right of existence in the realm of representation [*des Vorstellens*]" (p. 90, citing *Encyclopedia*, sect. 459; Derrida's brackets). (Derrida also cites passages in Hegel's *Aesthetics* that emphasize the privilege of speech.)

[28] Jacques Derrida, "The Pit and the Pyramid: Introduction of Hegel's Semiology", in *Margins of Philosophy*, tr. Alan Bass (Chicago: University of Chicago Press, 1972), 88. Further references will be given in the text.

Corresponding to the privilege of speech over writing is Hegel's elevation of alphabetic (phonetic) writing over the alternatives of Egyptian hieroglyphics and Chinese ideograms. Derrida provides a close survey of Hegel's critique of these systems, along the way deconstructively noting where the critique falls into contradiction or incoherence. He concludes with some reflections on Hegel's rejection of the Leibnizian "pretensions of mathematical symbolism and of arithmetic, the operations of formal understanding" (p. 105). Since symbolic language is entirely non-phonetic, it is, for all its technical uses, still in Hegel's view a remnant of the "less-developed" hieroglyphic and ideographic languages of non-European civilizations. As Derrida points out, this sort of technical ("machine") language has a role in Hegel's account. It is, in fact, the dialectical contrary of thought and, as such, must be *relevé* into a synthesis with it. Incoherence arises if, like Leibniz, we constitute "this moment of unthought . . . as an ideal model". In what reads like an anticipatory critique of much analytic philosophy, for Hegel "if this other of thought, calculation, became the ultimate finality, then paralysis would become regression". As a result, "Philosophy would fall back into childhood. The philosophers fascinated by the 'perverted mathematical formalism' are dreaming of a 'puerile incapacity'" (p. 106, citing *Logic and Existence*, 214).

As so often happens with Derrida, this paper is likely to leave the reader a bit at sea as to its ultimate conclusion. We are expecting a "criticism" of Hegel, there are hints of various directions from which this might come, but no clear sign of any decisive thrusts. There are a couple of passages of apparent criticism that commentators have taken as the paper's main point. For example, Christina Howells[29] highlights a fairly early paragraph (p. 79) where Derrida notes the contradictions that arise from the sign's being both productive and intuitive. But in the next paragraph Derrida transforms what seems to be an objection into questions that suggest that the apparent contradictions may be overcome dialectically: "Is this contradiction dialecticity itself? Is dialectics the resolution of the sign in the horizon of the nonsign, of the presence beyond the sign?" (p. 80). He goes on to propose that we "cover over this horizon in order to come back to it along the detour of our text" (p. 80), but there is no clear point in the following pages where he does this.[30]

Deborah Chaffin cites the passage I referred to just above (about dialectics resolving the sign in "the presence beyond the sign"), in which she thinks Derrida is claiming that "Hegel's semiology remains within the chain of a dialectic tied to the *Aufhebung*";[31] in other words, that Hegel never escapes from the metaphysics of presence.

[29] Christina Howells, *Derrida: Deconstruction from Phenomenology to Ethics* (Cambridge: Polity Press, 1999), 46–7.

[30] Howells (*Derrida*, 47) also rightly notes that Derrida finds various contradictions in Hegel's diatribes against non-phonetic languages, but it is hard to see how these could affect the heart of his metaphysical system.

[31] Deborah Chaffin, "Hegel, Derrida, and the Sign", in Hugh J. Silverman (ed.), *Derrida and Deconstruction* (London: Routledge, 1989), 82.

Even if that were Derrida's view (as we will see directly, it does not seem to be), this would only establish that Hegel holds the traditional position Derrida wants to question; it does not provide any grounds for questioning it.

But if we read "The Pit and the Pyramid" as an example of Derrida's Hyppolitean alteration of Hegel in the direction of an "endless task", his approach becomes much less puzzling. The text does, in fact, imply a quite straightforward way of criticizing Hegel. It begins with an explanation of how traditional metaphysics has always viewed both the subject and the object of knowledge as fully present: the object is given in its fullness to the subject, which in turn is given fully to itself in self-consciousness. As a result, the sign for metaphysics always has a merely "provisional" character: "the site of transition, the bridge between two moments of full presence" (p. 71). Since Hegel is regarded as the culmination (the "fulfillment . . . end and accomplishment") of metaphysics, we therefore expect that his philosophy will express the constraints of this way of thinking of signs in their "most systematic and powerful form, taken to their limits" (p. 73). With this expectation, we see Derrida closely follow Hyppolite's reading, which emphasizes that linguistic signs are essential in Hegel's system at every stage; even absolute knowledge must be expressed in a language—although presumably not any human language. Combining Derrida's initial placement of Hegel in the tradition with the Hyppolitean view of Hegel on language, it is natural to assume that the point of his paper is to show how Hegel's effort to synthesize all reality in the final self-presence of absolute consciousness is undermined by the ultimately linguistic nature of consciousness. Such a reading of Derrida would fit well with his suggestion (p. 82) that his treatment here of Hegel parallels his earlier treatment of Husserl on signs in *Speech and Phenomena*. It also fits with his promise, in *Of Grammatology*, some day to show how Hegel is "the last philosopher of the book [where "the book" stands for a totalizing presence] and the first thinker of writing [which is irreducible to presence]".[32]

But such a criticism is never formulated in Derrida's text, even though it hovers throughout in the background. In the first half of the essay, Derrida's takes off from Hyppolite's analysis of Hegel on signs and language to an exposition that reveals something of the complex depths of Hegel's view. But when this exposition comes to the point where it would seem natural to move to the criticism, Derrida instead turns to further complexities, centering on Hegel's subordination of writing to speech (and, correspondingly, of phonetic to alphabetic writing). This apparently marginal issue is, however, connected to more "central" Hegelian topics such as the meaning of *Aufhebung*, the relation of space to time, and Hegel's critique of Leibniz. The discussion of speech leads to a mention of the crucial place of metaphysical presence in Hegel's thought, which would seem a natural launching point for the "obvious" criticism, but the opportunity is not pursued.

[32] Jacques Derrida, *Of Grammatology*, tr. G. C. Spivak (Baltimore: Johns Hopkins University Press, 1976).

It is not that Derrida is shy of direct criticism of other philosophers. He was quite forthright in his attack on Foucault's treatment of Descartes in the *History of Madness*, and we shall see that he had no reluctance in confronting what he saw as Sartre's philosophical failings. But Derrida distinguishes between two sorts of thinkers. On the one hand, there are those for whom "a certain kind of rigorous analysis could render their texts accessible and exhaustible". These include "the great French thinkers", who have, he says, his "profound respect", but whom he would obviously have no hesitation in criticizing based on a thorough understanding of their views. On the other hand, there are thinkers (Greek and German, it seems) of whom he says that, when he reads them, "I feel that I am confronting an abyss, a bottomless pit in which I could lose myself".[33] He explicitly mentions Plato and Heidegger, but would surely also have in mind Hegel (and Nietzsche). Regarding such thinkers, there is for Derrida never a question of decisive refutations; there is only an interminable process of probing deeper and deeper, suggesting new questions and new responses. To any easy dismissal (or any ultimate dismissal at all) of philosophers such as Hegel and Heidegger, his response is always, "But it's more complicated than that". With them, we never escape from the abyss.

However, the very act of finding interminable complications in a thinker is not only a way of elaborating and appreciating the richness of that thought. It is also a way of challenging its "mastery". So Derrida's relentless pursuit of Hegel's semiology, tracking it through endless twists and turns, has, in addition to much else, the critical function of clogging the dialectical gears of the System with endless complications, postponing ("deferring", as "Derrida would say) the final vindication of Hegel's thought indefinitely. Such complications are as close as Derrida comes to a "philosophical method", and it is, in particular, his way (developed further in his essay on Hegel and Bataille and carried out *in exclesis* in *Glas*) of philosophizing without falling into a metaphysics of Hegelian presence. Although the method affects one of Hyppolite's alternations of Hegel, Derrida primarily derives it from his reading of Nietzsche. In Chapter 5 we will see how he simultaneously extracts the method from and applies it to Nietzsche's texts about woman and truth.

[33] See the discussion with Derrida in Richard Kearney (ed.), *Dialogues with Contemporary Continental Thinkers* (Manchester: Manchester University Press, 1984), 113.

3

Footnotes to Heidegger?

Before turning to the ways in which Foucault, Derrida, and Deleuze employed Nietzsche to escape from Hegel, we need to look at two other philosophers who were important in the background of French thought of the 1960s. In this chapter, I examine—and reject—the claim that Heidegger was the dominant influence in this period, and in the following chapter I reflect on what appears to be the nearly total eclipse of Sartre in the mature work of philosophers who grew up in an intellectual world where Sartre's existentialism held sway.

French Heidegger

How should we understand Heidegger's role in French philosophy? According to Tom Rockmore, "Like a massive, yet rarely visible dark star, Heidegger shapes and determines the nature and course of French philosophical debate". He goes on to endorse Michael Roth's claim that "Heidegger's influence on French philosophy can scarcely be overestimated". Employing a term the French themselves are fond of using, Rockmore asserts that Heidegger is "the master thinker of French philosophy".[1]

The French themselves seem to concur. Sartre, his enthusiasm momentarily overcoming his atheism, wrote in his diary that his discovery of Heidegger was "providential", that Heidegger "taught me about authenticity and historicity at the very moment when the war made these notions indispensable for me".[2] Foucault enthused, "My entire philosophical development was determined by my reading of Heidegger", although he quickly added, "I nevertheless recognize that Nietzsche outweighed

[1] Tom Rockmore, *Heidegger and French Philosophy: Humanism, Antihumanism, and Being* (London: Routledge, 1995), pp. xi, 19. Michael Roth, *Knowing and History: Appropriations of Hegel in Twentieth-Century France* (Ithaca, NY: Cornell University Press, 1988), 60.

[2] Jean-Paul Sartre, *The War Diaries: November 1939–March 1940* (New York: Pantheon, 1984), 182.

him [*c'est Nietzsche qui l'a emporté*]".[3] We have already noted Derrida's comment that when he reads Heidegger, "I feel that I am confronting an abyss, a bottomless pit in which I could lose myself".[4] And more directly: "Nothing I have tried to do would have been possible without the opening of Heideggerian questions."[5]

Heidegger himself was quite comfortable with such assessments. "When they [the French] think", he told *Der Spiegel* in a posthumously published interview, "they speak German, being sure that they could not make it with their own language".[6]

As Sartre's diary entry indicates, Heidegger was important in the development of existentialism in the 1930s and 1940s. After the Second World War, despite a general distaste for the Germanic enemy and knowledge that Heidegger in particular had joined the Nazi party and made embarrassingly pro-Hitler statements, French philosophers maintained and even strengthened their regard for Heidegger. They received him with respect and even enthusiasm at a ten-day conference on his work at Cerisy organized by Jean Beaufret in 1955, as well as in visits (organized by the poet René Char) to the University of Aix-en-Provence in the following three years.[7] There were, from the beginning, periodic attacks on Heidegger for his Nazi affiliations, culminating in the storm caused by Victor Farias's book in 1987, but Heidegger remained highly influential in French philosophy. On the whole, the French seemed to maintain the distinction between the character of the man and the quality of his philosophy.

On the other hand, French translations of Heidegger's works came very slowly. Amazingly, there was no full translation of *Being and Time* until 1985. When Sartre was writing *Being and Nothingness*, he had, to supplement his intermediate German reading ability, only the 250 pages of Henry Corbin's 1939 collection of about 50 pages from Division Two of *Sein und Zeit*, of the conclusion of *Kant und das Problem der Metaphysik*, and of the essays "Was Ist Metaphysik?", "Vom Wesen des Grundes", and "Hölderlin und das Wesen der Dichtung". As Alain Renaut notes: "This small volume . . . remained for a long time the only fairly substantial access [*quelque peu consistant*] to Heidegger's thought in France."[8] This lack of translations may have been connected with the relative lack of interest in Heidegger at the Sorbonne, where, for example, Jean Beaufret, the leading proponent of Heidegger, was, despite repeated efforts, never able to secure a professorship.

[3] Michel Foucault, "The Return of Morality", interview (1984) with G. Bardette and A. Scala, in Lawrence Kritzman (ed.), *Politics, Philosophy, Culture: Interviews and Other Writings, 1977–1984* (New York: Routledge, 1988), 250, 251. Other translators render "a emporté" as "prevailed over" or "led me to".

[4] In Richard Kearney (ed.), *Dialogues with Contemporary Continental Thinkers* (Manchester: Manchester University Press, 1984), 113.

[5] Jacques Derrida, *Positions*, tr. Alan Bass (Chicago: University of Chicago Press, 1981), 18.

[6] "Only a God Can Save Us: *Der Spiegel*'s Interview with Martin Heidegger", tr. M. P. Alter and J. D. Caputo, *Philosophy Today*, 20 (1976), 282.

[7] For details, see Dominique Janicaud, *Heidegger en France* (2 vols; Paris: Albin Michel, 2001). i. 149–62, 174–5.

[8] Alain Renaut, *Sartre: Le Dernier Philosophe* (Paris: Grasset, 1993), 29 n. 2. Courbin's translation, entitled *Qu'est-ce que la métaphysique?*, appeared in 1939.

Of course, since an interest in Heidegger was without a great deal of official support, he may well have been all the more attractive to bright philosophy students with a disdain for the establishment. In any case, their interest in Heidegger seems to have been piqued less by their professors than by highly regarded literary figures attracted by Heidegger, particularly René Char and Maurice Blanchot. Also, the new, post-war generation, as we shall see, found Heidegger's anti-humanism (in his "Letter on Humanism") an attractive counter to the Sartrean influence that threatened to overwhelm them in their early years.

The important question, of course, is what effect did Heidegger have on French philosophers and how deep did it go? To answer this question, we need to begin with a general assessment of what Heidegger had to offer his French audience. This question is quite different from the question of what Heidegger's various texts actually mean or what his overall philosophical achievement was. Most French philosophers read only a small part of his work, and even that with very specific preconceptions and preoccupations. Our question is as much about what the French were looking for in Heidegger as about what was actually there.

Sartre and Heidegger

I begin with the Heidegger–Sartre connection, both because Sartre was sometimes put down as largely derivative from Heidegger and because Heidegger's attack on Sartre in his "Letter on Humanism" was, at least among the younger generation, widely regarded as a decisive refutation of existentialism.

We have already seen that Sartre himself acknowledged a great debt to Heidegger, and, in his famous talk "Existentialism Is a Humanism", placed himself with Heidegger as a representative of atheistic existentialism. This was because Sartre read Heidegger as a practitioner of Husserl's phenomenology who offered compelling descriptions of states (joy, boredom, anguish before death, authentic individuality in a world of mindless conformity) that evoked the core of human existence. Sartre had been impressed by the vivid concreteness of Husserl's phenomenological descriptions, which he saw as returning us to the richness of our immediate experience of the world, in contrast to the intellectualist abstractions of his neo-Kantian teachers (Brunschvicg et al.) and even of the excessive self-reflection of Proust. This is apparent in his 1939 reaction to the doctrine of intentionality, by which, he claimed, "Husserl has restored to things their horror and their charm". As a result, "we are delivered from Proust" and from our obsessions with "internal life". Following Husserl, "it is not in some hiding-place that we will discover ourselves; it is on the road, in the town, in the midst of a crowd, a thing among things, a man among men".[9] Given this sort of reaction to Husserl, who most often directed his phenomenological analyses to rather stodgy epistemic phenomena (for example, the perspectival nature of

[9] Jean-Paul Sartre, "Intentionality: A Fundamental Idea of Husserl's Philosophy", tr. Joseph Fell, *Journal of the British Society for Phenomenology*, 1 (1970), 4–5.

perception, the distinction between empty and fulfilled intentions in our judgments), it is not surprising that Sartre was even more taken with Heidegger, who focused on compelling "existential themes" such as anguish and death.[10]

The idea, however, that Sartre's philosophy is mostly warmed-over Heidegger is not persuasive. Sartre cared more for the idea of concretely describing existential phenomena than he did for the specific content of Heidegger's descriptions. In his diary, as we saw, he mentioned authenticity and historicity as two Heideggerian notions that were decisively important for him. In *Being and Nothingness*, however, Sartre emphasizes the differences between Heidegger's account of Dasein's historicity and his own parallel account of the for-itself's temporality, noting that he himself gives priority to the present (the locus of all the for-itself's free acts), whereas Heidegger gives priority to the future toward which Dasein directs its projects.[11] As to authenticity, whereas Heidegger has a well-worked-out account of this notion (which Sartre criticizes as, despite Heidegger's protests, ethical rather than ontological), Sartre merely gestures in the direction of the authenticity that he wants to contrast with bad faith, postponing any meaningful treatment of it to his announced (but never completed) ethical treatise *L'Homme*.

As to other characteristically Sartrean existential descriptions, some—like those of bad faith and the various "concrete relations with others" (sexual desire, masochism, sadism, and so on)—have no counterpart in Heidegger. Others, most prominently Sartre's descriptions of nothingness and of our basic encounter with the Other, run deeply counter to Heidegger's. Where, for example, Heidegger presents nothingness as the source, independent of *Dasein*, of its experiences of negation, Sartre maintains that consciousness itself (the for-itself) is the ultimate source of nothingness, which, as he says, it "secretes" from its fundamental non-identity with itself. Similarly, Heidegger sees the commonality of a shared world (*Mitsein*, being with) as the ontological structure underlying personal relations, but Sartre strongly rejects this idea in favor of his claim that "conflict is the fundamental meaning of being-for-others".

Heidegger and Humanism

Heidegger himself denied any suggestion that he and Sartre were engaged in anything like a common enterprise, maintaining rather that his project, even in *Being and Time*, was entirely opposed to what Sartre called existentialism. He expressed this view

[10] Even so, Sartre was initially put off by what he calls "the revulsion I felt against assimilating [Heidegger's] barbarous and so unscientific philosophy, after Husserl's brilliant, *scholarly* synthesis" (*War Diaries*, 183). This reflects one of the ways in which Sartre was (and remained) a Cartesian philosopher and, as Derrida emphasized, a product of the French educational system.

[11] Alain Renaut argues that this difference is insignificant, since the for-itself's free actions are themselves directed to the future, and concludes that Sartre is straining to find a difference to distinguish his view from Heidegger's (*Le Dernier Philosophe*, 46–52). This, however, ignores the fundamental difference in the ways Sartre and Heidegger relate present freedom to future possibilities. For Sartre, my future possibilities are constituted by my presently chosen fundamental project, whereas Heidegger sees future possibilities as at least partially determined by the world I live in.

vigorously in his "Letter on Humanism", directed specifically to a French audience (the initial publication, in 1946, was in French translation). Writing in response to questions posed by Jean Beaufret, Heidegger marks a sharp distinction between existentialism and his position. He formulates the difference in terms of humanism, which periodically returned as a topic of heated debate in France. His focus is Sartre's "Existentialism is a Humanism", and he shows no sign of having seriously studied any other of Sartre's writings. Evoking Sartre's title, Beaufret had asked Heidegger: "How can we restore meaning to the word 'humanism'?"[12] Heidegger immediately responds: "This question proceeds from your intention to retain the word 'humanism.' I wonder whether that is necessary" (p. 219), and goes on to argue that a commitment to humanism is precisely the mistake that separates Sartre's existentialism from his view.

Here, of course, it is crucial to understand what Heidegger means by "humanism". He is not concerned with ethical or religious questions about the value of human beings in relation to other beings (for example, Is the value of humanity grounded in its relation to God? or Is humanity itself the source of all values?). Rather, he takes humanism as a metaphysical position in his own special sense of "metaphysical". In Heidegger's terminology, metaphysics is a distinctive (and distinctively wrong) approach to the question of fundamental ontology (inquiry into the nature of being). For metaphysics, which has dominated ontological thought since Plato, *being* is to be understood in terms of *beings*. What it means to be is reduced to the being of some privileged being or class of beings—for example, Platonic forms or the God of medieval ontotheology. Humanism, from this standpoint, is the metaphysical view (opposed to both Platonism and theism) that human reality is ontologically fundamental; that what it means to be can ultimately be understood in terms of the existence of human beings. In particular, Sartre's humanism leads him to center his "phenomenological ontology" on the for-itself, his term for finite human consciousness. In opposition to any such metaphysical view, Heidegger insists that ontology must be based on what he calls the "ontological difference": the fundamental distinction between *being itself* and the *beings that have being*.

Heidegger focuses on Sartre's expression of the core of existentialism through the formula "existence precedes essence". Admittedly, this superficially resembles the claim in *Being and Time* that "the 'essence' of Dasein lies in its existence" (cited p. 229) or that "The 'substance' of man is existence" (cited p. 233). But Heidegger emphasizes the difference between his use of "existence" and Sartre's. In Sartre, "existence" has its standard metaphysical meaning of the actuality of a being, contrasted to the potentialities defined by its essence. Previous metaphysicans (for example, Plato, Leibniz) had held that essence precedes existence—that, in other words, the fact that a being actually is (its existence) is one specification of the essential nature that defines it as a being. Sartre reverses this claim, maintaining that human beings (man) first simply exist as freedom of choice and that this choice determines whatever essence they have.

[12] Martin Heidegger, "Letter on Humanism", in *Martin Heidegger: Basic Writings*, ed. David Farrell Krell (rev. and expanded edn, New York: Harper Collins, 1993), 219. Further references will be given in the text.

Further, this choice also determines the meanings (essences) of all other beings in my world. But, according to Heidegger, "the reversal of a metaphysical statement remains a metaphysical statement" (p. 232), and Sartre has merely found a new way of understanding *being* in terms of *a being* (now man rather than God).

By contrast, for Heidegger, existence refers to man's (*Dasein*'s) essential standing-out-toward ("ek-sistence") the being that is prior to any particular being. When he says "The 'essence' of Dasein is existence", this means that "man occurs essentially in such a way that he is the 'there' [*das 'Da'*], that is, the clearing of Being. The Being of the *Da*, and only it, has the fundamental character of ek-sistence, that is, of an ecstatic inherence in the truth of Being" (p. 229). The point comes through more clearly in terms of Heidegger's understanding of existence as ek-sistence: "Ex-sistence, thought in terms of *ecstasis* [ecstasy, being 'out of' oneself], does not coincide with existentia [*existence* in the traditional metaphysical sense] . . . In terms of content ek-sistence means standing out into the truth of Being" (p. 230). The point is that, for Sartre, human reality is, just in its own right, the ontological basis of the meaning of being; for Heidegger, *Dasein* is the opening to the meaning that must be provided by being itself.

There is no doubt that Heidegger successfully distinguishes his ontological position from Sartre's existentialism. (It is, of course, another question whether this position was unequivocally expressed in *Being and Time* and the other writings Sartre was familiar with.) There is a clear difference between Sartre's view of man as the ultimate source of the meaning of being and Heidegger's view that man must await being's revelation of itself. But the "Letter" offers no philosophical reasons for preferring Heidegger's position to Sartre's. It shows that existentialism is a metaphysics in Heidegger's sense of a view that understands being in terms of a being (in this case, man) but it makes no case for rejecting metaphysics in favor of his ontological view. Heidegger simply assumes the superiority of his position, so that, once he shows that Sartre's position differs from his, he claims victory. It is hard to see how anyone not already predisposed against Sartre's humanism would have rejected it in the light of Heidegger's "Letter".

Heidegger's critique of metaphysics

Nonetheless, *Being and Time* itself could be plausibly read as a critique of the metaphysics that had dominated modern Western thought at least since Descartes and of which Sartre's position was arguably an example. Specifically, *Being and Time* could be taken as a highly effective criticism of the metaphysical (and epistemological) division between the mind as subject and the world as object. Against this, Heidegger argued that the fundamental reality is rather *Dasein* as being-in-the-world: not a subject starting from its entirely subjective consciousness and having somehow to connect with an entirely objective world, but, from the beginning, a being seamlessly integrated into a world that can no more exist apart from *Dasein* than *Dasein* can exist apart from the world.

Read in this way, Heidegger provided, variously, a critique of consciousness as the privileged starting point of philosophy, of presence as the fullness of being and immediacy of knowledge that guaranteed metaphysical stability and epistemic certainty, and of the Kantian notion of man as the simultaneously transcendental and empirical center of modern thought. This Heideggerian line of thought might well be deployed against Sartrean existentialism, and such a move was implicit in many attacks on traditional metaphysics in the 1960s. There were, for example, Lacan's psychoanalytic critique of consciousness, Derrida's critique of the metaphysics of presence, and the critique of man as a transcendental–empirical doublet in Foucault's *The Order of Things*. But these critiques were never developed explicitly and in detail against Sartre, and it remains an open question whether they would be effective against his own distinctive views. (We will return to this question in Chapter 4.)

Regardless of Sartre, however, there is no doubt that Heidegger's critique of consciousness-centered metaphysics was important for the new philosophers of the 1960s. At the same time, the critique of consciousness could be (and was) launched using resources quite independent of Heidegger. One prominent tack arose from new ways of thinking about language. Traditionally, language had been viewed as secondary to conscious experience, which was our immediate access to meaning and truth, with language merely a derivative means of giving experience a public form. This view was challenged by the linguistic theory of Ferdinand de Saussure, which presented meaning as entirely a matter of structural differences between the basic signs of a language. On this account, the meanings of any given linguistic sign derives entirely from its role in the overall system of linguistic signs and so requires no relation to consciousness or experience. Saussure's linguistics, introduced to French philosophy students through Merleau-Ponty's lectures at the Sorbonne after the Second World War, was central to the work of Lévi-Strauss, Lacan, Derrida, and Foucault that called into question the traditional centrality of the conscious subject. The priority of language over consciousness was also supported, in a quite different way, from the view of poets such as Mallarmé that poems were written not so much by poets as by the language into which the poet was born. Beyond considerations about language, there was another source for the critique of consciousness in the psychoanalytic theory of the unconscious, which, as we shall see, Foucault cited (along with language) as one of the central facts for which phenomenological philosophies of consciousness could not give an adequate account.

Derrida and Heidegger

There is no doubt that Heidegger is always a major force in Derrida's thought, so it will be particularly instructive to reflect on his role in Derrida's critique of metaphysics, carried out by undermining its central notion of presence. Derrida does often cite Heidegger's critique of presence, but his own most thoroughgoing development of it is in his early book on Husserl, *Speech and Phenomena*. Focusing on Husserl's account of the nature of signs, he argues that this account undermines the phenomenological goal of knowledge based on the direct intuition of, as Husserl puts it, "the things themselves". Derrida's central point, developed through admirable close (and sympathetic) readings of Husserl's text, is that there is no possibility of an expression of knowledge that is purified of the contingent and varying features of the signs needed to formulate it. Accordingly, the grounding intuitions of phenomenology cannot present the pure (undistorted) truths Husserl requires; in fact, the very idea of such truths is incoherent. Put another way, consciousness cannot be the totally transparent presence to its object that phenomenological certainty requires.

Although Derrida seldom explicitly mentions Heidegger (four short references according to the index of the English translation[13]), there is no doubt that the general thrust of his critique reflects Heidegger's insistence that Dasein is essentially embedded in the world and incapable of the objectifying distance that would be required to attain the idealized knowledge sought by phenomenology. As Derrida incidentally remarks in a footnote three-fourths of the way through his text, "we appeal to Heideggerian motifs in decisive places".[14] But, unlike Heidegger, Derrida does not proceed by providing a rival description of our epistemic and metaphysical situation vis-à-vis the world; rather, he teases the point out of Husserl's own discussion, showing how successive resolutions of key unclarities and omissions force us away from Husserl's ideal of knowledge. Whereas Heidegger typically imposes from the beginning his own problems, vocabulary, and method of analysis, Derrida is entirely respectful of Husserl's approach and shows how the Heideggerian conclusion arises from an attentive thinking from within Husserl's standpoint. He is content to evoke the generally Heideggerian nature of his conclusions by occasional allusions to Heidegger's terminology. Later, when he requires language that goes beyond Husserl's, he introduces his own expressions—for example "supplement" and the soon-to-be-famous *différance*—which stakes out his own distance from Heidegger.

But does any of this show that Derrida's critique is not just Heideggerianism by other means? Must we not agree that Derrida's philosophical conclusions, however distinctive his way of expressing them, are essentially taken over from Heidegger? This is the view of Luc Ferry and Alain Renaut, who summarize their position in the (admittedly crude) formula: "Derrida = Heidegger + Derrida's style".[15] A bit less starkly, their thesis is that "Derrida's work is limited to recapitulating the problematics of ontological difference". His many writings differ from Heidegger's—and from one another—only in the literary means chosen for their expression. As Ferry and Renaut put it in a succinct section title: "All the rest is literature".[16]

[13] In accord with the (unfortunate) standard French practice, there is no index of terms in the French original.

[14] Jacques Derrida, *Speech and Phenomena and Other Essays on Husserl's Theory of Signs*, tr. David Allison (Evanston, IL: Northwestern University Press, 1973), 74 n. 4.

[15] Luc Ferry and Alain Renaut, *French Philosophy of the Sixties: An Essay on Antihumanism*, tr. Mary H. S. Cattani (Amherst, MA: University of Massachusetts Press, 1990), 123.

[16] Ferry and Renaut, *French Philosophy of the Sixties*, 126. Ferry and Renaut acknowledge that Derrida maintains that his notion of *différance* is not reducible to Heidegger's ontological difference because, as he repeatedly tries to demonstrate, Heidegger's development of this difference sometimes falls back into

This assessment, however, is based on the implausible assumption that creative philosophizing requires putting forward original theses. Suppose that, using the analytic techniques of contemporary anglophone philosophy, I managed to offer effective cases for some of Thomas Aquinas's main metaphysical theses: that, for example, there is a real distinction between essence and existence, that there is a principle of efficient causality leading to a sound proof of Go's existence, and that all beings act for goals corresponding to their essences. It would be churlish to deny that I had achieved something philosophically important and original. Similarly, taking an example closer to our current topic, many have been struck by strong similarities between Heidegger's thought in *Being and Time* and Wittgenstein's later philosophy; for example, their critiques of the Cartesian view of the mind, their rejections of foundationalism, their emphasis on the importance of the social context of thought and knowledge. (Newton Garver makes excellent use of such similarities in his introduction to the English translation of Derrida's *Speech and Phenomena.*) Suppose we learn that Wittgenstein wrote his *Philosophical Investigations* after a careful reading and assimilation of *Being and Time*. It is hard to see how, given the distinctive way that Wittgenstein develops his position, this would justify giving up our opinion that he was an importantly creative philosopher.

Further, it is important to note that Derrida's agreement with Heidegger is primarily on the rejection of certain alleged mistakes in previous philosophy. Essentially, he asserts, along Heideggerian lines, the failure of metaphysics in the traditional sense (the metaphysics of presence). But he does not share Heidegger's view that the proper response to this failure is taking on the solemn task of waiting for being to reveal itself. On the contrary, he exalts in the world of perpetual intellectual play that this failure opens up. To cite Richard Rorty's deft formulation: "Whereas Heidegger's words express his reverence for the ineffable, the silent, and the enduring, Derrida's express his affectionate admiration for the proliferating, the elusive, the allusive, the ever-self-recontextualizing."[17] This accounts for Derrida's very unHeideggerian way of engaging with historical and contemporary texts—from his careful, respectful, but devastating unpacking of every nuance of Husserl's theory of signs in *Speech and Phenomena* to his exuberant, endlessly energetic circus of reading Hegel via Genet in *Glas*. Ferry and Renaut may take this as simply a difference in "style", but Derrida's diverse ways of writing express a philosophical attitude that takes him far from Heidegger; here the style makes the philosopher. If we must place Derrida under the Heideggerian banner, he is (as Rorty also suggests) a "far-left Heideggerian", in contrast to the master's firmly "right Heideggerianism". Derrida no doubt follows Heidegger to the end of Western metaphysical thought, but he leaps with abandon into the abyss at the end of the path, rather than waiting with Heidegger for being itself to fill the gap.

metaphysics. But they dismiss this move as one by which "the heir becomes parricide" only for the sake of "attempting to be fundamentally more Heideggerian than Heidegger himself" (pp. 128, 130).

[17] Richard Rorty, "Deconstructionist Theory", in *The Cambridge History of Literary Criticism*, viii. *From Formalism to Poststructuralism* (Cambridge: Cambridge University Press, 1995).

Foucault and Heidegger

What is true of Derrida, the most immersed in Heidegger of all recent French philosophers, is all the more true of others, for example, Foucault, who, although he acknowledges a strong influence, wrote nothing explicitly about Heidegger. Also, despite the "tons of notes" he took while reading Heidegger, there were vast gaps in his knowledge of his work: "I knew practically nothing of *Being and Time*, nor of the things published recently."[18] Heidegger for Foucault is not a matter of immediate and detailed concern but instead a part of the deep background of his work, someone who marked certain paths as no longer viable but had little to tell him about how positively to proceed. For Foucault, as for most French philosophers, the great message from Heidegger was that the conceptual framework that had defined philosophy since Plato and particularly since Descartes—the framework that posed questions about naturalism vs theism, materialism vs dualism, how to refute skepticism about knowledge, and how to ground ethical principles—was no longer viable. But, though the young French philosophers of the 1960s generally (Deleuze is a major exception) accepted this negative judgment that we had reached the "end of philosophy" in the traditional sense, they had no interest in following Heidegger in his mystical vigil of Being and set out on their own to find new directions. Only Derrida found elements of Heidegger's approach that he could use for his own still quite original project.[19]

This end-of-philosophy view is behind Foucault's rejection of Sartre as someone from "the great philosophical epoch of contemporary philosophy ... when a philosophical text ... should tell you with finality what life, death, and sexuality are, whether or not God exists, what freedom is, how to live your political life, how to act towards others, etc".[20] Foucault was among the most radical in this rejection, since, unlike Derrida, Deleuze, and, later, Badiou, he sought no way of thinking that could plausibly present itself as the legitimate successor of traditional philosophy (metaphysics in Heidegger's sense). As a result, he proposed a new kind of history that, although it had no pretensions to anything like philosophical truth, could, he thought, function in the critical role philosophy had, since Socrates, played in Western societies. Given Foucault's move away from traditional philosophy, we may perhaps not be overreading his oft-cited comment about the influence of Heidegger by noting that he emphasizes Heidegger as his main *philosophical* influence: "For me Heidegger has

[18] Foucault, "The Return of Morality", 250.

[19] We can roughly compare the role of Heidegger in French philosophy from the 1960s on to the role of Quine in anglophone philosophy during roughly the same period. Just as Quine was widely perceived to have undermined the previously dominant logical positivist approach to philosophy, so Heidegger was perceived to have undermined traditional metaphysics. But in neither case did this perception set the agenda for the positive approaches taken by philosophers. Indeed, although among analytic philosophers there were a good number who pursued a broadly Quinean naturalism, there were few French philosophers who pursued Heidegger's *Seinsfrage*.

[20] Michel Foucault, "Foucault répond à Sartre", interview with J.-P. Elkabbach in *Quinzaine littéraire* (Mar. 1968), 20–2; repr. in Michel Foucault, *Dits et écrits* (4 vols; Paris: Gallimard, 1994), i. 662.

always been the essential *philosopher*... My entire *philosophical* development was determined by my reading of Heidegger." Since Foucault took more the path of a historian than that of a philosopher, this can be plausibly read as saying that Heidegger helped him realize that he needed to move in a direction other than traditional philosophy, not that he was a strong influence on the historical work Foucault in fact undertook. Then, his following remark, that Nietzsche's influence "outweighed" (*a emporté*) Heidegger's can be readily taken as an allusion to his "genealogical" approach to history.[21]

None of this is to deny that there are strong affinities between Foucault and Heidegger. Hubert Dreyfus has shown informative and fruitful parallels between Heidegger's being and Foucault's power, as well as between the two thinkers' conceptions of the subject and freedom.[22] As Dreyfus points out, where Heidegger helps us "understand how in our modern world things have been turned into objects", Foucault helps us understand how "selves... became subjects". Further, Heidegger presents his understanding through "a history of being, culminating in the technological understanding of being, in order to help us understand and overcome our current ways of dealing with things as objects and resources", while Foucault "analyses several regimes of power, culminating in bio-power, in order to help us free ourselves from understanding ourselves as subjects" (p. 30). So far, of course, the similarities are due largely to the highly abstract level of our description: both Heidegger and Foucault are describing a certain form of transformation (thing to object and self to subject) and are doing so through a historical account that culminates with the triumph of a certain sort of "technology" that operates on what has been transformed.

To give more substance to the parallels, Dreyfus adds further correlations between the key terms of the two accounts. *Being* and *power*, he says, are each presented as "an understanding of reality" effected through a certain set of "practices". Changes in the understanding result from "a leap [*origin* for Heidegger, *emergence* for Foucault] of marginal practices to center", after which the leap is "stabilized into a series of disclosive spaces [*epochs* for Heidegger, *regimes* for Foucault]", which "must be described historically [via *recollection* for Heidegger, via *genealogy* for Foucault] in order to free us from our current style" (p. 45, table).

But even this expansion remains at a high level of abstraction since it leaves room for major differences in the two thinkers' understandings of the corresponding terms. And, in fact, there are fundamental differences, starting with the fact that Heidegger's practices and the understanding they correspond to are global features of epochs extending through many centuries. By Dreyfus's own account, the main Heideggerian

[21] Foucault in his final work, on ancient sexuality, at last finds himself comfortable with the role of philosopher, but now in the old Greek sense of one concerned with practical living rather than theoretical insight.

[22] Hubert L. Dreyfus, "Being and Power Revisited", in Alan Milchman and Alan Rosenberg (eds.), *Foucault and Heidegger: Critical Encounters* (Minneapolis, MN: University of Minnesota Press, 1993). References will be given in the text.

epochs are pre-Socratic Greece, Greece after Plato, the Roman Empire, the Middle Ages, and the Modern Age (beginning with Descartes). Foucault's histories almost always focus on much briefer and more recent periods: the Renaissance (sixteenth century), the Classical Age (roughly 1650–1800), and the Modern Age (1800–mid-twentieth century). Even more important, Foucault's characterizations of his periods typically concern quite specific features: how the mad were treated, how medicine was practiced, how criminals were punished, how sexuality was regarded. The only work that suggests a more global characterization is *The Order of Things*, and even here Foucault's primary concern is a restricted range of disciplines concerned with life, labor, and language, viewed as predecessors of the modern "human sciences". (And Foucault explicitly rejected the idea—admittedly suggested by some of his formulations—that he was trying to characterize the Classical Age, and so on, *tout court.*) Heidegger, by contrast, is quite explicitly concerned to characterize the *general* way of thinking about *everything* (it is, after all, thinking about being) for periods close to millennia. It is no doubt true that being and power pervade in an entirely comprehensive way the societies whose practices they sustain. But Heidegger's concern with being is precisely on this comprehensive level, while Foucault always restricts himself to quite specific and localized aspects of power. This, moreover, is entirely natural, given that, as Dreyfus points out, Heidegger treats Being as a principle of unity and stability, whereas Foucaultian power (or, better, the multiple loci of power dispersed throughout a society) is a principle of division and instability. Heidegger's being has no parallel to Foucault's "micro-physics of power".[23]

The differences are especially marked when we compare Heideggerian recollection—the overcoming of the forgetting of being—with Foucaultian genealogy. Recollection is no doubt a mysterious matter, but it is in any case some sort of ontological thinking (thinking about being). Genealogy, however, is a method of historical investigation—an essentially factual inquiry, governed by the same basic rules of objectivity and evidence required of any other historical investigation. In Heidegger's terms, it is *ontic* not *ontological*, operating of the level of beings, not of being.

Dreyfus's comparison is on its strongest footing when he draws parallels between what he calls "the last two stages in the history of being and power"—between Heidegger's "age of the world picture" followed by an "age of technicity" and Foucault's "age of man" followed by an "age of bio-power" (p. 45, table). Foucault's treatment of man and the "death of man" in *The Order of Things* is his most Heideggerian moment, a highly philosophical, ontologically loaded critique of Kantian and post-Kantian metaphysics and epistemology. As such, however, it is very atypical within

[23] Dreyfus does maintain that something like Heideggerian unity appears in Foucault "when he talks, for example, of the totalizing tendency of a carceral society" ("Being and Power Revisited", 37). But even the carceral society is an "archipelago", made of disparate power centers, each modeled somehow on the ideal of the prison; and Foucault would not have been happy with a characterization of his history of this archipelago as "totalizing".

Foucault's corpus—and even within *The Order of Things* itself, which is mostly a historical study in the manner of Canguilhem's history of concepts. The difference is signaled by Foucault's uncharacteristic discussion of philosophers and philosophical problems, contrary to his usual practice and to his boast—just a few pages before his treatment of the death of man—that he had learned what he knows about the question "What relation is there between language and being?"... more clearly from Cuvier, Bopp, and Ricardo than from Kant or Hegel".[24] Precisely because this section of *The Order of Things* is quite Heideggerian,[25] it is very different from almost everything else Foucault wrote.

The parallel between Heidegger's treatment of technology and Foucault's of bio-power also has a certain depth, because of the fact that it touches on a point of convergence between Foucault's focus on selves and Heidegger's focus on things. As Foucault himself puts it, bio-power is precisely a *technology of the self.* It is perhaps not surprising that two acute observers of the modern scene agree to a significant extent about the dangers of modern technologies, including, as Dreyfus puts it, "the devastation that would result if technicity enabled us to solve all [our] problems" (p. 46). Agreement about a pressing contemporary problem does not eliminate the deep differences that we have seen in the paths that led Foucault and Heidegger to their diagnoses. Moreover, Dreyfus himself recognizes the major difference between the ways that the two thinkers propose to "resist" the evils of technicity. Foucault embraces what he calls "hyper- and pessimistic activism"—exemplified, for example, by the agitations of his Groupe d'Information sur les Prisons—whereas Heidegger's recommendation is to "preserve the marginal practices [threatened by technicity] and wait for a new cultural paradigm" (a "new god") (p. 47).[26] These are not just two different tactical judgments; they express the deep differences between Foucaultian power and Heideggerian being.

My point has not been to reject the many helpful comparisons Dreyfus calls to our attention. They remain valuable reminders of ways that Heidegger's and Foucault's paths sometimes run along one another and sometimes even cross, and in some cases suggest that Foucault indeed did have an eye on a thinker he at one point had studied seriously and admired greatly. My point—which I have no reason to think that Dreyfus would deny—is just that the parallels do not show Foucault to have been anything like a disciple of Heidegger or even that Heidegger is the primary influence on the bulk of Foucault's work.

[24] Michel Foucault, *The Order of Things*, tr. A. Sheridan (New York: Random House, 1970), 306, 307.

[25] Even here there is a major difference with Heidegger, who sees the "modern age" as essentially Cartesian, whereas Foucault insists on a sharp distinction between the Classical age of Descartes and the modern age that begins around the time of Kant.

[26] Dreyfus says that this minimal recommendation corresponds to "Middle Heidegger" and that "for Later Heidegger... there is more we can do". This more is a matter of producing "temporary, self-enclosed, local worlds that resist the totalizing and dispersing effects... of technicity". Examples of this "resistance" are "the gathering of local practices around things such as a jug of wine or a family meal". But this sort of passive resistance is far from Foucault's "hyper-activism".

Deleuze and Heidegger

Heidegger is far less a presence for Deleuze than for Derrida or Foucault. He accepts the broad lines of Heidegger's critique of traditional metaphysical systems, but rejects the conclusion that this means the end of philosophy or even of metaphysics. As he told an interviewer: "I've never been worried about going beyond metaphysics or any death of philosophy."[27] Instead, he returns to the metaphysical tradition, including some figures, such as Hume and Spinoza, to whom Heidegger had paid little attention. Deleuze proposes new ways of reading these philosophers, and from these readings tries to renew the metaphysical tradition with his construal of being as difference. There are several pages in *Difference and Repetition* where he summarizes and comments on Heidegger's treatment of difference, but the tone is that of someone comparing his own independently developed ideas with another thinker in the same general area. Deleuze's conclusion is that Heidegger, after some clarifications, eventually arrives at something like Deleuze's difference and accordingly winds up "giving renewed splendour to the Univocity of Being". But he questions whether Heidegger "truly disengages" from any subordination of being to "the identity of representation", saying that he doubts it "given [Heidegger's] critique of the Nietzschean eternal return".[28]

Deleuze also has some indicative comments regarding the relation of Foucault to Heidegger.[29] He links Heidegger's influence on Foucault to that of Merleau-Ponty: "Foucault found great theoretical inspiration in Heidegger and Merleau-Ponty", particularly regarding his notion of the fold, which comes up in some of Foucault's early literary essays, especially on Raymond Roussel. This notion—which Deleuze himself found of particular interest—is meant to replace the sharp separation of subject and object with an internal self-relation by which something (depending on context, the self, time, being) folds (doubles) over on itself (Merleau-Ponty's "chiasm" or "interlacing" and Heidegger's "between-two" are examples). Although Deleuze acknowledges Heidegger's influence here on Foucault (and presumably on himself), he maintains that Foucault's treatment of the fold is a significant advance on Heidegger's—primarily because Foucault has thought the matter through in Nietzschean terms. In this connection, Deleuze emphasizes the importance of "Foucault's declaration that Heidegger always fascinated him, but that he could understand him only by way of Nietzsche and along side Nietzsche" (p. 113).[30] Then, speaking at least for himself, he says, "Heidegger is Nietzsche's potential, but not the other way around, and Nietzsche did not see his potential fulfilled" (p. 113), presumably meaning that

[27] Gilles Deleuze, *Negotiations: 1972–1990*, tr. Martin Joughin (New York: Zone Books, 1995), 136.

[28] Gilles Deleuze, *Difference and Repetition*, tr. Paul Patton (New York: Columbia University Press, 1994), 66.

[29] Gilles Deleuze, *Foucault*, tr. Seán Hand (Minneapolis, MN: University of Minnesota Press, 1988), 110–13. References will be given in the text.

[30] The second clause seems to be Deleuze's reading of Foucault's claim (which he cites) that, for Foucault, Nietzsche's importance "outweighed" Heidegger's (see n. 3 above).

Heidegger could have but did not develop important truths implicit in Nietzsche's work (which, we can also presume, Deleuze did develop). Overall, Deleuze's occasional comments about Heidegger show respect for someone Deleuze regards as an important thinker with whom he has some affinities but who has not been one of his primary influences.

The master-thinker in French philosophy

Younger philosophers who came to prominence in the 1980s have been well trained in Heideggerian thought and swim expertly in its sea. Alain Badiou, who offers an alternative ontology of difference to Deleuze's, seems to have much the same attitude toward Heidegger as Deleuze does. Some, like Luc Ferry and Alain Renaut, have rebelled against Heidegger in the name of a humanism that returns in important respects to Kant. Others, like Jean-Luc Marion, have integrated their Heidegger into a revival of phenomenology—but one that takes it in religious directions that might have disconcerted both Husserl and Heidegger.

In every case, apart from the small circle around Jean Beaufret, French philosophers have recognized Heidegger as a master-thinker, but without following him as disciples. This distinction is crucial for understanding French philosophy since the 1960s. French philosophical education works, as we have seen, against the creation of disciples and instead leads students to learn from a variety of master-thinkers of the past. Whereas disciples work to mine the riches of their unique master, French students learn to engage with a range of major thinkers and to develop their own original position through interaction (both appreciative and critical) with them. This approach avoids both the vapidity of discipleship and the ahistoricity common among analytic philosophers.

But why then have none of the master-thinkers of French philosophy since Sartre been French? Why the dominance of Hegel, Nietzsche, Husserl, and Heidegger? For one thing, the nineteenth century simply failed to produce any world-class French philosophers, and the French emphasis on quality admirably refused to privilege their own simply because they were their own. The first half of the twentieth century did produce Bergson and Sartre, both at least candidates for the status of major thinkers. Bergson, for all his flair and brilliance, was too much of a pre-war figure, a philosopher, as Hyppolite put it, of "final serenity" through communion with nature.[31] The terrors of two world wars made such optimism unpalatable if not ludicrous, and philosophers of the second half of the century turned to thinkers like Heidegger with a sensibility for the tragedy and absurdity of existence.[32] It may also be, sad to say, that Bergson's elegant and limpid prose posed insufficient challenge to the sharply honed hermeneutic

[31] Jean Hyppolite, "Du Bergsonisme à l'existentialisme", in his *Figures de la pensée philosophique* (2 vols; Paris: Presses Universitaires de France, 1971), i. 453.

[32] Characteristically, Deleuze found major inspiration from Bergson. Cf. his *Bergsonism*, tr. Hugh Tomlinson and Barbara Habberjam (New York: Zone Books, 1988).

skills of *normaliens*. Sartre met the criteria that excluded Bergson, but, as our discussion so far has suggested, his case is complex, and we will look at it more closely in Chapter 4.

In any case, French philosophy deserves praise for sticking to its judgments of philosophical greatness even when that meant pointing their students across the Rhine for their primary intellectual nourishment. This is why the philosophers we are discussing engage with Hegel, Nietzsche, and Heidegger more than they do with Comte, Bergson, and Sartre.

Heidegger and French style

On the other hand, the Germanic turn had a devastating effect on French philosophical style. It appeared very quickly, between the mere eleven years that separate Bergson's last book, *Two Sources of Morality and Religion* (1932), and Sartre's first major book, *Being and Nothingness* (1943). Bergson's work is a model of lucid classical French prose; philosophers and non-philosophers alike read it with pleasure and understanding. Sartre's book, for all its occasional flair, is a struggle for any reader, a dense network of obscure technicalities that specialists continue to sort out; it has spawned generations of guides, introductions, and companions to which even the most acute philosophical readers turn hopefully for assistance. And Sartre's obscurity almost immediately became the norm, so that students of late-twentieth-century philosophy can only shake their heads (or give a Gallic shrug) when they hear the old saying: "What is not clear is not French."

In Germany, of course, philosophical style, at least among the dominant voices, had been going downhill since Kant's first *Critique*. Hegel, who was just starting to make headway in France in Sartre's time, was a strikingly bad influence. But it was Heidegger above all, who gave instant legitimacy to a mode of writing that had scarcely existed in France before Sartre picked up *Being and Time*.[33] Badiou argues that the new philosophical concepts introduced from Sartre required new ways of philosophical writing.[34] No doubt, but did they require so much *bad* philosophical writing? Do the army of commentators who so heroically explicate the master-thinkers fail in their explications precisely to the extent that they achieve a reasonable level of clarity?

I would suggest that, beyond the example of Heidegger, the French move to obscurity reflects an as yet little explored connection of French philosophers to modernism. Badiou emphasizes this in another context, without connecting it to their style of writing. But if, as Badiou plausibly claims, "French philosophers evinced a profound attraction to modernity" and were particularly drawn to "non-figurative painting, new music and theatre, detective novels, jazz, and cinema",[35] it would be more than likely that they would want

[33] Nietzsche, of course, can be a remarkably good writer, but he is a poor model for imitation, and his effect on his French emulators was mainly to introduce an offputting note of hysteria into their convoluted prose.

[34] Alain Badiou, "The Adventure of French Philosophy", *New Left Review*, 35 (Sept.–Oct. 2005), 71.

[35] Badiou, "The Adventure of French Philosophy", 77.

to emulate the high modernist writing of Proust, Joyce, and Eliot. One characteristic of such writing is, to put it crudely, its unreadability—it is typically too long, too complex, too erudite, too profound to be read without special assistance from scholarly commentators. Hegel and the other idealists, taking off from Kant, had created a proto-modernist mode of expression in philosophical German, but, later, neo-Kantians and positivists (not to mention Nietzsche) pretty much eradicated it. Heidegger, however, just around the time modernist literature came to full bloom, reinvented a philosophical version of it, which Sartre picked up and younger Turks like Deleuze and Derrida took to an even higher level.

"Unreadability" is a relative term, and great writers such as Proust, Joyce, and Eliot are able to coax readers to their level and the effort turns out to be entirely worthwhile. But it is by no means obvious that the difficulty of recent German and French philosophical writing has similar redeeming value. We will return to this issue in Chapter 10.

4

Whatever Happened to Existentialism?

Sixty-eight years after Sartre's *Being and Nothingness*, existentialism seems to survive only as a popular topic in undergraduate courses in philosophy or literature. Indeed, by 1960, when Sartre's *Critique of Dialectical Reason* appeared, the movement had faded, with Sartre himself recasting his thought to accommodate the Marxism that he had even three years earlier called "the unsurpassable philosophy of our time".[1] Even this retreat from pure existentialism was not enough for rising structuralists, such as Claude Lévi-Strauss, whose *Savage Thought* (1962) concluded with a scathing critique of Sartre's new book. Lévi-Strauss's fundamental objection is that Sartre still gives the conscious subject (the cogito) a privileged role, remaining "the prisoner of his Cogito", even though it is now "sociologized".[2] Although allowing that the phenomenological level of consciousness corresponds to a localized truth that needs to be respected in our final account of human reality, Lévi-Strauss insists that the full truth of man is attained only through analysis of the unconscious structures underlying the phenomena of consciousness. Our idea that the conscious subject has some ultimate control over its history is itself just a contingent feature of one stage of that history, which is in the end controlled by the objective psychoanalytic and anthropological truths not accessible to conscious reflection. Accordingly, Sartre's claim for a privileged role for consciousness is on a par with the claims of the "thousands" of societies in different times and places, each claiming that "it contains the essence of all the meaning and dignity of which human society is capable". Here Sartre's thought is on a par with that of "a Melanesian savage"; his "philosophy (like all the others) affords a first-class ethnographic document, the study of which is essential to an understanding of the mythology of our own time".[3]

Lévi-Strauss at least paid Sartre the courtesy of offering a detailed critique in his book. The new generation of French philosophers largely ignored Sartre, apart from occasional

[1] Jean-Paul Sartre, *The Search for a Method*, tr. Hazel Barnes (New York: Knopf, 1963; first French publication, 1957).

[2] Claude Lévi-Strauss, *The Savage Mind* (Chicago: University of Chicago Press, 1966), 249.

[3] Claude Lévi-Strauss, *The Savage Mind*, 249 and n.

dismissive or patronizing remarks in interviews. Foucault, for example, dismissed Sartre's *Critique of Dialectical Reason* as "the magnificent and pathetic [*pathétique*—'touching' might be a more precise translation] effort of a man of the nineteenth century to think the twentieth century. In that sense Sartre is the last Hegelian and, I would say, the last Marxist." When asked to respond to Sartre's criticisms of *The Order of Things*, Foucault responded: "Sartre has work . . . that is too important to allow him time to read my book. He has not read it."[4]

Derrida is far harsher. He admits that as a student Sartre "played a major role for me" (indeed, was "the unsurpassable horizon"), but he immediately adds that Sartre was a "model that I have since judged to be nefarious and catastrophic". Similarly, he acknowledges that he read Husserl, Heidegger, and Blanchot "thanks to [Sartre] but especially against him". He marvels that "a man who, in his own way, rejected or misunderstood so many theoretical and literary events of his time—let's say, to go quickly, psychoanalysis, Marxism, structuralism, Joyce, Artaud, Bataille, Blanchot—who accumulated and disseminated incredible misreadings of Heidgger, sometimes of Husserl, could come to dominate the cultural scene to the point of becoming a great popular figure".

Derrida goes on, "I sometimes share the almost familial affection that many feel for this man whom I have never seen", but concludes that Sartre "does not belong to the age of those works that matter for me".[5] He also disagrees with those who say that Sartre "escaped or resisted" the influence of the University, maintaining instead that "university norms determined his work in the most internal way" and that Sartre is "an enormous screen of French culture", who needs to be understood in terms of "the models and the history of education, the *lycée*, the *khâgne*, the Ecole Normale, and the *agrégation*". The interviewer tries to sum up the indictment: "So, in short, you see in Sartre the perfect example of what an intellectual should not be", to which Derrida responds, "I didn't say that", though he does go on to say that, regarding intellectuals and political affairs, "Sartre's example . . . incites one to prudence" and to decry the "formidable authority, the authority that was not granted to stricter and more interesting analysts" but was given even to Sartre's "most impulsive remarks".[6]

Deleuze had a much more generous response to Sartre, apparent in the brief notice "He Was My Teacher" ("Il a été mon maître"), written in 1964 on the occasion of Sartre's refusing the Nobel Prize for literature. Deleuze says that "for us twenty year olds during

[4] Michel Foucault, "Foucault répond à Sartre", interview with J.-P. Elkabbach in *Quinzaine littéraire* (Mar. 1968), 20–2; repr. in Michel Foucault, *Dits et écrits* (4 vols; Paris: Gallimard, 1994), i. 662. Foucault subsequently objected in a letter to the editor of *La Quinzaine littéraire* to the publication of this and several other remarks that he maintained were given off the record. He ended by saying: "I think that Sartre's immense work and his political action mark an epoch. It's true that some people today work along different direction from his. I would never accept that anyone compare—even to contrast them—the trivial [*petit*] historical and methodological spadework I have tried to do to a work like his" (i. 670).

[5] Jacques Derrida, "Unsealing ('the Old New Language')", interview with Catherine David, in Jacques Derrida, *Points . . . : Interviews, 1974–1994* (Palo Alto, CA: Stanford University Press, 1995), 122.

[6] Derrida, "Unsealing ('the Old New Language')", 123.

the Liberation" Sartre was "the only one [who] knew how to say anything new".[7] He recalls "the initial astonishment we felt for Sartre's renewal of philosophy" (p. 79), when they first read *Being and Nothingness*. He also insists that *Critique of Dialectical Reason* (published in 1960) "is one of the most beautiful books to have come out in recent years" and provided the needed social ("collective") complement to the individual subjectivity of *Being and Nothingness* (p. 79). In conclusion: "It is [Sartre's] peculiar destiny to circulate pure air when he speaks, even if this pure air, the air of absence, is difficult to breathe" (p. 80).

For all his praise, Deleuze says very little, for or against, Sartre's specific philosophical views (though we will later note some comments about Sartre on the Other). Foucault and Derrida, however, have some substantive discussions that are worth examining.

Foucault and Sartre

Although Foucault almost never mentions Sartre in his formal publications, there are numerous references in interviews, particularly from the days of his early fame after the publication of *The Order of Things*, which was rightly seen as an implicit challenge to Sartre.[8] To a great extent, Foucault's case against Sartre is his case against phenomenology. As he put it in an interview with Gérard Raulet:

> The problem of language appeared, and it was clear that phenomenology was no match for structural analysis in accounting for effects of meaning that could be produced by a structure of the linguistic type, in which the subject (in the phenomenological sense) did not intervene to confer meaning.... Psychoanalysis—in large part under the influence of Lacan—also raised a problem which, though very different, was not unanalogous. For the unconscious could not feature in any discussion of a phenomenological kind.[9]

This case is strong against phenomenology strictly construed, namely, as requiring that all knowledge be entirely derived from the givens of lived experience. But Foucault ignores the fact—which he was surely aware of—that both Sartre and Merleau-Ponty (before his death in mid-career in 1961) were centrally concerned with expanding the phenomenological standpoint to take account of linguistics and psychoanalysis. As Foucault himself points out, it was Merleau-Ponty's lectures that introduced Saussure's linguistic structuralism to the French scene. Merleau-Ponty's bridge from phenomenology to structuralism is sketched in his essay on Lévi-Strauss (derived from his presentation of Lévi-Strauss for membership in the Collège de

[7] Gilles Deleuze, *Desert Islands and Other Texts, 1953–1974* (Los Angeles: Semiotext(e), 2004), 77. Further references will be given in the text.

[8] According to Didier Eribon, at the proof stage the book contained many explicit criticisms of Sartre that Foucault omitted in the published version (Didier Eribon, *Michel Foucault*, tr. Betsy Wing (Cambridge, MA: Harvard University Press, 1991), 156).

[9] Michel Foucault, "Structuralism and Post-Structuralism: An Interview with Michel Foucault", tr. Jeremy Harding, in Lawrence Kritzman (ed.), *Politics, Philosophy, and Culture: Interviews and Other Writings, 1977–1984* (New York: Routledge, 1988), 21.

France): "For the philosopher, the presence of structure outside of us in natural and social systems and within us as symbolic function points to a way beyond the subject–object correlation which has dominated philosophy from Descartes to Hegel."[10] Because structures are both objective realities, independent of any mind, and meanings informing the lives of individuals, they are the vehicle of the concrete unity of man-in-the-world. But we cannot limit ourselves to the study of structures alone. We also need to understand how structures enter into the lives of individuals. "The surprising logical operations attested to by the formal structures of societies must certainly be effected in some way by the populations which live these . . . systems" (for example, the kinship systems studied by Lévi-Strauss). Accordingly, for any given structure, we must look for "a sort of lived equivalent of that structure. . . . The variables of anthropology . . . must be met with, sooner or later, on the level at which phenomena have an immediately human significance." In fact, Merleau-Ponty suggests, "this process of joining objective analysis to lived experience is perhaps the most proper task of anthropology, the one which distinguishes it from other social sciences such as economics and demography."[11]

This process is also what Sartre has in mind when he proposes his *Critique of Dialectical Reason* as the basis for "a structural, historical anthropology".[12] In a 1969 interview, responding explicitly to Foucault's *The Order of Things*, Sartre agrees that "man is . . . a product of structures", that he "receives structures insofar as he himself is engaged in history". His point, he says, is merely that this cannot be the entire story, since the received structure has been "worked by man and bears the traces of man". So, for example, Sartre admits that, on one level, language is "an autonomous system, reflecting a social unification. . . . The linguist takes this totality of relations as an object of study and is right to do so, since it is already constituted. This is the moment of structure."[13] Sartre accepts the structuralists' Saussurean distinction of *langue* and *parole*, translating the distinction into his own terminology of the practico-inert vs praxis. But, just as Saussure, despite his tactical focus on language as a formal system (*langue*), had to allow for the essential role of actual speech acts (*parole*), so Sartre insists that there must also be a moment of praxis, where we recognize that ultimately language itself exists only because we speak it. It is hard to see how Foucault, whose work, after all, is ultimately designed to provide us with the intellectual tools we need to develop as free individuals, could disagree with this.[14]

[10] Maurice Merleau-Ponty, *Signs*, tr. Richard McCleary (Evanston, IL: Northwestern University Press, 1964), 123.

[11] Merleau-Ponty, *Signs*, 119.

[12] Jean-Paul Sartre, *Critique of Dialectical Reason*, vol. i, tr. Alan Sheridan-Smith (London: New Left Books, 1976), 822.

[13] "Jean-Paul Sartre répond" (interview), *L'Arc*, 40 (1966), 89.

[14] Foucault, in fact, in a lecture in Japan, gave an excellent summary of Sartre's response: "Jean-Paul Sartre objects that . . . if there was no speaking subject to continually take up language . . . if there was not this element of human activity, if there was not speech at the very heart of the language system, how could language evolve?" (*Dits et écrits*, ii. 422).

In a 1967 interview, Paolo Caruso presses Foucault on a similar point, suggesting that, if he refuses to acknowledge even a prereflective cogito, "the phenomenologists could argue . . . that you are forgetting (or hiding) the genesis of your own viewpoint. In your analysis, there is a kind of methodological forgetting of the subject that carries out this very analysis."[15] Foucault responds, very oddly, that this objection assumes that a method of analysis "is justified only to the extent that it can take account of the 'totality'".[16] This leads him to a long discussion of the idea that philosophy is designed to give a comprehensive account of all reality (à la Hegel), an idea that, he says, thrived in the nineteenth century but has been mostly abandoned by twentieth-century philosophy after Husserl. Just as we begin to wonder what this has to do with Sartre's insistence on an irreducible role for the subject, Foucault compounds our confusion by concluding: "I don't believe Sartre still thinks that philosophical discourse is a discourse about totality."[17] In the end, Foucault seems to have no coherent response to the claim that his position here does not differ significantly from Sartre's later thought. In any case the very issues on which he claims phenomenology had failed are the ones that Sartre and Merleau-Ponty were addressing with considerable success. By arbitrarily restricting phenomenology to the (Husserlian) claim that everything needs to be reduced to transcendental subjectivity, Foucault ignores important options whereby Sartre and Merleau-Ponty could and did dissolve his objections.

As to psychoanalysis, Foucault's comments seem based on a misunderstanding of Sartre's position (even in the high existentialist text of *Being and Nothingness*). As Thomas Flynn points out, the "prereflective awareness" of *Being and Nothingness*, along with the "comprehension" (of *Critique of Dialectical Reason*) and the "lived experience" (of the Flaubert biography), are "functional equivalents of the classical unconscious".[18] So, for example, Sartre's famous woman is in bad faith because she reflectively constructs versions of herself and her companion ("just friends", "intellectual soul-mates") that are contrary to her prereflective orientation (desire for erotic attention). His problems are with what he sees as the ontological crudity of Freud's formulation, not with the idea of some sort of fundamental split between levels of awareness. Existential psychoanalysis is a redescription, not a rejection, of the Freudian data. Indeed, each of Sartre's biographies is dedicated to ferreting out truths that its subject "knows" but represses: "When I show how Flaubert did not know himself and how at the same time he understood himself admirably, I am indicating what I call [lived] experience [*vécu*]—that is to say, life aware of itself, without implying any thetic knowledge or consciousness."[19] None of this is to say that Foucault might not have found good grounds for disagreeing with Sartre's way of coming to terms with the

[15] Foucault, *Dits et écrits*, i. 609.
[16] Foucault, *Dits et écrits*, i. 610.
[17] Foucault, *Dits et écrits*, i. 612.
[18] Thomas Flynn, "Sartre at One Hundred: A Man of the Nineteenth Century Addressing the Twenty-First? (Jean-Paul Sartre and Michel Foucault)", *Sartre Studies International*, 11 (2005), 9.
[19] Jean-Paul Sartre, *Life/Situations* (New York: Pantheon, 1977), 127–8.

unconscious, but he was wrong to think that existential phenomenology simply had no resources for such an enterprise.

Why did Foucault, like most other French intellectuals of his generation, come to see structuralism as not a complement but a stark alternative to existential phenomenology? On one level, the explanation lies in the rivalry between Lévi-Strauss and Sartre. Lévi-Strauss's explicit, even virulent, challenge to Sartre's dominant position (as we saw in the concluding chapter of *La Pensée sauvage*) left no room for cooperative inquiry. If Merleau-Ponty, with his close ties to Lévi-Strauss (he dedicated *The Savage Mind* to Merleau-Ponty), had lived long enough and succeeded Sartre (whose interests were becoming much less narrowly philosophical) as the leading existential phenomenologist, the relations between structuralism and phenomenology may well have been very different. This may have been particularly true for Foucault, who seems to have had considerably more respect for and sympathy with Merleau-Ponty than he did for Sartre.

In any case, Foucault's comments on Sartre betray a clear anxiety of influence, as the dismissive remarks we cited at the outset show. More seriously, Foucault strongly resisted even plausible suggestions of similarities between his views and Sartre's. For example, an interviewer once noted Foucault's idea that "one is to create oneself without recourse to knowledge or universal rules" and asked how this differs from Sartrean existentialism. Foucault replied that Sartre's notion of "authenticity" implicitly contradicts his existentialist "theory" that there is no pregiven self and turns back to the "idea of the self as something that is given to us . . . to the idea that we have to be ourselves—to be truly our true self". This is an obvious distortion of Sartre's conception of authenticity, which involves total acceptance of the fact that any self (essence) we have is our own free creation. Foucault then goes on to say that we can avoid Sartre's mistake by substituting creativity for authenticity and recognizing that "we have to create ourselves as works of art". This is a puzzling suggestion, since Sartre himself offers precisely this aesthetic model of self-making in his famous lecture "Existentialism Is a Humanism".[20] Foucault ignores this well-known text and, when his interviewer comments that the aesthetic model recalls Nietzsche (whose views on this point are quite similar to Sartres's), he merely comments: "Yes. My view is much closer to Nietzsche's than to Sartre's."[21]

Perhaps the most fruitful path toward a meeting of the Sartrean and Foucaultian minds is their shared emphasis, pointed out by Thomas Flynn, on the notion of experience. On the one hand, Foucault speaks of "experience" throughout his writings, even those that most directly challenge the centrality of the subject and of consciousness. Even in The *Order of Things* he evokes an "experience of order"

[20] Jean-Paul Sartre, "Existentialism Is a Humanism," trans. P. Mairet, in Walter Kaufmann (ed.), *Existentialism from Dostoyevsky to Sartre* (New York: Meridian, 1975), 364.

[21] Michel Foucault, "On the Genealogy of Ethics: An Overview of Work in Progress" (interview with Hubert Dreyfus and Paul Rabinow), in *Essential Works of Foucault 1954–1984*, ed. Paul Rabinow, vol. i, ed. Paul Rabinow (New York: New Press, 1997), 262. The last few paragraphs have made use of material from my article "Foucault's Philosophy of Experience", *boundary 2*, 29 (2002), 69–85.

associated with an episteme, and his final work on ethics requires a notion of the self and even, as Flynn points out, a relationship of the self to itself, which can hardly be understood except in terms of some sort of self-awareness. Also, one of Foucault's last essays was an exploration of life and experience in the thoughts of his mentor, Georges Canguilhem, in which he develops his own conception of experience in some detail. This continuing theme of experience should be no surprise, given Foucault's admission (noted above) that his critique of the subject is by no means intended to deny that there is a realm of phenomenological consciousness. The point is rather to situate this realm in relation to other dimensions (linguistic, psychoanalytic) that are ignored if we make consciousness the source of all meaning.

On the other hand, Sartre, as we have seen, moved away from a hegemony of phenomenological consciousness precisely in order to account for factors such as the linguistic and psychoanalytic dimensions Foucault emphasizes. Sartre's central notion of praxis in *The Critique of Dialectical Reason* went a long way in this direction. And, as Flynn notes, his later understanding of "lived experience" (*le vécu*), developed in his biography of Flaubert, goes even further, leading Sartre to suggest that his notion of lived experience has no need for the opposition of "subjectivity" and "objectivity" that was assumed in *Being and Nothingness*.[22] For these reasons, Flynn plausibly concludes, looking at the overall development of each man's thought, Foucault's "use of 'experience' maps onto that of Sartre".[23]

Derrida and Sartre: early dismissals

In addition to the anti-Sartre swipes of his interviews (and some similar comments in *Glas*), Derrida offers two more serious assessments, one in his 1968 essay "The Ends of Man", and another in his 1996 article in *Les Temps modernes*. The treatment in "The Ends of Man" is, nonetheless, quite different from the meticulous close readings Derrida is famous for. Like Heidegger, he presents Sartre as a representative of "humanism", which he takes to be obviously unacceptable because it is based on metaphysics. He opens by rebuking Sartre for misreading (or perhaps not reading) Heidegger, represented by his accepting and popularizing Corbin's translation of *Dasein* as *realité humaine*, which conveys a humanist connotation quite inappropriate for Heidegger, even in *Being and Time*. Derrida acknowledges that "human reality" was intended as a neutral term that would avoid the presuppositions of "a certain intellectualist or spiritualist humanism which had dominated French philosophy (Brunschvicg, Alain, Bergson)", which, Derrida notes, Sartre had ridiculed in *Nausea* in the pathetic figure of the Autodidact.[24] Nonetheless, he says, Sartre offers no critical analysis of

[22] Jean-Paul Sartre, *Beyond Existentialism and Marxism*, tr. John Mathews (Pantheon Books, 1983), 35.

[23] Flynn, "Sartre at One Hundred", 8.

[24] Jacques Derrida, "The Ends of Man", in *Margins of Philosophy*, tr. Alan Bass (Chicago: University of Chicago Press, 1982), 115. Further references will be given in the text.

"man" as such but rather takes "the unity of human-reality" as the "ground and horizon" of his phenomenological ontology, which accordingly "describes the structures of human reality" and so is "a philosophical anthropology" (pp. 115–16).

None of this seems out of line as a broad statement of the existentialism of *Being and Nothingness*, particularly given Sartre's subsequent claim that it is a humanism and the obvious fact that it is based on a description of the fundamental reality of human beings (and so in Heidegger's sense, if not Sartre's, a metaphysics). But why think, as Derrida clearly does, that there is something wrong with this sort of humanism and this sort of metaphysics? The question is compelling not only because Derrida offers no criticisms of Sartre's specific form of metaphysical humanism but especially because he makes no effort to explicate the sense in which Sartre is a humanist and a metaphysician. Surely, we cannot assume that Heidegger has shown that any position that can be labeled humanist and metaphysical is untenable.

A hint of a reason appears when Derrida says that, although Sartre's anthropology may be different from the "classical anthropologies" (for example, those of Bergson et al. mentioned just before), "there is an uninterrupted metaphysical familiarity with that which, so naturally, links the *we* of the philosopher to "we men", to the *we* in the horizon of humanity" (p. 116). But for this to be a criticism we would need to see why there is something wrong about speaking of "we men" in the sense of all humanity and how Sartre's "metaphysical" descriptions of human reality commit him to such a pernicious usage.

The next sentence—rather abruptly—raises the issue of historicity. According to Derrida, although history is an important theme in Sartre, he offers little in the way of the "history of concepts". In particular, "the history of the concept of man is never examined" (p. 116). Here we may begin to glimpse (or construct) a serious line of critique. If, as Sartre himself thinks, "classical" humanisms go wrong in positing a fixed, atemporal human essence, it might seem to follow that his own ahistorical phenomenological description of human reality, which delineates unchanging structures of the for-itself and its world would seem itself to be essentialist. Derrida develops this objection by actually venturing into the details of Sartre's text.

Characteristically, he focuses on an apparently marginal text, Sartre's brief, highly programmatic, and puzzling speculations in the conclusion of *Being and Nothingness* (pp. 787–90) about the origin of being-for-itself from being-in-itself.[25] (Presumably, this passage strikes him since Sartre labels his speculation here as "metaphysical", not ontological.) Derrida notes that this metaphysical question is about the "unity of Being" (p. 116) (Sartre himself speaks of it as about "unifying the *givens* of ontology".[26]) Derrida goes on to say, "it goes without saying that the mystical unity of being, as the totality of the in-itself and the for-itself, is precisely the unity of human-reality in its project" (p. 116). Further, according to Derrida, although Sartre purports to characterize this

[25] Jean-Paul Sartre, *Being and Nothingness*, tr. Hazel Barnes (New York: Pocket Books, 1966), 287–790.
[26] Sartre, *Being and Nothingness*, 790.

unity "in a ... neutral and undetermined way", he is actually referring to "the metaphysical unity of man and God". What Derrida has in mind here is Sartre's famous claim that the ultimate project of the human being (being-for-itself), the final goal of its freedom, is to achieve the self-identity of being-in-itself, while still remaining a self-aware being-for-itself. To achieve such a state would be to become God: a being that is simultaneously the fullness of all perfection and a free consciousness. For Sartre, of course, such a state is logically impossible (hence God cannot exist), so that our ultimate desire is unattainable: "man is a useless passion".[27] Derrida comments that Sartre's "atheism changes nothing in this fundamental structure" and concludes that "Sartre's project remarkably verifies" Heidegger's claim that humanism is always based in a metaphysics—and in the precise Heideggerian sense of an "ontotheology" (p. 116).[28]

Derrida gives no reason for thinking that Sartre's ontotheological description of human reality does not have its own accuracy as an account of conscious life as Sartre and his contemporaries encounter it. (In this regard, it would seem to be on an equal footing with Heidegger's descriptions of the inauthenticity of Dasein's "average everydayness".) The problem is rather that Sartre raises "no questions" about "the history of this concept of negativity as a relationship to God" or about "the meaning and origin of the concept of (human) reality" (p. 116 n. 5). In short, Sartre fails to realize that his description may not delineate the essence of human reality but merely catch a contingent historical stage of human reality.

A first point to note is that, even if Derrida is right, Sartre is not contradicting his existentialist rejection of essentialism. The essential structures of consciousness do not correspond to essence in the sense of a psychological self or a human nature that predetermines or limits the free choices of the for-itself, and Sartre rejects essences only to the extent that they restrict human freedom. Freedom itself exists only because the ontological structure of consciousness involves a specific sort of non-self-identity (being what it is not and not being what it is). Accordingly, the point of Derrida's critique must be Sartre's failure to recognize the radically historical character of human reality.

[27] Sartre, *Being and Nothingness*, 784.

[28] It is not clear why Derrida highlights Sartre's sketchy, odd, and opaque comments about the "metaphysical" origin of the for-itself from the in-itself, particularly since these comments do not give priority, as Derrida suggests, to the for-itself but to the in-itelf, which Sartre says would somehow "have to be originally a presence to itself—i.e., it would have to already have consciousness". It would have to be (although Sartre's ontology can make no sense of this) "as if the in-itself in a project to found itself gives itself the modification of the for-itself" (*Being and Nothingness*, 789–90). The (correct) claims Derrida makes about Sartre's giving priority to human reality have to do not with this metaphysical speculation about the causal origin of the for-itself but with Sartre's description, in ontological terms, of consciousness's attempt to overcome the instability of not being what it is (and being what it is not) by becoming an in-itself, which is simply what it is. Sartre formulates this view before and quite independently of his metaphysical speculations, and the key passage Derrida quotes (about the for-itself as a useless passion seeking to be God) is not part of his concluding discussion of "metaphysical implications". In any case, Derrida's critique of Sartre does not change if it is separated from the metaphysical discussion, since it concerns only the ontotheological priority of the for-itself.

But if this is the point, it is odd that Derrida focuses on the human project of "becoming God", which is the fundamental manifestation of bad faith and inauthentic behavior. For Sartre makes it entirely clear that bad faith and inauthenticity are not inevitable features of human reality. In *Being and Nothingness* he at several key points emphasizes that it is possible for human beings to avoid bad faith and live authentically, even though the description of this sort of existence falls outside the scope of his present discussion. In other places, he maintains that inauthenticity is practically unavoidable only within the socio-economic structure of bourgeois society. Critics have maintained that Sartre's ontology leaves no room for authentic existence, which, they say, is why he was never able to write his promised ethical treatise, *L'Homme*. But Sartre certainly thought he knew of concrete cases of authentic behavior (for example, by heroes of the Resistance) and would have rejected any feature of his ontology that contradicted this. For this line of criticism to strike home against Sartre, it would have to be shown that the defining features of his ontology entail bad faith as a permanent human condition, something that Derrida obviously does not even attempt.

If there is an effective criticism of Sartre in Derrida's "The Ends of Man", it would have to be simply that there are no essential structures of human reality, so that every aspect of Sartre's phenomenological ontology is a contingent feature of his historical situation. But Derrida says nothing to support this, and it is hard to see how his Heideggerian presuppositions could accord with such a claim. Does not Heidegger see Dasein's relation to Being as essential to its existence? Is it not necessary that the language in which Dasein exists be "the house of Being"? Are not the structures of ordinary everydayness described in *Being and Time* at least *permanent possibilities* of human existence, possibilities sustained by the essential ontological structures of being-in-the-world?

It is, therefore, very difficult to see any effective critique of Sartre that even begins to be formulated in Derrida's "The Ends of Man". There are other possible modes of critique that we can imagine him offering. It is, in particular, very tempting to think of him as trying to apply to Sartre the critique of the metaphysics of presence launched against Husserl in *Speech and Phenomena*. But the fact is that this is not what Derrida does in "The Ends of Man" or, as far as I know, anywhere else. Nor is it obvious how such a critique would be effective, since Sartre's description of consciousness rigorously avoids positing it as a fullness of being or a transparent presence to itself. A critique in terms of presence would be effective only if it could come to terms with Sartre's transformation of Descartes's cogito into a non-substantial, non-self-identical nihilation of being. The fascinating question, which it would have been very exciting and informative to see Derrida take up, is whether Sartre's conception of consciousness in terms of negation could be reduced to an instance of metaphysical presence. Or does it rather function along the same lines as Derridean *différance*?

Although Derrida never pursued this question, commentators have. Christina Howells, in particular, has made a strong case for the convergence of Sartre and Derrida on consciousness.[29] Howells begins by emphasizing that Sartre's understanding of the "self-presence" of consciousness (being-for-itself, *pour-soi*) involves a negativity that sharply distinguishes it from the "fullness of being" asserted by standard versions of the metaphysics of presence. For Sartre, the very fact that consciousness is present to itself means that "it is not entirely itself" (p. 332). For Sartre, consciousness always implies separation, so that self-consciousness requires separation from self. As Howells puts it, "presence is precisely what prevents identity" (p. 332).

Because of this, she goes on to argue, "Sartre's analysis of the self-presence of the *pour soi* anticipates Derrida's deconstruction of Husserl's *Logical Investigations*" in *Speech and Phenomena* (p. 333). Derrida, for example, examines Husserl's treatments of internal time consciousness and of consciousness's interior "dialogue" with itself and concludes that in neither case can Husserl "maintain consistently the self-coincidence of the present". Just as Sartre argues that *belief* is *consciousness (of) belief*, although the two are "radically different though within the indissoluble unity of one and the same being", so Derrida argues against Husserl that "the present of self-presence is not *simple*... it is constituted in an originary irreducible synthesis" (p. 333).

Howells also maintains that the main functions of Derrida's *différance*—which he introduces to undermine metaphysical conceptions of presence—correspond to functions of Sartrean consciousness: deferring, differentiating, and producing meaning through linguistic and conceptual differences. "*Différance* may be intended as part of a radical deconstruction of the conscious subject, but its function at times appears remarkably similar" (p. 334). Given this, it is not surprising that Derrida from the beginning qualified the rejection of the subject, claiming that "he had never maintained that... there was no subject" merely that "the 'punctual simplicity' of the classical subject cannot be found" (p. 347).

Howells further notes that, in a 1989 interview with Jean-Luc Nancy, Derrida says that it was never a question of eliminating the subject. For Lacan, Althusser, and Foucault, for example, "the subject is perhaps reinterpreted, resituated, reinscribed, it is certainly not liquidated" (p. 348, citing *Après le sujet qui vient?*). He goes on to discuss recent efforts to rethink the subject by those "who might say... what we mean by 'subject' is not absolute origin, pure will, self-identity or the self-presence of consciousness, but rather this noncoincidence with self". We may, he says, ask: "By what right may this be called a subject?" But, on the other hand, "by what right may we forbid this to be called a subject?" He goes on to explain that he is talking about "those who want to reconstruct, today, a discourse on the subject that has no longer the form of self-mastery, of self-adequation, center and origin of the world, etc., but which would rather define the subject as the finite experience of non-self-identity, of the inderivable interpellation that comes from the other, from the trace of the other" (cited p. 349).

[29] Christina Howells, "Conclusion: Sartre and the Deconstruction of the Subject", in Christina Howells (ed.), *The Cambridge Companion to Sartre* (Cambridge: Cambridge University Press, 1992), 318–52. References will be given in the text.

Howells is amazed at this statement: "it is extraordinary to see what could well be a description of the subject of *Being and Nothingness* envisaged as a possible attempt to come to terms with the subject in a way that does not fall short of the work already carried out by deconstruction" (p. 349).

Howells makes an excellent case that Sartre's subject is seriously different from the classical Cartesian or Husserlian subject that sustains the metaphysics of presence. She is right that its intrinsic self-division and non-identity call for comparison with Derridian *différance* and that there is something puzzling in Derrida's avoidance of this comparison. But there are still aspects of Sartre's account that do not sit well with Derrida's position and suggest a (perhaps more sophisticated) version of the metaphysics of presence. True, Sartre's consciousness is fissured, separated from itself, "is what it is not and is not what it is", a status that clearly distinguishes it from the steady presence of Kant's or Husserl's transcendental ego. Nonetheless, this inner negation is the source of the nothingness whereby it constitutes all the meaning there is in the world. Sartre has substituted negative instability for positive structure, but the function of consciousness remains that of bringing intelligibility to an otherwise senseless world. The *pour-soi* is, as many have noted—and Sartre no doubt learned from Jean Wahl—a human unhappy consciousness, as conflicted and torn as Hegel's spirit prior to the stage of absolute knowledge but just as much master of its domain. Out of the division of consciousness comes the unity of the world.

Truly irreducible otherness for Sartre comes from the Other—the existence of other consciousnesses. Here Deleuze offers a perceptive reading of what Sartre has and has not achieved.[30] In one sense, he says, "Sartre is here the precursor of structuralism, for he is the first to have considered the Other as a real structure or specifically irreducible to the object and the subject". Although the Other is an object within "my" perceptual field, it also escapes from this field by its perceived ability to assert itself as a subject and make me an object. At the same time, it is "subjectivity" and is (like mine) open to objectification by rival subjects. This is why Deleuze says that "Sartre's theory in *Being and Nothingness* is the first great theory of the Other, because it transcends the [exclusive] alternative of being either an object or a subject".

But, Deleuze points out, Sartre "fell back into the categories of object and subject" when he defined the structure of the Other in terms of the look, a subject-centered event if ever there was one. The Other "constitutes me as an object when he looks at me", just as I constitute the Other as a object by looking at him. There is no structure of Otherness, for Sartre, outside of the domain of the look, which means that his account of the Other is in the end based on the constituting activity of the subject. A truly structuralist account—one that decisively broke with the metaphysics of presence—would show how "the structure Other precedes the look", while the look itself merely "marks the moment at which *someone* happens to fill the structure". To break

[30] Gilles Deleuze, *The Logic of Sense*, tr. M. Lester and C. Stivale (New York: Columbia University Press, 1990), 366 n. 12. All citations here are from this passage.

decisively with a metaphysics of subjective presence, we must show how "the look brings about only the effectuation or the actualization of a structure which must nonetheless be independently defined". Because Sartre has no way of independently defining this structure—precisely because he is committed to the existentialist assumption that all structure is constituted by consciousness—his account remains based in the presence of a subject.

Derrida and Sartre: later ambivalence

After many years of offering mainly casual sneers at Sartre, Derrida finally dealt with him at length and with characteristic subtlety—but also considerable diffuseness, vagueness, and ambivalence. This was in a piece he wrote, sixteen years after Sartre's death, for the fiftieth anniversary issue of *Les Temps modernes*, the journal Sartre had founded in 1946. Perhaps disappointingly, Derrida does not engage directly with the obviously philosophical writings; we get no Derridean dissection of the central concepts and theses of *Being and Nothingness* or the *Critique of Dialectical Reason*—the books are scarcely mentioned. Instead, he focuses on Sartre's initial "Presentation" of *Les Temps modernes* in its first issue, a kind of manifesto in which Sartre puts forth the motivation and goals for his journal.

Avoiding even the appearance of a standard essay, the piece presents itself as a long letter to Claude Lanzmann, the current editor of *Les Temps modernes*, apologizing for Derrida's failure to submit an article he had not quite promised ("I had . . . promised to try") for the anniversary issue. To the letter (written, he insists, while traveling and in difficult circumstances) Derrida appends what he describes as "some notes" he had made for the never completed article. These—and even much of the material in the "letter"—are a bit of a jumble, disconnected and underdeveloped. Nonetheless, what Derrida sent Lanzmann constitutes a substantial reaction to the journal and, especially, to Sartre as a major figure in Derrida's background as a writer and a thinker. The result is a subtle, personal, and ambivalent close reading, which, although not a genuinely philosophical engagement with Sartre's thought, still tells us something about why there was no such engagement.

We can find the ambivalence in what may well have been Derrida's first encounter with Sartre, when, as a 17-year-old student in the *classe de philosophie*, he read Sartre's first novel, *Nausea*. He recalls reading it

> in a certain ecstatic dazzlement . . . seated on a bench in Laferrière Square, looking up every so often at the tree roots, the flowering shrubs, or the thick-leaf plants, as if to verify the excess of their existence, but also with intense surges [*mouvements*] of 'literary' identification: how to write like that and, above all, how not to write like that?[31]

[31] Jacques Derrida, "Il courait mort: salut, salut", *Les Temps modernes* 51 (1996), 16-17. Further references will be given in the text (my translations).

From the beginning, Sartre was the model that could not be a model.

Such ambivalence—in various forms—pervades the *Temps modernes* piece. Certainly, there is the celebratory tone of an anniversary greeting (addressed, however, primarily to the journal, not to its founder): "Long live *Les Temps modernes*! Greetings [*Salut*] to you! Yes, I would like to salute [*saluer*] your future—your future as *ours*" (p. 7). But scruples and qualifications immediately enter: does Derrida have the right to say "ours" with Sartre's journal when "in a thousand ways I have never been, as they say, one of the *Temps modernes* group [*quelqu'un des* Temps modernes]". But still it would, he says, be "stupid" to conclude that he was "against *Les Temps modernes*"—"it is so much more complicated" (p. 8). Then, once Sartre is mentioned and a passage quoted from him, Derrida asks: "Why do I still love what he says . . . when I'm not always ready to go along with [*souscrire à*] it?" (p. 9). Later, after quoting a passage from Sartre (concluding "One must write for his own epoch, as all great writers have done"), Derrida says: "On reading this, as is almost always the case, I enter into [*partager*] and well understand [the text]; I even believe it—his feeling [*sentiment*]—as the truth of his desire. But I don't accept a single word of what he writes" (p. 32). This is typical of his reactions to Sartre: a deep sympathy and even affection, but total intellectual rejection. Writing the piece generates further levels of ambivalence. His close readings of Sartrean texts uncover complex connections and complexities; texts he finds outrageously wrong are contradicted by other texts; he finds himself insisting that he can do little more than list the topics and passages he would someday like to discuss in detail—leading to the exclamation: "It's necessary to reread everything!" (p. 42).

The need to reread Sartre is also the climax of a delightful self-parody, included in the "notes" appended to his letter to Lanzmann, where Derrida constructs an imaginary interview, in which he reduces himself to repetitive mumbling when challenged to say why he rejects Sartre.

> INTERVIEWER: "In spite of your eloquently stated admiration and the amicable gratitude you express in so many ways, you are still not ready to follow Sartre . . . What are the reasons? Can you finally say why you remain so reserved on this point, despite your claim—made with such insistence and conviction—of your closeness and solidarity?"
>
> DERRIDA: "Uh . . . literature . . . but I've explained that elsewhere . . . "
>
> INTERVIEWER: "Really? Is that it? Sartre's literature?"
>
> DERRIDA: "Almost all his literature, except maybe *Nausea*, but especially literature and the experience of language *for* Sartre . . . His scholastic models and his rhetoric. . . . "
>
> INTERVIEWER: "And what else? Psychoanalysis?"
>
> DERRIDA: "Uh . . . yes, and philosophy . . . His scholastic models and his rhetoric, I've explained that elsewhere. But it's Sartre . . . philosophy . . . his scholastic models and his rhetoric, I've explained that elsewhere." [Then, finally] "I want to re-read him, to re-read everything differently." (p. 44)

Despite this overall impression of conflict, ambivalence, and a need to reread, Derrida's *Temps modernes* piece does offer, in its opening pages, some specific insight into his dissatisfaction with Sartre's humanism. In contrast to the thoroughly Heideggerian philosophical discussion in "The Ends of Man", Derrida here is concerned with questions of literary and, especially, political engagement. He starts with Sartre's declaration that "salvation [*salut*] is achieved on this earth, that it is of man as a whole by man as a whole, and that art is a meditation on life, not on death" (cited p. 11). Derrida claims (as he did in "The Ends of Man") that the humanism endorsed here—as well as in "Existentialism Is a Humanism"—is the same view that Sartre's character Roquentin dismantled in *Nausea*. "Sartre is sometimes this Roquentin," Derrida says, "and sometimes his most identifiable target" (p. 11). And, as Derrida notes, in the novel Roquentin himself "yields", in the final pages, to the vision of humanist salvation, anticipating the split, after 1945, between the Sartre who "denounced the discourse on the fraternity" of man and the Sartre who wanted "to *save* [*sauver*], to redeem [*racheter*], or, more precisely, deliver [*délivrer*]" man (p. 10).

Derrida, like Sartre, emphasizes the term "deliver", connecting it to Sartre's refusal, in his "Présentation", of the "antinomy", posed by contemporary political thought, between a socialist communitarianism that leads to the state's domination of individuals and a libertarian individualism that leads to the horrors of capitalism. Sartre asserts that "a man, even though his situation totally conditions him, can be a center of irreducible indetermination" and that this core of freedom can be maintained in the context of a new social order that is itself the outcome of individual free choices. "If society makes the person . . . the person makes society." For Sartre, the very idea of deliverance entails that those delivered are intrinsically free. As Derrida puts it: for Sartre "we can speak of 'deliverance' only when we refer to a being that is free and able to exercise its freedom [*capable de sa liberté*]" (p. 11).

What Derrida objects to is the idea that freedom has an absolute status that allows man's deliverance without having to come to terms with the antinomy between capitalist oppression and socialist totalitarianism. He sees an antinomy in Sartre's rejection of this antinomy. This is first because the antinomy is real and cannot be just declared invalid: "antinomy in the antinomy, antinomy without antinomy". But there is also an antinomy in Sartre's blithe assumption that he is authorized to speak for all of us on this matter, when, for example, he says "we, for our part, refuse to let ourselves be torn [*écarteler*] between the thesis and the antithesis", thereby speaking "in the name of a 'we' (a term worth another long letter) [that includes] himself and his heirs, whether or not they consent". Derrida suspects that it is precisely this antinomy, which Sartre "formulates and sharpens" while rejecting totalitarianisms of both the right and the left, that we need to avoid totalitarianism. This very antinomy is one of Sartre's achievements to which Derrida says he would "like to think of himself as the heir". But Sartre's rejecting it makes him worry that Sartre "risks paving the way for totalitarianism" masking as "a soteriology of deliverance" (p. 14).

Having expressed his reservations about Sartrean deliverance or saving (*salut*), Derrida briefly turns, in a more appreciative mood, to the scene near the end of *Nausea* ("this great work of fiction . . . which I still admire") where Roquentin listens "for the last time" to a favorite recording of "Some of these Days" and sees the composer and the singer as "saved" from death by their art. Here, Derrida says, he is not trying "to advance anything that counts [*compte*], in itself or for itself, but just to awaken what, by a dizzying metonymy, could be called 'the voice of Sartre'" (pp. 14–15). Toward the end of his sensitive appreciation, he notes with approval the tentative language ("as if", "perhaps") that Sartre introduces to characterize claims about the death and salvation of the Jew and the Negress who wrote and performed the song. He says that this language gives a certain tentative, "spectral" characterization of death—and, by implication, of life. This, he thinks, fruitfully "complicates" if it does not entirely "ruin" Sartre's later troubling claim that historical epochs have an "absolute life" that is "always right as long as it exists" (p. 17). But Derrida's efforts to develop this point, which takes up most of the rest of his "letter", collapse under the complexities of the analyses for which he can here do little more than gather the materials, by quoting key Sartrean texts and underlying crucial terms that he would someday like to discuss *in extenso*. For better or worse, he never got beyond the disjointed ambivalence of this response.

What might have been?

The banality of the inevitable Oedipal take on Sartre's rejection by the 1960s generation does not undermine its fundamental truth. Sartre was such a powerful figure in French philosophy after the war that the new wave of philosophers needed drastic action to maintain their individuality. But there were other factors that made marginalizing him a viable response. His separation from the university world left him without an institutional basis for winning disciples, and his political and literary activities put much of his effort out of the realm of academic philosophy. His dogged commitment to an increasingly questionable Communist Party in the early 1950s, followed by his much more nuanced but increasingly *démodé* endorsement of Marxism, also alienated students who were moving in other, often more radical, political directions. The unfashionable topic of *The Critique of Dialectical Reason* (1960) made the garrulous complexity of the book much more of an obstacle than it would otherwise have been. Also, despite his moves toward a position compatible with a good dose of structuralism, the early existentialism that had made him famous was the perfect whipping boy for the attack on subjectivity. There is really no surprise that the new generation could and did turn its back on him.

How much was lost by this is hard to say. I have argued against Howells's strong claim that Sartre anticipates much of the new anti-humanist turn, so I do not think the basic projects of Foucault, Derrida, and Deleuze would have been enhanced by deeper engagement with another great mind moving in the same direction. At the same time, I think there is some truth to the picture of Sartre moderating his strong existentialism and Foucault and Derrida modifying, in the opposite direction, their strong anti-subjectivism, thereby converging to a suitably more complex, nuanced, and—in some sense—truer position. And the thought that Sartre and his younger friends might have had lively but civil and profitable exchanges is humanly satisfying. But it is by no means obvious that convergence to the mean, no matter how solidly golden, is the best path to philosophical progress. It may be that great thinkers are more valuable when they are pushing "crazy" ideas to the limit than when they are toning them down for the sake of correctness. If truth is the goal of philosophy, then perhaps the disciples and the commentators, with more care and common sense than sheer creative genius, are the ones meant to attain it. Since there are many more of us and we have, as a group, much more time, it may well have been for the best that Sartre and his unruly children never made peace.

5

How They All Are Nietzscheans

We have seen how the French philosophers of the 1960s seek something like Hegelian results (accounts of history that give us some sort of ethical political guidance) by something other than Hegelian means. This is why they are anti-Hegelian but also—since, as Hegel showed us, opposition recognizes and so legitimates—Hegelian. We have also seen how these philosophers typically develop their ideas through encounters with other thinkers. This chapter suggests that Nietzsche has a special role in the efforts of Foucault, Deleuze, and Derrida to plot an anti-Hegelian course. In this sense, they are "all Nietzscheans", which is not to say that they are nothing else nor, especially, to say that they all engage with the same Nietzsche. But, for each of these philosophers, there is a Nietzsche who is the primary historical antecedent to his anti-Hegelianism, a privileged lens through which to view his philosophical orientation.

Deleuze's Nietzschean confrontation with Hegel

Deleuze shares what he sees as Nietzsche's fundamental opposition to Hegelianism: "What I most detested was Hegelianism and dialectics."[1] He rejects the view of some commentators that Nietzsche knew little of Hegel and was not especially concerned with his thought. "We have every reason to suppose that Nietzsche had a profound knowledge of the Hegelian movement, from Hegel to Stirner".[2] Admittedly, Hegel's name is not often mentioned in Nietzsche's texts, but Deleuze maintains that his importance is evident from the "apologetic or polemical directions of [Nietzsche's] work itself". Indeed, "We will misunderstand the whole of Nietzsche's work if we do not see 'against whom' its principal concepts are directed. Hegelian themes are present in this work as the enemy against which it fights" (p. 162). "Anti-Hegelianism runs through Nietzsche's

[1] Gilles Deleuze, *Negotiations: 1972–1990*, tr. Martin Joughin (New York: Columbia University Press, 1995), 6.

[2] Gilles Deleuze, *Nietzsche and Philosophy*, tr. Hugh Tomlinson (New York: Columbia University Press, 1983), 162. Further references will be given in the text.

work as its cutting edge" (p. 8). On Deleuze's reading, Nietzsche's attack focuses on Hegelian dialectic: "we must take seriously the resolutely anti-dialectical character of Nietzsche's philosophy" (p. 8). Deleuze presents Nietzsche's critique in terms of his theory of forces. This theory, in turn, he explains in terms of Nietzsche's general project: to introduce "the concepts of sense and value into philosophy".

Nietzsche agrees with Kant that the project of philosophy must be critique but is convinced that Kant himself (and those who followed him—especially Hegel) did not push the project far enough and in fact produced only "a new conformism and new forms of submission" (p. 1). Deleuze first puts Nietzsche's project of critique in terms of a philosophy of values. Here Nietzsche's great idea is that we need to reverse the standard relation between values and evaluations. We typically think of values as given principles that are the basis for evaluating "phenomena". But in fact "it is values which presuppose evaluations, 'perspectives of appraisal', from which their own value is derived" (p. 1). We might say, the value of values depends on the value of the evaluation that produces it. But here the "values" of evaluation are not really values but "ways of being, modes of existence of those who judge and evaluate" (p. 1). Think of it this way: someone claims that a given practice (for example, democracy) is good, that is, it conforms to some pre-given standard of value (for example, freedom). The idea is that we should all agree that freedom is a value and that, as such, it grounds the evaluation of democracy as good; that is, we can show that democracy is good by showing that it promotes freedom. Nietzsche, though, points out that this case for democracy simply assumes the value of freedom itself, an assumption that is grounded in nothing other than our evaluation of freedom as good. The basic point seems to be that values have no objective, simply given status; they depend on our positive attitude, our "approval" of them, and so have some sort of non-cognitive status. But Nietzsche goes on to claim that evaluations themselves can be assessed—as "base" or "noble", for example. Base/noble (or high/low) "are not values but represent the differential element from which the value of values themselves derives" (p. 2).

Deleuze illustrates Nietzsche's point in terms of the standard Kantian and utilitarian moralities. Kant accepts certain moral actions (for example, truth telling) as simply valuable in their own right; the utilitarian sees (generally the same) actions as valuable for everyone (desired by all). In both cases, the moralist is "indifferent" to the origin of our acceptance (evaluation) of the value. The Kantian claims that this acceptance has nothing to do with the value's being valuable, the utilitarian finds the acceptance relevant but just a matter of "a simple causal derivation" (it is valuable because we all value it). Neither allows any room for critical inquiry into the specific historical roots of our evaluation (acceptance of a value). Nietzsche's project for a genealogy of morality is precisely an insistence on such an inquiry. We need, he claims, to look at what mode of being or existence leads us to accept certain values. Depending on whether this mode of being is "noble" or "base", we will judge the values as worthy or not.

Deleuze emphasizes that genealogy as critique is not an essentially negative enterprise. Of course, it will reject certain values as "unworthy", but this is not an expression of mere rejection (a matter of "revenge, grudge, or *ressentiment*"). It is not a matter of merely saying no, a reaction to a positive evaluation. Rather, it is "the active expression of an active mode of existence" (p. 3). It is critical only because it is first *creative*.

On Deleuze's reading, Nietzsche gives evaluation priority over values, but he does not fall into a relativity of evaluations. Some evaluations are better than others (nobler, higher) because they express superior modes of existence. But in virtue of what are some evaluations better? Nietzsche cannot appeal to values (objective givens) to support such claims, since he denies that there are any such values. But neither can he simply cite his own evaluation of the mode of existence that leads to a certain evaluation, since this would directly raise the question of the value of the mode of existence that leads to this meta-evaluation, and lead to an infinite regress in evaluations of evaluations. Deleuze never raises this obvious question, but his implicit response seems to be that the superiority of a given mode of existence (and hence of the evaluations to which it gives rise) is grounded in the values that are created in the very act of critique. Genealogical critique is creative, and what it creates are the values that sustain its preference for certain evaluations. As Deleuze says, "Nietzsche has high expectations of this conception of genealogy: a new organization of the sciences, a new organization of philosophy, a determination of the values of the future" (p. 3).

Nietzsche's genealogy concerns both values and sense (meaning); it not only evaluates but also interprets. Interpretation is the means by which genealogy arrives at evaluations. Nietzsche sees everything we encounter (all "phenomena") as in the grip of various forces, and these forces determine the sense (meaning) of the phenomena. "We will never find the sense of something . . . if we do not know the force which appropriates the thing, which exploits it, which takes possession of it or is expressed in it" (p. 3). Phenomena are not appearances (of underlying essences) but *signs* of the forces that produce them. Further, the sense (meaning) of signs is pluralistic—and in two ways. The senses of phenomena change over time, as different complexes of forces struggle for control over them, and, at any given time, the same phenomenon will have different senses. "There is no event, no phenomenon, word or thought which does not have a multiple sense" (p. 4).

But this pluralism does not imply a relativism. We can, in fact, still speak of the *essence* of a phenomenon. "The thing itself is not neutral and will have more or less affinity with the force in current possession . . . Essence . . . will be defined as that one, among all the senses of a thing, which gives it the force with which it has the most affinity" (p. 4). Accordingly, interpretation—the art of weighing the various possible senses of a phenomenon and deciding which it most accords with—is a fundamental task of philosophy. In the case of religion, for example, "Nietzsche asks which force gives religion the chance of acting 'in its own right and as *sovereign*" (199 n. 4, citing *Beyond Good and Evil*, sect. 62).

To say that the thing (phenomenon) is not neutral is to say that "it itself is force, expression of force". Consequently, the forces acting on things are acting on other forces. "Nietzsche's concept of force is therefore that of a force which is related to another force" (p. 7). There is no question of forces acting on essentially inert objects (for example, "on muscles or nerves, still less on 'matter in general'" (p. 7)). It is at this point that Nietzsche introduces his notion of will (will to power), which he defines as precisely a force that acts on (or is acted on by) another force. In contrast to Schopenhauer—and in accord with his fundamental pluralism—he insists that there is a plurality of wills (forces acting on one another). There is a hierarchy of wills, expressing which dominate and which are dominated. Genealogy begins with interpretation, the discovery of sense; that is, of a thing's "relation to the force [will] which takes possession of it". Once a phenomenon is interpreted, genealogy examines the domination relations of the forces that constitute it, seeing the extent to which its own forces dominate or are dominated by other forces. This leads to a genealogical *evaluation* of the phenomenon. Roughly, the idea is that a phenomenon has value to the extent that its own forces are dominant.

Although Deleuze insists that Nietzsche is an arch anti-Hegelian, we may wonder why his struggle of forces for domination is not a form of dialectic. Deleuze's response is that, contrary to dialectic, there is no essential role for negation in Nietzschean struggle: "the essential relation of one force to another is never conceived of as a negative element in the essence." A dominating force does "make itself obeyed", but in so doing it does not "deny the other" forces; it simply "affirms its own difference and enjoys this difference" (p. 8). In Hegel's dialectic, by contrast, an active (affirming) force must always be synthesized with an opposing reactive force. As we will see shortly, Hegel's master–slave dialectic is a paradigm example of the essential place of reactive force in his dialectic.

Here we arrive, in the context of his reading of Nietzsche, at the central point of Deleuze's critique of Hegel (already apparent, as we saw, in his 1954 review of Hyppolite's *Logic and Existence*): difference must be understood as an affirmation of itself, not as a negation of some other. A force (or will) is *different* to the extent that it actively asserts itself, not to the extent that it negates some other force. Retrospectively, we can, of course, say that a dominating force has overcome and in that sense negated the force that it dominates. But this contrast between the dominant and the subjected force does not express the essential nature of the dominant force. The negative concept of the force "is only a subsequently-invented pale contrasting image in relation to its positive basic concept—filled with life and passion through and through" (p. 9, citing *Genealogy of Morality*, i. 10). We might put it this way: whereas the driving power of Hegel's dialectic is negation, the driving power of Nietzsche's play of forces is affirmation; and, whereas for Hegel affirmation (synthesis) is a by-product of an essentially negative power, for Nietzsche negation is the by-product of an essentially affirmative power. As Deleuze puts it, "for the speculative element of negation, opposition or contradiction Nietzsche substitutes the practical element of difference, the object of affirmation and enjoyment" (p. 9).

Deleuze contrasts the "empiricism" of Nietzsche's view to the "rationalism" of Hegel's. First, Nietzsche's empiricism is pluralistic because it accepts the irreducible conflict of forces that results in hierarchical subordination, in contrast to Hegel's unification of opposing elements in a higher synthesis. Second, Nietzsche's empiricism is based on the immediacy of feeling, in contrast to Hegel's mediation through reflective thought: "the empirical feeling of difference, in short hierarchy, is the essential motor of the concept, deeper and more effective than all thought about contradiction" (p. 9).

From Nietzsche's standpoint, Hegel's dialectic is itself an example of forces dominated by other forces. It is "the speculation of the pleb, the way of thinking of the slave", in which "the abstract thought of contradiction . . . prevails over the concrete feeling of positive difference, reaction over action, revenge and *ressentiment* take the place of aggression [positive self-assertion]" (p. 10). Hegel, of course, has a famous analysis of the master–slave relation as dialectical, so it might seem odd that Nietzsche would try to criticize Hegel for thinking in terms of this relation. Nietzsche's point, however, is that the master–slave relation appears to be dialectical only from the perspective of the slave, who sees the dominance of a force (will to power) as a matter of its representation in a way that wins the recognition of others. Such recognition fits the dialectical schema, since it is a matter of two opposites, master and slave, coming together in mutual recognition (the master recognizes the value of the slave and the slave delights in this recognition). But this positive evaluation is based on already "established values" (p. 10), which means that it expresses the slave's (and the master's) domination by those values, not the creative self-affirmation of new values. Correspondingly, Hegel's dialectical thinking is just a way of accepting the established values (artistic, religious, political) of contemporary society. Dialectical thinking merely reacts to what it is given and does not actively affirm its own power.

The weakness of dialectical thinking derives from its abstraction, which cuts it off from the concreteness required for effective production: "Opposition can be the law of the relation between abstract products, but difference is the only principle of genesis or production" (p. 157). Hegel, of course, argued that it is empiricism—based on sense certainty—that is an empty abstraction. But Nietzsche's empirical phenomena are not the bare, unanalyzable particulars of traditional sense-data empiricism; they have a rich historically developed content (the forces constituting them) that is open to genealogical investigation and interpretation. Moreover, this content cannot be exhausted through a dialectic that "flattens" it into what can be consistently combined with its opposite in a higher synthesis. At the same time, Nietzschean phenomena do not fall into the abyss of ineffability. They cannot be expressed by the abstract resources of dialectic, but they can be expressed by the interpretative evaluations of genealogy.[3]

One of Nietzsche's most concrete criticisms of Hegel is his assimilation of Hegelian unhappy consciousness to the bad conscience of his own *The Genealogy of Morality*. Anticipating Jean Wahl's interpretation, Nietzsche, according to Deleuze, thinks "the discovery dear to the dialectic is the unhappy consciousness, the deepening, the

[3] For an excellent discussion of Deleuze's empiricism as a challenge to Hegelian dialectic, see Bruce Baugh, *French Hegel* (London: Routledge, 2003), 154–6.

resolution and glorification of the unhappy consciousness" (p. 159). Indeed, "unhappy consciousness is the subject of the whole dialectic" p. (196). But what is unhappy consciousness except the triumph of "reactive forces that express themselves in opposition" (p. 159)? The unhappiness of the unhappy consciousness consists precisely in its feelings of alienation and incompleteness because it desires to be something that it is not and cannot be, because, in other words, it defines itself in terms of something it is not. Such nihilistic thinking is "a fundamentally Christian way of thinking", trapped in an endless cycle of self-questioning and self-reproach, "powerless to create new ways of thinking and feeling" (p. 159).

To this the Hegelian response would no doubt be that Nietzsche ignores the significance of the final stage of absolute knowledge, in which the divisions that torment the unhappy consciousness are revealed as due to a limited, incomplete stage of consciousness that is unaware of the fundamental identity of the "divided" elements. As Deleuze says, "we are informed, in the Hegelian manner, that man and God, religion and philosophy, are reconciled" (p. 158). But, he goes on to ask, "what is this reconciliation if not the old complicity, the old affinity of will to nothingness and reactive life?" (p. 159). The dialectician (here Deleuze has Feuerbach as much as Hegel in mind) tells us that "God becomes Man, Man becomes God" (p. 158). But such syntheses ignore the underlying fact that Man and God still remain what they have always been: Man "is always the reactive being, the representative, the subject of a weak and depreciated life". God "is always the supreme Being as the means of depreciating life" (p. 158). Dialectic can interchange or intermix these two concepts, but it cannot escape from the essential negativity of their content, their reactive denial of life's self-affirmation. The practical proof of Hegel's failure is his ready acceptance of the established values of society: his "dialectic was quick to be reconciled with religion, Church, State. . . . We know what the famous Hegelian transformations mean: they do not forget to preserve piously" (p. 161). It is, then, no surprise that "Nietzsche never stops attacking *the theological and Christian character of German philosophy* (the 'Tubingen seminary')" (p. 162, emphasis in original).

At this point Deleuze's exposition of Nietzsche's anti-Hegelianism converges with the anti-humanism of 1960s French philosophy. At the deepest level, Nietzsche's objection to Hegel is that he provides no way of overcoming Man, who remains in his essence a merely reactive being. Deleuze emphasizes that, although there are ambivalences and complexities in Nietzsche's treatment of "the higher man" (in *Zarathustra* IV), in the end his position is that even man at his "highest" (most active) remains captive to the reactive forces of negation. "Nietzsche presents the triumph of reactive forces as something essential to man and history" (p. 166). Admittedly, "even the history of man seems to include active periods", such as Greece (before Socrates), Rome, and the Renaissance, and "Zarathustra sometimes evokes his true men and announces that his reign is also the reign of man". But "each time that Nietzsche speaks of active men, he does so with the sadness of seeing the destiny to which they are predetermined as their essential becoming"—their inevitable overthrow by reactive forces such as Socratic theory, Pauline Christianity, and the Reformation. At first "men's activity appears to be generic [essential to their kind]" with "reactive forces... grafted onto it, perverting it from its course". But "more deeply, what is truly generic is the becoming reactive of all [human] forces" (p. 167). Even in his highest forms, Man is doomed to reactive failure. "The product itself is botched, not because of accidents which happen to it, but because of its nature, because of the kind of goal that it is" (p. 168).

Hegelian dialectic is nothing other than the movement of this failure. "The movement of reappropriations, dialectical activity, is nothing more or less than the becoming-reactive *of* man and *in* man" (p. 168, emphasis in original). By contrast, Nietzsche's Overman must not, Deleuze insists, be understood as "a man who surpasses himself" but as the destruction and replacement of man. This destruction is, however, not driven by negation but by affirmation, the affirmation of the Overman's creative difference for its own sake, which, in its sheer positivity, sweeps away the reactive negation of the human, all-too-human. "Affirmation is only manifested above man, outside man, in the Overman which it produces and in the unknown that it brings with it" (p. 177).

This mention of "the unknown" refers to a central feature of the "transmutation" from Man to Overman. What is knowable—that is, what falls under the concepts of dialectic—remains merely human, trapped in the web of unhappy consciousness. The move to the Overman is a matter not of knowing but of being (*ratio cognoscendi* vs *ratio essendi*), where "being" means creative affirmation, in which the legislator replaces the scholar and "creation takes the place of knowledge itself" (p. 173). This is not, however, a falling-back into the unthinkable, the ineffable that Hegel rightly criticized. It is, rather, a new way of thinking that does not receive (represent) what is given to it but is the creation of what it thinks. For Nietzsche, thinking is "not affirmation as acceptance but as creation; not man but the Overman as a new form of life" (p. 185).

Deleuze emphasizes Nietzsche's connection of affirmation to his doctrine of the eternal return. Commentators typically distinguish between a metaphysical and an ethical sense of eternal return in Nietzsche. Metaphysically, return would mean the literal recurrence (repetition) in the future of what has happened in the past. Some of Nietzsche's unpublished speculations based on the science of his day suggest such a view, but it seems ultimately ungrounded either in Nietzsche's published texts or in empirical science. Ethically, affirming eternal return says nothing about what will in fact happen in the future but is rather a commitment to the permanent value of our present life (in opposition, in particular, to religious subordinations of this life to a supernatural afterlife). To affirm eternal return is to endorse our present existence to the extent of being willing to live it over and over again.

Deleuze's reading suggests a third interpretation that maintains but transforms both the metaphysical and the ethical views. First of all, Deleuze insists that "there is no return of the negative.... Only that which affirms or is affirmed returns" (p. 189). But what is it to affirm? "Affirmation is the enjoyment and play of its own difference" (p. 188), where difference is understood not in the Hegelian sense of opposition or negation but in the Nietzschean (and Deleuzian) sense of "multiplicity, becoming, and change" (p. 189). Hegel's dialectic reflects on difference but in a way that inverts its true sense. "For the affirmation of difference as such it substitutes the negation of that which differs; for the affirmation of the self it substitutes the negation of the other, and for the affirmation of affirmation it substitutes the famous negation of the negation" (p. 196).

To understand Nietzchean–Deleuzian difference, we must stop thinking of difference as a matter of being essentially *other than* or *opposed to*. Difference is instead a matter of positive multiplicity, of overflowing diversity. As such, difference endlessly "repeats" itself, but here repetition cannot mean reproduction of the same, since such reproduction would destroy the very difference of difference. The repetition (return) of difference must, therefore, involve radical novelty, not the mere recurrence of the same.

Here Deleuze is proposing a quite novel concept of repetition, treating it not as a matter of something's conforming to (resembling) a previous state—of itself or of something else—but rather of something's effecting a new expression of its reality. On this view, to repeat is not to duplicate what I have been but to become something new that is, nonetheless, still me. Repetition would no longer be a matter of qualitative resemblance or quantitative equivalence; not, that is, a matter of replacing something with something else that is equivalent to it. Rather, it would be a matter of something that is irreducibly singular producing a novel version of itself.[4]

Understood in terms of this new concept of repetition, Nietzsche's eternal return has both metaphysical and ethical significance. Affirming the "return" of difference is a practical or ethical endorsement (evaluation) of difference, but it is also an assertion of the unending creativity of difference, which, once negation has been overcome, will express itself in an eternal series of ever-new affirmations of itself. "It is in the nature of affirmation to return or of difference to reproduce itself" (p. 189).

One can readily quarrel with what can seem to be Deleuze's imposition of a systematic metaphysics on Nietzsche's aphoristic texts, particularly since his interpretation often relies on the enigmatic poetry of *Zarathustra* and the fragments of works he never finished or published that others gathered into the non-book entitled *The Will to Power*. But the interest of the Nietzsche book for us is its adumbration of Deleuze's own anti-Hegelian ontology. In keeping with Deleuze's pluralism, he offers many other ways of formulating this ontology, first through complementary interpretations of Hume, Spinoza, Leibniz, and Bergson—all major figures outside the ambit of critical and dialectical philosophy. In his two great books of the 1960s, *Difference and Repetition* and *The Logic of Sense*, Deleuze undertook more direct formulations of the same fundamental ontology, and other works developed various aspects of his "system" through analyses of art, literature, and film. His massive collaborations with Félix Guattari (*Anti-Oedipus* and *A Thousand Plateaus*) developed his thought in social, economic, and political terms. All these efforts combine to offer a direct challenge to

[4] I will develop this reading of Deleuze more fully in Chapter 10.

Hegel's thought on its own ground of a comprehensive metaphysical account. As we shall see, Foucault and Derrida are more circuitous in coming to terms with Hegel.

Foucault, Nietzsche, genealogy

Foucault published only one extended treatment of Nietzsche, an essay on the project of genealogy, which appeared in a collection posthumously honoring Jean Hyppolite.[5] This essay is modeled on the traditional French pedagogical assignment of a close *explication de texte*, which make it a distinctly appropriate means of honoring Foucault's former teacher, but should also warn us against taking it as simply a manifesto of what Foucault himself meant by genealogy.[6] But reading the essay in the context of Foucault's own practice of genealogy can provide considerable insight into his own views. In particular, it can show us how Foucault finds genealogy an alternative to Hegelian dialectic.

The anti-Hegelian perspective shows up immediately in Foucault's opening insistence on the "relentless erudition" (p. 370) required of genealogical studies. Precisely because of its commitment to "gray, meticulous, and patiently documentary" research "on a field of entangled and confused parchments" (p. 369), "genealogy does not oppose itself to history as the lofty and profound gaze of the philosopher might compare to the molelike perspective of the scholar". Quite the contrary, says Foucault, genealogy "rejects the meta-historical deployment of ideal significations and indefinite teleologies. It opposes itself to the search for 'origins'" (p. 370). Here we have an implicit rejection at the outset of Hegel's effort to provide a *teleological* account in terms of a dialectic of *ideal meanings* that provides a philosophical account of the *origins* of historical realities.

In his second section, Foucault presents a Nietzschean distinction between two senses of "origin": *Ursprung* (which Foucault continues to call "origin") versus *Herkunft* (which he calls "descent"). Although Nietzsche sometimes uses the terms interchangeably, in key passages, such as the preface to the *Genealogy of Morality*, he uses *Ursprung* to denote the "attempt to capture the exact essence of things, their purest possibilities, and their carefully protected identities"—an endeavor entirely at odds with Nietzschean genealogy, although quite in accord with Hegelian dialectic.

To *Ursprung* Nietzsche opposes *Herkunft*, which has connotations of social and even biological derivation. "It is the ancient affiliation to a group, sustained by bonds of blood, tradition, or social class" and "often involves a consideration of race or social type" (p. 373). In Nietzsche's use, however, according to Foucault, this sense of origin

[5] Michel Foucault, "Nietzsche, Genealogy, History", in *Essential Works of Foucault 1954–1984*, ed. Paul Rabinow, vol. ii, ed. James D. Faubion (New York: New Press, 1998), 369–91. References will be given in the text.

[6] See Gary Gutting, *Foucault: A Very Short Introduction* (Oxford: Oxford University Press, 2005), 43–4, for more on this point.

is not a "category of resemblance". In tracing back the social and biological roots of, for example, the German people, the genealogist does not find a "coherent identity" (the German soul or self) but rather a "dissociation of the Me" in "numberless beginnings". "Liberating a profusion of lost events", this diversity reveals the self or soul as an "empty synthesis" (p. 374). Contrary to Hegelian dialectic, genealogical *Herkunft* undoes apparent syntheses: "it fragments what was thought unified; it shows the heterogeneity of what was imagined consistent with itself." "What convictions", asks Foucault, "and, far more decisively, what knowledge can resist it?" (p. 375). Even, it would seem, the pretensions of absolute knowledge fall to genealogical analysis.

Herkunft cuts particularly against Hegelian idealism by taking the body as the locus of history: "the body—and everything that touches it: diet, climate, and soil—is the domain of the *Herkunft*". Nor is this body as *aufheben* by spirit. Genealogy treats the body in its weaknesses and failures ("in faulty respiration, in improper diets") and shows how these very defects led to the invention of "the contemplative life" and produced the "thinker and prophet" (p. 375).

The anti-Hegelian theme is particularly clear in Nietzsche's treatment of *Entstehung*—the "emergence, the moment of arising" (p. 376) of something new from its causes. Emergence is never a matter of a "struggle among equals" resulting in a dialectical unification of opposing forces. Rather, the struggle is between "adversaries [who] do not belong to a common space" (p. 377) and can end only in the domination of one force by another. Contrary to Hegelian reconciliation, "humanity does not gradually progress from combat to combat until it arrives at universal reciprocity, where the rule of law finally replaces warfare". Rather, "humanity installs each of its violences in a system of rules and thus proceeds from domination to domination". The sytheses and mediations of rational rules are, therefore, themselves instruments of violence: "rules are empty in themselves, violent and unfinished; they are impersonal and can be bent to any purpose" (p. 378).

Foucault makes the anti-Hegelian point explicit by evoking the central idealist concept of interpretation. "If interpretation were the slow exposure of the meaning hidden in an origin, then only metaphysics could interpret the development of humanity". But, if human history is to be thought of as a series of interpretations, then interpretation must be a matter of "the violent surreptitious appropriation of a system of rules, which in itself has no essential meaning" (p. 378). Genealogy is the history of interpretations in this sense. This will be "the history of morals, ideals, and metaphysical concepts, the concept of liberty or the ascetic life". But (in stark contrast to Hegelian dialectic), this history will be one of unending violent appropriations with no reconciling end but merely ever new "substitutions, displacements, disguised conquests, and systematic reversals", each designed to "impose a new direction, to bend . . . to a new will, to force . . . participation in a different game" (p. 378).

History in this genealogical sense, which Nietzsche calls "effective history" (*wirkliche Historie*) or "historical sense", differs from traditional history in three characteristics: discontinuity, chance, and perspective—all opposed to Hegelian features of traditional history. Traditional history "tries to compose the finally reduced diversity of time into a totality fully closed upon itself" by attaining a perspective "that implies the end of time, a completed development". It pretends, in other words, "to base its judgments on an apocalyptic objectivity". Effective history, however, "refuses the certainty of absolutes" and seeks a "dissociating view . . . capable of shattering the unity of man's being through which it was thought that he could extend his sovereignty to the events of his past" (p. 379). Accordingly, "history becomes 'effective' to the degree that it introduces discontinuity into our very being" and hence "deprives the self of the reassuring stability of life and nature". Its "knowledge is not made for understanding; it is made for cutting" (p. 380).

Next, effective history recognizes that "the forces operating in history do not obey destiny or regulative mechanisms, but the luck of the battle. . . . They always appear through the singular randomness of events. Traditional historians "confirm our belief that the present rests upon profound intentions and immutable necessities". But "the true historical sense confirms our existence among countless lost events, without a landmark or a point of reference" (p. 381).

Finally, whereas traditional historians "take unusual pains to erase the elements in their work which reveal their grounding in a particular time and place", Nietzsche's history "is explicit in its perspective" and admits that "its perception is slanted". It eschews the "discreet effacement" of neutrality and does not hesitate to prescribe its own "antidote" for what it sees as "poisonous traces". Effective history does not pretend to defer entirely to what it is studying but "gives equal weight to its own sight and to its objects" (p. 382). But acknowledging its perspective does not mean reducing it to a relativized common denominator with all other perspectives. Nietzsche (and, clearly, Foucault) insist that the studied neutrality of traditional history "in fact exhibit[s] a total lack of taste" and fails to distinguish between what is noble and what is base. In fact, the alleged "neutrality" belies "a certain crudity that tries to take liberties with what is most exalted, a satisfaction in meeting up with what is base". Efficient history, by contrast, is based on a proper sensitivity to "those things which should be repugnant" (p. 383) and what merits respect.

I have emphasized the anti-Hegelian elements of Foucault's explication of Nietzsche's genealogy. But skepticism toward the excesses of a philosophical view need not imply a philosophical counter-position, and we can plausibly read Foucault's employment of genealogy as a way of carrying out a historical project without philosophical baggage, corresponding to our earlier suggestion that Foucault avoids Hegelianism by avoiding philosophy. But in the final section of "Nietzsche, Genealogy, History", Foucault seems to move in a philosophical direction by associating genealogy with a counter-philosophy that would try to undermine traditional notions of reality, identity, and truth. This seems to go beyond a merely skeptical questioning of the need for Hegelian assumptions about dialectic and absolute knowledge to propose an alternative positive philosophical account.

Foucault on Deleuze

We might, of course, argue that these indications of substantive philosophical positions are merely part of Foucault's presentation of Nietzsche and that his own appropriation of genealogy has no need of such metaphysical support. Such a dismissal may well, in the end, be correct. But before we can go along with it, we need to notice another and much stronger indication that Foucault subscribes to a Nietzchean metaphysics. This is his apparent endorsement of Deleuzean ontology in his enthusiastic 1970 review of *The Logic of Sense* and *Difference and Repetition.*[7]

Foucault's essay explores a variety of "paths" into Deleuze's philosophy. I will follow just one, the Deleuzian transformation of the traditional understanding of the distinction between difference and repetition, which has close ties to what we have already seen of Deleuze's metaphysics in his study of Nietzsche.

Foucault starts from Deleuze's (Nietzschean) idea that every philosophy is a form of anti-Platonism (even Plato's own, he says, if we think of the self-critique of the *Sophist*). But Deleuze does not, like so many, oppose Plato merely "by reinstating the rights of appearances" as opposed to the essential Forms they imitate. On Deleuze's reading of Plato, the function of the Forms is to distinguish between two levels of appearances: the privileged appearances that more or less adequately represent the Forms (for example, the institutions of a just state) and the "false appearances" or "simulacra", which "submerge appearance and break its engagement to essence" (p. 345). Deleuze's radical anti-Platonism elevates not appearances in general but the simulacra themselves. It challenges, in the name of what Plato rejects as "false appearances", not only the Forms but also the appearances that share in their "solidity and meaning". Here, as Foucault puts it, "the sophist springs up, and challenges Socrates to prove that he is not the illegitimate usurper" (p. 345).

Deleuze associates the Platonic simulacrum with what he calls the *event*, the vehicle of his new conceptions of difference and repetition. True to the spirit of simulacra, these new conceptions derive from a challenge to the morality of "good will" and "good sense". This morality imposes a "pedagogical model" for which "every real problem has a solution" that will be apparent to anyone who is not stupid and works according to the rules we have learned for interrogating the world. Following this epistemological morality will lead to a consensus by which we come to "think 'in common'" with other men of good will and good sense. Foucault says that the "function" of this "disreputable morality . . . in our society is easy to decipher" and that we must "pervert . . . this morality" and "liberate ourselves from [its] constraints" (p. 355).

[7] Michel Foucault, "Theatrum Philosophicum", in *Essential Works of Foucault*, ii. 343–68. The enthusiasm is apparent from Foucault's opening declaration that, in virtue of these two books, "perhaps one day, this century will be known as Deleuzian" (p. 165). Further references will be given in the text.

The disreputable morality of good sense is based on a traditional view of difference as existing only in the context of a prior unity—the unity of a group within which we can distinguish differences that separate individuals that are, nonetheless, essentially the same. Differences exist only between things that fall under the same concept; they "must be specified within a concept, without overstepping the bounds" set by the concept. Different things are, therefore, repetitions of the same general concept. Good sense is a matter of putting each in its proper category and knowing the individual features that distinguish it from other examples of its kind. Priority is given to the general concept, and individuals are, with only relatively minor variations, repetitions of the concept. As Foucault sardonically puts it: "Underneath the ovine species, we are reduced to counting sheep" (p. 356).

But suppose we turn away from common sense and toward "the mad flux and anarchical difference" that lies outside the realm of shared concepts. "What if [thought] conceived of difference differentially, instead of searching out the common elements underlying difference"; that is, what if we treated difference in itself as primary and did not subordinate it to an underlying sameness? Then, Foucault says, difference would become "a pure event", a sheer differing within itself, not a secondary differentiation between things that are essentially the same. Correspondingly, repetition "would cease to function as the dreary succession of the identical, and would become displaced difference" (p. 356); that is, it would be a new and *different* expression of difference.

Deleuze's reconception of difference and repetition also involves a rejection of the epistemology of *representation*. On the traditional view, a concept can "master difference" because our perceptions "apprehend global resemblances" (p. 356) and thereby represent to the mind the common nature that corresponds to the concept. Then, only within the shared space of conceptual representation, we can distinguish different instances of the common nature. And, of course, "it is good sense that reigns in the philosophy of representation", as it "assimilates and separates" the individuals that fall under a given concept. Deleuze, Foucault points out with relish, calls on us to "pervert good sense" from this representationalist function "and allow thought to play outside the ordered table of resemblances". Such thought will be a play of "pure difference", that is, of the intensity of a singularity that "displaces and repeats itself"—not with the banality of repetition of the same but with the ever-renewing novelty of difference itself. Thought in this sense will be an "intensive irregularity" that, to come back to Foucault's recurring desire, will bring about the "dissolution of the Me" (p. 357).

It might seem that dialectics, with its emphasis on negation, provides a way out of representationalism's prioritization of sameness. But in fact, Foucault points out, "dialectics does not liberate differences" (p. 184). Negation is always a negation of the same, so that difference, understood as negation, always presupposes the same. Moreover, the operation of the dialectic always insures that no difference ever effects a "successful subversion of the Other" but is rather synthesized with it, thereby assuring "the salvation of identities" (p. 358).

The genuine "freeing of difference requires thought without contradiction, without dialectics, without negation" (p. 358). This means thinking in terms of affirmations that are different but not because they have conceptual contents that are denials of one another. They are, we might say (although Deleuze and Foucault do not use this language), *incommensurable affirmations*. Together, they constitute a multiplicity that cannot be analyzed and "resolved by the clear distinctions of a Cartesian idea" or by "the Hegelian negative". In short, we are dealing with events that escape "the logic of the excluded third" (either P or not-P). We are dealing with "a multiple affirmation" that "is not subject to the contradiction of being and non-being, since it is [simply] being" (p. 359).

At the deepest level, Deleuze's ontology of pure difference (free of negation) requires the elimination of all ontological categories, since, ultimately, it is these categories that allow us to differentiate things in negative terms (*a* is different from *b* because *a* is a C and *b* is not). Such categorical differentiations "establish the legitimacy of resemblances within representation, and guarantee the objectivity and operation of concepts". As such, "they suppress anarchic differences" (p. 359). To overcome this suppression, we must reject all ontological categories (different ways of being, as Aristotle said) and join Duns Scotus and Spinoza in asserting the radical univocity of being. However, Foucault notes that, unlike Scotus and Spinoza, for whom univocity is a way of maintaining the fundamental unity (sameness) of being, Deleuze identifies being with difference. As a result, he cannot reduce the univocity of being to, say, Scotus's general concept of being or Spinoza's unity of substance. For Deleuze, being is univocal because to say that something (some event) is is simply to say that it is a recurrence (repetition) of difference. To be different is the only way that something can be.

The penultimate paragraph of Foucault's review sums up what he takes to be the significance of these two books: "a lightening storm was produced which will, one day, be given the name of Deleuze: new thought is possible; thought is again possible" (p. 367). But how closely is this new thought tied to the new, genealogical histories Foucault proposes to write? The genealogist, we must remember, reads dusty manu-scripts line-by-line in order to tease out complexly intertwined micro-causes. This is due to a conviction that what he needs to know is in these highly localized details, not in any sweeping accounts of what things, in general, are, or should be, like.

Nonetheless, as we saw in our discussion of what led the young Foucault away from both Hegel and phenomenology, his intellectual work was motivated by a personal desire to perpetually throw off any fixed identity, always to become someone other than who he had been. Human experience as rendered by both Hegelian dialectic and phenomenological description merely reinforced the constraints of alleged essential structures. For an alternative he turned, even as a student, to two avant-garde literary figures, Georges Bataille and Maurice Blanchot, who then referred him to Nietzsche, who, "because of the way the Nazis had used him . . . was completely excluded from the academic syllabus".[8] "What struck me and fascinated me about those authors", Foucault tells us, "and what gave them their capital importance for me, was that their problem was not the construction of a system but the construction of a personal experience". Whereas "phenomenological work consists in unfolding the field of possibilities, related to everyday experience", the personal experiences constructed by Bataille, Blanchot, and Nietzsche are "limit-experiences" that "have the function of wrenching the subject from itself, of seeing to it that the subject is no longer itself, that it is brought to its annihilation or its dissolution". This is what Foucault calls "the project of desubjectivation" (p. 241), which informs all his books: "however boring, however erudite my books may be, I've always conceived of them as direct experiences aimed at pulling myself free of myself, at preventing me from being the same" (pp. 241–2).[9]

His passion for such extreme experiences certainly explains his affinity for Deleuze's metaphysics. At one point in "Theatrum Philosophicum", he even describes with vivid and meticulous strokes how LSD and opium (each, he explains, in its own distinctive way) can evoke an experience of a Deleuzian world. Nonetheless, limit-experiences themselves play little role in Foucault's books. The *topics* of these books are things associated with extreme experiences: madness, sickness and death, crime and punishment, sexuality. Even the apparently more sober topic of knowledge (in *The Order of Things*) deals with radical differences in fundamental frameworks of thought (as in Borges's fictional "Chinese encyclopedia", of which "we apprehend in one great leap . . . the stark impossibility of thinking *that*").[10] But, despite a certain amount of evocative prose (for example, in the original preface, later dropped, of *History of Madness*), the bulk of Foucault's discussion is about how (quite ordinary) people in various ages viewed madness, death, sex, not the actual limit-experiences of the mad, the dying, the sexually ecstatic. Since, according to Foucault, perceptions of madness and the like were, no longer ago than the eighteenth and nineteenth centuries, radically different from our own, his explications of these perceptions can help shake us out of the dogmatic doze that hides alternatives to our conventional ways of thinking. But such increased alertness to possibilities is far from the explosion of

[8] "Interview with Michel Foucault" (by D. Trombadori, 1978), in *Essential Works of Foucault 1954–1984*, ed. Paul Rabinow, vol. iii, ed. James D. Faubion (New York: New Press, 2000), 248. Further references will be given in the text.

[9] Even on a more mundane level, he expressed lack of interest in the ordinary pleasures of daily life: "I'm not able to give myself and others those middle-range pleasures that make up everyday life. Such pleasures are nothing for me and I not able to organize my life in order to make place for them. . . . A pleasure must be something incredibly intense. . . . Some drugs are really important for me because they are the mediation to those incredibly intense joys that I am looking for" ("Michel Foucault: An Interview by Stephen Riggins" (1982), in *Essential Works of Foucault 1954–1984*, ed. Paul Rabinow, vol. i, ed. Paul Rabinow (New York: New Press, 1997), 129). So it is not surprising, particularly given his desire for self-surpassing, that limit-experiences would be singularly important for him.

[10] Michel Foucault, *The Order of Things*, tr. A. Sheridan (New York: Random House, 1970), p. xv.

identity Foucault says he was seeking. Even if the process of writing his books had such an effect for him, this was not expressed in their contents.

Rather than evocations of limit-experiences, we typically find analyzes of the deep rational structures that Foucault eventually calls epistemes: conceptual systems underlying the thought and language of a given historical period. As we have seen, in his earlier works—up through *The Order of Things*—Foucault ignores questions about the transition from one system to another, restricting his discussion to the excavation of the implicit cognitive rules (hence his label, "the archaeology of knowledge"). After *The Order of Things*, beginning with *Discipline and Punish*, Foucault finally turned to questions about the diachronic, causal development of thought, questions he had earlier avoided because he found the standard ways of treating them—by evoking a broadly Hegelian "spirit of the times", Marxist references to technological and social changes or academic historians' appeals to intellectual influences—were "more magical than effective".[11] His rejection of the first two approaches also no doubt reflect his fear of slipping into the totalizing syntheses of the Hegelian system or similar "grand narratives". Eventually, however, Foucault developed, under the broad inspiration of Nietzsche, his genealogical method for explaining changes in ways of thinking.

This method, as we have seen, decisively escapes Hegelianism by insisting on explanations that are multiple, contingent, and corporeal. Epistemes shifted, Foucault claimed, not because of pervasive monolithic forces such as spirit's elimination of contradiction (or Marxist materialist equivalents), but because of the chance convergence of specific practical techniques for, for example, teaching children how to write, training soldiers in the use of their rifles, making factory workers more efficient producers. As a result, however, genealogy restricts itself to the relentlessly mundane experiences of daily life (handwriting, military drills, assembly lines), not the limit-experiences that connect to Deleuze's philosophy of radical difference.

Foucault's genealogical studies (*Discipline and Punish* and the first volume of his *History of Sexuality*) do work out of a view of power (schematically outlined in *History of Sexuality I*) that has clear affinities with the Deleuzian–Nietzschean metaphysics of differential forces. Like the fields of Nietzsche's forces and Deleuze's differences, Foucaultian power is a pluralistic, dispersed, non-dialectical complex in no way under the sway of any unifying principle of sameness. But Foucault need not—and does not—present this sketch as a counter-Hegelian ontology. Its function in his genealogical studies is strictly to delineate a topology of the *historical ground* that leaves no room for Hegelian, Marxist, or other unifying grand narratives. There is nothing in Foucault's genealogical projects that calls for an ontological construal of his remarks about power.

The essential point is that there is no connection in principle between Foucault's histories, which constitute the major part of his intellectual achievement, and the drive

[11] Foucault, *The Order of Things*, p. xiii.

toward limit-experiences that he tells us motivated his work. Deleuze's philosophy is an ontology of limit-experiences and, if Foucault's histories had a point only on the assumption that such experiences have a vital role in our lives, then his work would require a philosophical "certification" from a philosophy such as Deleuze's. But Foucault's histories have a point for anyone who thinks that: (i) there are unacceptable contemporary constraints on human actions; (ii) these constraints are in part due to ways of thinking that present themselves as inevitable but actually are not; and (iii) showing by historical investigation that these constraints are not inevitable helps remove them. There are various grounds for thinking that contemporary constraints (associated with, for example, psychiatry, clinical medicine, penal justice, and sexuality—to cite Foucault's main topics) are unacceptable. Foucault clearly thought that one major reason they were unacceptable was that they keep us from the limit-experiences needed to prevent us from falling into a fixed identity. But there are many other, less radical, reasons for objecting to the sorts of constraints that Foucault analyzes. The most domesticated liberals, for example, can invoke Foucault's histories to challenge what they view as unacceptable violations of human rights.

We can, accordingly, separate Foucault's work as a historian or genealogist from Deleuzian ontology. Foucault himself may have found this ontology philosophically compelling, and it certainly resonated with his personal predilection for limit-experiences. But he never went beyond his appreciation of Deleuze's work and occasional undeveloped hints (especially in his essays on literary figures such as Bataille, Blanchot, and Klossowski, and in some passages of *The Order of Things*) as to what a parallel Foucaultian ontology might look like. Moreover, the penultimate section of "Theatrum Philosophicum" suggests the dangers latent in an ontology of Deleuzian difference.

In this section Foucault notes that, once we move, as Deleuze urges us to, beyond the domain of categorical classifications, there are no longer criteria for judging our beliefs or actions correct or mistaken. We can, nevertheless, have a totally muddled view of things; we can, like Flaubert's clueless pair, Bouvard and Pécuchet, be *stupid*. "Within categories, one makes mistakes; outside of them, beyond or beneath them, one is stupid. Bouvard and Pécuchet are acategorical beings" (p. 361). (We might think here of the Wittgensteinian point that someone who claims, for example, that the sum of 21 and 23 is 41,557, can hardly be said to have "made a mistake" in addition.)

There is, therefore, a signal risk "in wanting to be free of categories; no sooner do we abandon them than we face the magma of stupidity". Specifically, "we risk being surrounded not by a marvelous multiplicity of differences, but by equivalences, ambiguities, the 'it all comes down to the same thing', a leveling uniformity" (p. 361), which Foucault compares to the thermodynamic heat-death of the universe. The hope, of course, is that this confrontation with stupidity, with its "lassitude, immobility, excessive fatigue, obstinate muteness, and inertia", will lead to a thought that "suddenly dissipates" (p. 362) it and presents us with "the shock of difference" (p. 363).

Foucault thinks Andy Warhol's art produces such an effect. His banal, repetitive forms begin by confronting us with a stupidity that says, "Here or there, it's always the same thing; what difference if the colors vary, if they're darker or lighter. It's all so senseless—life, women, death! How stupid this stupidity!". But then, Foucault says, "in concentrating on this boundless monotony, we find the sudden illumination of multiplicity itself. . . . Suddenly, arising from the background of the old inertia of equivalence, the zebra stripe of the event tears through the darkness, and the eternal phantasm informs that soup can, that singular depthless face" (p. 362).

More strikingly, Foucault notes how LSD almost simultaneously "eliminates the supremacy of categories" and "tears away the ground of its indifference and disintegrates the gloomy dumbshow of stupidity" (p. 363). (Opium, he tells us, produces a similar result but in a quite different way.) His tentative conclusion is that drugs can trigger, beyond categories, a new way of thinking, a thought of difference: "Perhaps . . . drugs, which mobilize [stupidity], which color, agitate, furrow, and dissipate it, which populate it with differences and substitute for the rare flash a continuous phosphorescence, are the source of a partial thought—perhaps" (p. 363).[12] The process—whether involving drugs or not—whereby we can confront acategorical stupidity and experience the shock of difference is what Foucault means by the "philosophical theater" of his article's title.

Although this discussion maintains Foucault's high intellectual excitement for Deleuze's thought, its essential recognition of the possibility of losing ourselves (via drugs or otherwise) in the "black stupidity" (p. 361) in which all differences are leveled will constitute for many a decisive objection to the Deleuzian path. Certainly, anyone can appreciate the sort of limit-experiences evoked here if their effects are contained within a "theater" clearly separated from "serious life", if they occur in a world we can enter and leave at will. But if, as Foucault's (and Deleuze's) rhetoric suggests, the claim is that such separation must not be tolerated, that there is no ultimate worth to a categorical life, then it is hard to see the demand that we undergo the risk of "black stupidity" as anything more than a personal preference or, perhaps, obsession.

Foucault's flight from Hegelian philosophy does not, therefore, force him into a counter-Hegelian philosophy, such as that of Deleuze. He had found a way to pursue historical studies that, while it retained the critical thrust of philosophy—by challenging the authority of assumptions held to be rationally inevitable—did not depend on the development of any counter-Hegelian account. He no doubt saw Deleuze's achievement as proof that a non-Hegelian philosophy was possible, but such a philosophy was inessential to the practice of genealogical history.

Derrida reading Nietzsche

Derrida's preferred manner of philosophizing is the close reading, in his own distinctive manner, of a text he finds philosophically significant (which does not always mean a

[12] Here Foucault includes a note added by Gilles Deleuze: "What will people think of us?"

text by someone generally regarded as a philosopher). Sometimes, particularly in his early work on Husserl, these readings at least roughly fit the standard model of a critical commentary. More often, however, Derrida's readings seem to have little to do with this model and suggest that he is trying to find some alternative to the traditional mode of philosophical thinking—the mode that, as we have seen, he sees most fully articulated in Hegel. The stakes of this game are particularly high when Derrida engages with Nietzsche and Heidegger, the two philosophers he takes to have done the most to transform what it means to think philosophically. Here I examine his most important engagement with Nietzsche (which also pays serious attention to Heidegger's own engagement with Nietzsche).[13]

Nietzsche's writings include some famous misogynistic passages, as well as some that could be taken in a feminist sense. Also, he relates his discussion of "woman" (this abstract singular form is common with him) to the topic of truth. Derrida connects these two themes to the question of Nietzsche's style as a writer and ties his entire analysis to Heidegger's interpretation of Nietzsche.

After an epigraph of a few "bits" from a letter Nietzsche wrote to a woman friend right after the publication of *The Birth of Tragedy* (1872), Derrida gives us a brief opening section, "The Question of Style", where he suggests, without explaining, a connection (maybe an identity, maybe not) between style[14] and woman in Nietzsche, and also alerts the reader to the relation of his essay to other recent work on Nietzsche that he is willing to call "deconstructive" (meaning, he says, "affirmative"). The oxymoronic tone is further emphasized, as Derrida goes on to say that he "will not refer to [these recent works] individually (not even to *Version de soleil*)"[15] and that these works "have opened up that problematic field to the very margin in which (aside from those moments when I deviate from it) I shall remain" (p. 37). This bantering, bait-and-switch "style" remains a prominent feature of Derrida's text.

The next section, "Distances", begins with a succession of plays on words that introduce a range of concepts Derrida will be deploying in the rest of his essay. He begins with "style", which has etymological relations to words for *pointed objects* (stylus, stiletto), objects that can, however, be used for both attack and defense. Defense, of course, aims to keep an attack "at a distance, to repel it—as one bends or recoils before its force" (p. 37). A defensive maneuver may involve hiding (say behind veils) or fleeing on a ship powered by sails. Derrida takes advantage of the fact that in French *des voiles* can mean either "veils" or "sails". The singulars, though, differ in gender: *le voile* is

[13] Jacques Derrida, *Spurs: Nietzsche's Styles* (French–English edition, English translation by Barbara Harlow; Chicago: University of Chicago Press, 1979), References will be given in the text. For an excellent discussion of Derrida and Nietzsche (including a perceptive reading of *Spurs*), see Ernest Behler, *Confrontations: Derrida/ Heidegger, Nietzsche*, tr. Steven Taubeneck (Stanford, CA: Stanford University Press, 1991), ch. 7.

[14] It is worth emphasizing from the outset that "style" for Derrida means much more than the formal features of literary style and includes the attitudes, assumptions, and overall conceptual framework of a text.

[15] Derrida's reference is to Bernard Pautrat, *Versions de soleil: Figures et système de Nietzsche* (Paris: Seuil, 1971).

"veil", *la voile* is "sail", so the plurals "float between the masculine and the feminine" (p. 39)—and the *langue* ("tongue" or "language") experiences a—sexually ambivalent—pleasure (*jouissance*) in expressing the term. Nietzsche, Derrida assures us, would have "been familiar with all genres" (presumably, both genders and all manners of writing).

The nautical (and sexual) language leads Derrida back to the connection of style to "pointed objects". "Thus the style would seem to advance in the manner of a *spur* of sorts (*éperon*). Like the prow [*éperon*], for example, of a sailing vessel [*vaisseau voilé*]... Or yet again, and still in nautical style, the style might be compared to that rocky point, also called an *éperon*, on which the waves break at the harbor's entrance" (p. 39). But now, turning again to the defensive role of stilettos, etc., Derrida takes the wordplay in a more explicitly philosophical direction. "So, it seems, style also uses its spur [*éperon*] as a means of protection against the terrifying, blinding, moral threat (of that) which *presents* itself, which obstinately thrusts itself into view. And style thereby protects itself against the presence, the content, the thing itself, meaning, truth" (p. 39, translation modified). In other words, style, the way one writes, can work against (indeed, spurn—a verb Mallarmé suggests is related to "spur") the classic assumptions of the metaphysics of presence. One more twist: Derrida notes that the German *Spur* means "trace", one of the terms he uses (along with *différance*, supplement, and so on) to develop a language to counter the metaphysics of presence.

Tying together his images of defense and attack with his images of sails/veils, Derrida notes that "the spurring style [*le style éperonnant*]... perforates even as it parries. It... derives its apotropaic [adverting-evil] power from the taut, resistant tissues, webs, sails and veils which are erected, furled and unfurled around it." But, he concludes, with a wry reference to the Nietzschean fragment he will discuss in his final section: "It must not be forgotten, it [style as pointed, as a spur] is also an umbrella" (p. 41).

Finally, to connect the images to the question (and image) of woman in Nietzsche, Derrida quotes (and comments on) a long passage from a section of the *Gay Science* entitled "Women and their Effect in the Distance". In this passage, the speaker ("I") stands hearing the stupendous roar of the ocean (the song of the "old earth shaker" (p. 43), Poseidon), when he sees a large and beautiful "sailing ship (*Segelschiff*) gliding silently along like a ghost". He compares the ship, which seems to contain "all the repose and silence of the world" to his "happier ego, my second immortalized self... still not dead but also no longer living" (p. 45). The speaker then remarks that, when out of the "hubbub" of our lives he glimpses the "calm, enchanting beings" for which he longs, these beings "are women". But, no matter how beautiful the ship we are sailing in, there will still be the "noise and bustling" of life, and the enchantment of woman is, "to use the language of philosophers, an effect at a distance... an *actio in distans*; there belongs thereto, however, primarily and above all—*distance*!" (p. 47).

The next section, "Veils", picks up immediately on the pairing of woman and distance. Woman's power (her seduction) operates at a distance but, Derrida says, Nietzsche also suggests that one "needs to keep one's distance from her beguiling song of enchantment". This is "not only for protection against [her] spell . . . but also as a way of succumbing to it" (p. 49), as one man might advise another how to seduce a woman without himself being seduced.

But, Derrida suggests, it may be that the need to "keep one's distance from the feminine operation" is "because the 'woman' is not a determinable identity", not "some thing which announces itself from a distance" but a "non-identity, a non-figure, a simulacrum". Perhaps, in other words, woman is not a distant thing but "distance itself". Derrida says that we "are forced to appeal here to the Heideggerian use of the word *Entfernung*, the meanings of which include "divergence" and "distance" but also "the distantiation of distance, the deferment of distance"—hence "remote proximity", "the veiled enigma of proximation" (pp. 49–51). This oxymoronic language returns us to Derrida's (and Heidegger's) claim that the very concept of presence (for example, the idea of objects "simply given" to consciousness or of consciousness's "direct" awareness of its own states) is unstable, constituted by an undecidable tension between an absent present and a present absence.

The metaphysics of presence is closely tied to the classical notion of truth as simply "the way things are", so that the instability of presence is paralleled by the instability of truth. This is why Nietzsche suggests that woman, who has no essence or identity, who "out of the depths, endless and unfathomable . . . engulfs and distorts all vestige of essentiality, of identity, of property", *is* truth. (Here, of course, the famous passage is the opening of *Beyond Good and Evil*, which Derrida will soon cite.) Woman is not, however, the truth in which the "dogmatic philosopher" believes. "He has understood nothing of truth, nor anything of woman." Woman is woman "precisely because she herself does not believe in truth itself, because she does not believe in what she is, in what she is believed to be, in what she thus is not" (p. 53). Derrida's last comment in this section is: "How is it possible that woman, who is herself truth, does not believe in truth? And yet, how is it possible to be truth and still believe in it?" (p. 55)—after which he simply quotes Nietzche's passage about "supposing truth to be a woman".

The tie to woman has, then, made truth something that "will not be pinned down" (p. 55), that "diverges" from itself, that needs to be put in quotation marks (p. 56). And this destabilization of truth fits well with Nietzsche's (and Derrida's) critique of the traditional notion of truth. So far, then, Nietzsche's use of woman as an image has been favorable to her; the claims he has been making are "feminist propositions". But—all this being clear as we begin the section entitled "Truths"—how are we to reconcile this "with the overwhelming *corpus* of Nietzsche's venomous anti-feminism?" (p. 57). Derrida tells us that his "thesis in the present communication" is that the "congruence" of these two sets of texts, "feminist" and "anti-feminist", "although ineluctably enigmatic, is just as rigorously necessary" (p. 57).

What we need to be able to understand is that precisely "as truth" woman "is scepticism and veiling dissimulation" (p. 57). This is expressed in Nietzsche's comments about the "blushing modesty" of old women, who "believe in the superficiality of existence and in its essence, and all virtue and profoundity is to them only the disguising (*Verhüllung*) of this 'truth', the very desirable disguising of a *pudendum*" (p. 59). Without the veil of feminine modesty, it will be entirely clear that truth is merely "truth"; to remain "truth, profound, indecent, desirable", superficiality must be hidden, veiled.

But why, then, "the fear, the dread, the 'blushing modesty'?" (p. 59). Why should woman be afraid or ashamed of this essential veiling of truth, which is really just a discrete recognition of how much "truth" lacks the pretensions of the traditional notion of truth? The reason, Derrida tells us, in what might seem an abrupt shift in a Freudian direction, is that "the feminine distance abstracts truth from itself in a *suspension* of the relation with castration" (p. 59). Here Derrida is using "castration" in Lacan's sense, where it is a symbol for the loss of an ideal wholeness analogous to traditional notions of presence and truth. In sexual terms, woman's power (in, for example, the Oedipal relationship) comes from man's fear of castration and desire to keep his phallic "wholeness". But, according to Lacan's Freudianism, the phallus itself (that is, the wholeness it stands for) does not exist, wholeness is not a possibility. So woman's power is based on a "myth" that she herself sees through, which accounts for her fear and shame in trying to conceal it.

Derrida emphasizes that, for woman, there is no relevant difference between castration and anti-castration, between challenging and defending the privilege of the phallus. Whichever approach woman took, she would still "find herself trapped in phallocentrism" (p. 61); she would still have to live a life that revolved around concerns about the phallus. But the "truth" that woman knows is that neither castration nor anti-castration is an issue because there is no phallus, no possibility of the completeness it signifies. Derrida formulates this point as "woman knows that castration does not take place", but notes that "this formula must be manipulated with great prudence" because it "indicates that area where castration is no longer determinable" and "describes a margin whose very consequences are incalculable" (p. 61). In other words, woman's "truth" undermines the very framework (of phallocentrism) that has defined her and provided the site where, although—and because—she is subordinated, she still has power (that of the seductress) that is due to her (subordinate) role. There is no way to calculate what will happen once that framework is undermined.

Also undetermined, at least in this discussion, is the relation between the philosophical question of truth and the psychoanalytic question of castration (the phallus). Derrida's discussion can be taken as simply a comparison between these two questions, noting certain structural similarities between them, but implying no real (ontological) connection. But it can also be taken—as, presumably, Lacan would—as expressing the psychoanalytic origin of the philosophical question of truth. Derrida's text does not provide any way of choosing between these alternatives. More generally, Derrida leaves indeterminate the significance of his fundamental "comparison" in *Spurs* between the question of woman and the question of truth.

In any case (moving into the section called "Adornments"), Derrida is now in a position to explain how Nietzsche's positive view of woman is congruent with his denunciations of feminism. The essential point is that, for Nietzsche, "feminism is nothing but the operation of a woman who aspires to be like a man", that is, of a woman who, like the "masculine dogmatic philosopher... lays claim... to truth, science and objectivity in all their castrated delusions of virility" (p. 65). The feminist accepts the castration–anti-castration framework, thereby losing woman's distinctive "style", her pointed defense against the pretensions of presence and truth. Feminism—the demand to become equal to men—can in the end only maintain the framework that subordinates woman because it maintains the phallocentric illusions that underlie this framework. "Feminism too seeks to castrate. It wants a castrated woman" (p. 65). It seems, however, that Nietzsche's quarrel is with what is now called "equality feminism" and might perhaps be open to the "difference feminism" of, say, Luce Irigaray.

We can now see how misleading some of Nietzsche's apparently misogynistic passages can be, for example, when he says: "What is truth to a woman! From the very first nothing has been more alien, repugnant, inimical to woman than truth—her great art is the lie, her supreme concern is appearance [*Schein*] and beauty" (p. 67, citing *Beyond Good and Evil*, sect. 232). Here Nietzsche seems to condemn woman, but his "condemnation" in fact cites what he regards as her good qualities, her rejections of truth/presence and her affirmation of artistic style (the "spur" that pops the bubble of truth/presence). Derrida picks up this point in his next section, "Simulation", where he maintains that, for Nietzsche, "the entire process of the feminine operation takes place in the interval of this apparent contradiction" (p. 67, translation modified) between woman as the model of traditional truth and the Nietzschean "truth" of "dissimulation", the undermining of truth/presence. Derrida goes on to emphasize Nietzsche's connection of such dissimulation—and hence of woman—with the artist (and the Jew, another object of Nietzsche's apparent ambivalence). He concludes that "it is impossible to dissociate the questions of art, style and truth from the question of woman" and that, although "she is certainly not to be found in any of the familiar modes of concept or knowledge", still "it is impossible to resist looking for her" (p. 71).

Derrida has now considerably developed the question of Nietzsche's style(s) through its connection with truth and woman, but, he tells us (beginning the section "'History of an Error'"), to go further the "question of style must be measured against the larger question of the interpretation of Nietzsche's text". Indeed, the question is even wider—a question "of the interpretation of interpretation, the question of interpretation itself". Once this formidable question is posed, "either the question of style will be resolved, or its very statement will be disqualified" (p. 73). Derrida's portentous tone is soon explained when he says that taking up Nietzsche interpretation means discussing Heidegger, a thinker Derrida typically approaches with a high seriousness—particularly appropriate here given Heidegger's magisterial four volumes of Nietzsche studies.

Derrida begins by laying out some of Heidegger's basic principles for interpreting Nietzsche: warnings against confusing philosophy and art, against confusing "grand style" with "heroico-boastful style", and against neglecting to read Nietzsche in the context of "an unremitting interrogation of Western civilization"; claims that

Nietzsche wants to replace an aesthetics of consumers with an aesthetics of producers, that Nietzsche's thought on art is fundamentally metaphysical, that Nietzsche proceeds by "inverting" Platonism. Oddly, however, after presenting and commenting on Heidegger's ideas in some detail, Derrida turns away from them—he explains why only much later—and (in the next section, "Vita femina") goes back to his own discussion of woman and truth in Nietzsche.

His concern here is the famous passage on truth (in *Twilight of the Idols*) called "History of an Error", and he focuses on three words that Nietzsche underlines in the "second epoch" of his history: "it becomes female" (*sie wird Weib*).[16] The context shows that the "it" refers to "the idea": "Progress of the idea: it becomes more subtle, insidious, incomprehensible—*it becomes female*" (p. 89). Since "the idea is a form of truth's self-presentation", it follows that "truth has not always been a woman", that both truth and woman "have a history", in fact, a history that begins when the idea (escaping from identity with the philosopher, with Plato) becomes female. At this point, all the things that Derrida talked about at the outset of his essay enter the story of truth: distance, veils, woman. But then Nietzsche, "as if in apposition or as if to explain the 'it becomes female', adds there 'sie wird christlich'"—"it becomes Christian". This, Derrida says, initiates the theme of castration via a connection of the castrating woman (who cuts away truth) and the religion that enjoins "if thy eye offend thee, pluck it out" (and Nietzsche notes that it is not exactly the eye that is meant). The following section of *Twilight of the Idols*, "Morality as Anti-Nature", makes this explicit, denouncing Christianity as "castratism" (p. 91), dedicated to rooting out the passions and, as such, essentially opposed to life.

With the next section, "Positions", Derrida leaves behind specific textual commentary and begins a sustained reflection on what we can and cannot conclude about the nature of Nietzsche's philosophizing. He begins by emphasizing the "heterogeneity" of Nietzsche's texts on woman, which shows that "Nietzsche had no illusions that he knew the effects that are called woman, truth, castration—or the ontological effects of presence and absence" (p. 95, translation modified). Derrida characterizes this heterogeneity by distinguishing three different kinds of positions (propositions) that Nietzsche asserts about woman. The first two operate within the "economy of truth", the traditional view of truth/presence as the supreme ideal. In this context, Nietzsche will, as we have seen, sometimes condemn, in the conventional manner, woman as a deceiving seductress. But in the same traditional context, he sometimes presents woman as a symbol of the distant ideal of truth (recall the passage in *Gay Science* about the beautiful sailing ship). In rejecting the truth/presence ideal, Nietzsche is also condemning woman as a symbol of this ideal. But, finally, from the standpoint of

[16] Derrida notes that Heidegger, despite his detailed commentary on this section, never mentions these words—but insists that, in focusing on them, he is not "proceeding in a way counter to Heidegger's", which, in any case, "would only amount to [doing] the same thing" as Heidegger.

Nietzsche's critique of truth, woman, who "sees through" truth, is "recognized and affirmed as an affirmative power, a dissimulatress, an artist, a dionysiac" (p. 97).

It is possible, of course, that there is a "systematic unity" underlying these apparently inconsistent ways of speaking. If so, "the parodying heterogeneity of Nietzsche's style or styles could be masterable, reducible to the content of a single [consistent] thesis" (p. 99). Derrida, however, rejects this view, maintaining that the heterogeneous texts show that "Nietzsche himself did not see his way too clearly" and that "a regular, rhythmic blindness takes place in the text" (p. 101). "Simultaneously or successively, depending on the position of his body and the situation of his story", Nietzsche accepted all of these diverse views without reconciling them.

In the next section, "The gaze of Oedipus", Derrida moves from the irreducible heterogeneity (which he also calls the "undecidability") of Nietzsche's claims about woman to the general assertion that "there is no such thing as the truth of Nietzsche, or of Nietzsche's text". He cites Nietzsche's assertion (in *Beyond Good and Evil*—and in a paragraph about women!) that "these are only—*my* truths", and argues that, since "these truths" are "multiple, variegated, contradictory even", they are not really truths. "Indeed there is no such thing as truth in itself" (p. 103). Derrida concludes that, for Nietzsche, "the question of woman suspends the decidable opposition of true and non-true" and requires that we put in "quotation marks" (scarce quotes, no doubt) "every concept belonging to the system of philosophical decidability" (p. 107).[17]

At this point (in "Le Coup de don"), Derrida finally returns to Heidegger's interpretation, which, he says, "has been idling offshore . . . ever since it missed the woman in truth's fabulous plotting" (p. 109). Despite Heidegger's apparently ignoring the question of woman and truth, Derrida argues that Nietzsche's "numerous analyses" (he cites examples on p. 153–7 n. 14) of the "eternal war between the sexes", and so on, lead us back to Heideggerian ontology. These analyses present relations between the sexes as centered on "appropriation, expropriation, mastery, servitude, etc."; that is, on giving, taking, possessing, and being possessed. (For example, woman "gives herself" to man as her possessor, but can use this very act as a way of "appropriating" him as her own.)

Derrida maintains that, in the process of mutual giving and taking, men and women continually exchange dominance, with no resolution possible. "Man and woman change places. They exchange masks ad infinitum" (p. 111). Derrida calls this endless, undecidable process *propriation* and argues that, "because it is finally undecidable, propriation is more powerful than the question *ti esti*, more powerful than the veil of truth or the meaning of being". A further argument shows that "propriation is all the more powerful since it is its process that organized both the totality of language's process and symbolic exchange in general", which implies that propriation "also organized all ontological statements. The history (of) truth (is) a process of propriation" (p. 111). Failing to take account of the role of propriation, we remain in a "pre-critical relation to the signified, in the presence of the

[17] In Chapter 10 I will raise some critical questions about the force of Derrida's argument here.

spoken word, to a natural language, to perception, visibility, in a word, to consciousness, and its phenomenological system" (p. 113).

All this is relevant to Heidegger's interpretation, which holds that Nietzsche is the last of the metaphysicians, that, in particular, his thinking of will (will-to-power) "belonged to the history of metaphysics" (p. 115). This seems inconsistent with Derrida's reading in terms of propriation, which surely puts Nietzsche outside the metaphysical realm of truth, presence, and self-identical being. But, as always with Heidegger (and much else), Derrida thinks that things are more complicated than they seem. This is because Heidegger's own thinking of being was long tied to something close to propriation (to *Eigenlichkeit* in *Being and Time*, to *Ereignis* in the later works). Whenever this aspect of Heidegger's thought emergences, there is a *dehiscence*, a bursting-forth, that pushes to the limit the opposition of the metaphysical and the non-metaphysical. "Metaphysical questions and the question of metaphysics have only to be inscribed in the more powerful question of propriation for their space to be reorganized" (p. 119). In his next section, "Abysses of Truth", Derrida shows how this is just what occurs in the final chapter of Heidegger's *Nietzsche*. Here talk of being (*Sein*) flows into talk of propriation (*Ereignis*), and "truth, unveiling, illumination are no longer decided in the appropriation of the truth of being, but are cast into its bottomless abyss as non-truth, veiling and dissimulation". When this happens, "the history of being becomes a history in which no being, nothing, happens except *Ereignis*' unfathomable process" (p. 119). Derrida's suggestion is that "perhaps truth's abyss as non-truth, propriation as appropriation/a-propriation . . . is what Nietzsche is calling the style's form and the no-where of woman" (pp. 119–21). He also suggests that the "undecidable oscillation" of "the gift, which is the essential predicate of woman" (and, an expression of propriation) is similar to that involved in the giving or gift of being (*es gibt Sein*) in Heidegger. Along these lines, Derrida suggests in conclusion, Heidegger's reading of Nietzsche may open up into the "enormous field" (p. 123) of what he has found to be Nietzsche's thought.

Derrida's final section, "'I have forgotten my umbrella'", uses this isolated single sentence, included in the French translation of *Gay Science*, to reflect on the prospects of textual interpretation. He explores a variety of ways of understanding the text. Is it—as the quotation marks might suggest—a simple record of a piece of conversation Nietzsche heard? Is it—as the "forgetting" and the penetrating shape of an umbrella might suggest—open to a Freudian reading? Is it a secret code? In one sense, of course, everyone knows what this simple sentence "means"—someone, speaking in the first person, says that he/she forgot his/her umbrella. But what does the sentence mean in the context of Nietzsche's work as a whole? Given that we know almost nothing about the sentence's relation to this context, Derrida unsurprisingly concludes that we have no idea. Nor can we even conclude that there is a hidden, secret meaning to which we do not have access. Our ignorance is so great that, as far as we know, there might not be anything further to know about its meaning: "its secret is . . . the possibility that indeed it might have no secret, that it might only be pretending to be simulating some hidden truth within its folds" (p. 133).

Derrida generalizes this conclusion. No text in its totality has a context that allows us to penetrate its meaning. For example, "To whatever lengths one might carry a conscientious interpretation, the hypothesis that the totality of Nietzsche's text, in some monstrous way, might well be of the type 'I have forgotten my umbrella' cannot be denied" (p. 133). And this, Derrida says, "is tantamount to saying that there is no totality to Nietzsche's text"—or any text.

For example: this very text of Derrida's that we are just finishing reading. Perhaps, Derrida tells us, he has written the text so that it is "cryptic and parodying" (p. 137) and excludes any overall meaning. Indeed, whether or not he tells us this, it may or may not be so, since he could, either way, easily be lying. So there is no reason to say that *Spurs* is any more open to overall interpretation than is "I have forgotten my umbrella".

But this does not mean that reading is pointless, just that there is no reading that will reveal *the* meaning of a text: "there never has been *the* style, *the* simulacrum, *the* woman" (p. 139). The "truth" (in Nietzsche's in-quotes sense) of reading "must be in the interval between several styles . . . If there is going to be style, there can only be more than one" (p. 139). Derrida's conclusion is not skeptical but pluralistic.

Why be a Nietzschean?

While Derrida is, of course, a "more complicated" case, Deleuze and Foucault appeal to Nietzsche to support their opposition to Hegel. But what precisely is the problem with Hegel? Their objections are both philosophical and cultural (or ethical). Philosophically, they reject Hegelian "totalization", his claim to provide a comprehensive meaning for history, based on an account that purports to be the final (absolute) truth about reality. Culturally or ethically, they oppose institutions and practices (to a good approximation, the values of conventional, bourgeois society) that they think Hegel's philosophy supports. Since Hegel offers elaborate cases (especially in his *Phenomenology* and *Logic*) for his position, we might expect Foucault and Deleuze to offer detailed specific objections to these arguments. We find, however, hardly any trace of such an approach. They begin with the assumption that the Hegelian system must be rejected, and set out, along lines Foucault found suggested by Hyppolite, to develop alternatives (ontological or methodological) to them. Nor do they offer any critique (Marxist or otherwise) of bourgeois society; they merely register their obvious disdain and outrage at its deficiencies. It might well be that, in both instances, they regard the cases against what they oppose to have been conclusively made by other philosophers and social critics. (Deleuze, however, seems to regard explicit criticism as the sort of "reactive" movement he wants to replace with pure affirmation.) No matter, they come to their intellectual project with firm anti-Hegelian convictions that function as starting-points, not claims they need to establish.

I do not intend this point as a criticism. All philosophies are developed on the basis of pre-philosophical convictions of one sort or another. Philosophical inquiry often consists in the critical examination of these convictions (at least by testing their mutual consistency) and in development (refinement, extension, application) of them. Properly carried out, this process can provide important indirect support for the initial convictions by answering possible objections and showing the intellectual fruitfulness of the convictions. Philosophical inquiry becomes not a presuppositionless derivation of its conclusions but a persuasive elaboration of its presuppositions.[18]

In the case of Deleuze, the elaboration will not be of the simple denial of Hegelian ontology but of Deleuze's positive alternative ontology, his philosophy of difference understood as creative affirmation rather than negation. Although we cannot even touch its surface here, Deleuze's elaboration over the course of his career was impressive. He began by showing how elements of his ontological view could be developed from the work of a wide variety of philosophers: Hume, Spinoza, Bergson, Nietzsche. Then he showed, in *Difference and Repetition* and *The Logic of Sense*, how his approach could fruitfully transform our understanding of classical philosophical problems such as the plurality of being (one-many), causality, and the nature of representation, of sensation, of thought, etc. In other works, he demonstrated the power of his position to illuminate art, literature, psychology, economics, and politics. This sort of elaboration does not prove that the viewpoint is true (or otherwise to be preferred over alternatives), but it shows it to be a powerful way of thinking and so reinforces the convictions of those inclined to accept it and requires the attention of those who would dismiss it.

There is, of course, room for debate about just how persuasive Deleuze's elaborations are. But, at least in principle, he employs an approach capable of intellectually supporting his Nietzscheanism. There are, however, two points at which even many sympathetic readers are likely to balk. The first is the self-consistency of his basic notion of difference. One essential element of any successful persuasive elaboration, particularly when it introduces new, counter-intuitive ways of thinking, are ways of disarming claims that the new ideas are not logically coherent. In the case of Deleuze (and of many other recent French thinkers), this is a particularly sensitive issue—on the one hand, because many of his claims seem obviously absurd and, on the other, because of the reply that insistence on flat-footed notions of consistency begs the question against his radical challenge to common-sense thought. This is an important issue that I will take up in some detail in Chapter 10.

The second sticking point for many—and here the discussion will include Foucault as well as Deleuze—is the Nietzschean challenge to our deepest ethical commitments.[19] There are respectable readings of Nietzsche on which he does not challenge such values but rather defends them against the distortions of "morality". But Deleuze's and Foucault's readings at least suggest a Nietzsche whose views are as explosive as his

[18] I have developed this view of philosophical inquiry for the context of analytic philosophy in *What Philosophers Know: Case Studies in Recent Analytic Philosophy* (Cambridge: Cambridge University Press, 2009).

[19] This applies to Foucault only when—say through his focus on limit experiences—he commits himself to something like Deleuze's ontology of pure difference. As we noted above, the merely methodological Nietzscheanism of his genealogy can be entirely comfortable with a quite ordinary reformism.

most unguarded rhetoric. Here Nietzschean anti-humanism is an obvious focus. If what this calls for is a going beyond man (the human condition) *as such* to create new values that have no grounding in what "we" (who are still human to the core) are, then the commitment to a future "overman" could be to what even Foucault seemed to fear as a humanly unintelligible "black stupidity".

Derrida's Nietzscheanism is more complex because it neither pushes Nietzsche's thought to an anti-Hegelian ontology nor extracts from it a methodology that is more historical than philosophical. His methodology is itself philosophical, based on a firm commitment to what philosophical thinking can and should be. We have seen how Derrida both presents Nietzsche as a thinker whose view of truth implies the undecidability of our concepts and tries to show, through his reading, the undecidability of Nietzsche's own text. Roughly, this project (like all Derrida's deconstructive efforts) starts from the following pre-philosophical convictions: (1) the traditional concepts that embody the metaphysics of presence (dichotomies such as subject/object, true/false, fact/value, and so on) can never lead to a finally complete and coherent system, but will, under sufficient pressure, always eventually reveal their essential undecidability;[20] (2) there is, however, no decisive escape from these concepts of presence, so that we must always come back to thinking in their terms; (3) there is, nonetheless, substantial value in the never-ending effort to push our concepts to the point that reveals their essential undecidability.

As in the case of Deleuze and Foucault, these pre-philosophical convictions are not subject to direct proof. But they can be persuasively elaborated in a very straightforward way: by actually deconstructing any text that comes our way. What better way to show the "fruitfulness" of thesis (1)? Of course, this approach can never decisively establish the thesis. It can only take the form of Derridian undertaking to deconstruct any text presented. As the challenge is upheld in more and more cases, there begins to develop a "deconstructive induction" in support of thesis (1). Thesis (2) admits of a similar defense. Do we ever encounter a case of a thinker decisively escaping from the metaphysics of presence? Derrida's analyses—including those of Heidegger, the paradigm opponent of metaphysics—suggest not.

In both cases, any "proof in principle" would have itself to take a metaphysical form that would itself be subject to deconstruction, so there is no alternative to the brutely "empirical" proof by challenge. It will be pointed out that I am here assuming the need for a pragmatic level of practical history that escapes from deconstruction, a level where we can just proclaim as decided fact that such and such deconstructions have been carried out. But, without such a pragmatic level, our very lives would be shown incoherent by deconstruction; everything would have to be in scare quotes.[21] Derrida

[20] Undecidability: roughly, that the concept lacks the basic coherence to allow us to decide how it can be applied.

[21] This is the truth behind the perceptive humor of the *Onion*'s headline reporting Derrida's death: "Jacques Derrida 'dies'".

himself recognizes this sort of point in *Limited Inc.*, when he insists that even deconstructive readings (for example, his reading of Rousseau in *Of Grammatology*) must be based on a knowledge of "what interpretations are probabilistically dominant and conventionally acknowledged to grant access to what Rousseau thought he meant and to what readers for the most part thought they could understand".[22]

Derrida's "normative" claim (3) could presumably also be supported by practical demonstrations that deconstructive analyses have obviously good effects. This, I suggest, is what must be behind any meaningful defense of Derrida's claim that "deconstruction is justice".

"Nietzscheanism" as a characterization of the work of Deleuze, Foucault, and Derrida is by no means a univocal term. Each thinker approaches Nietzsche with his own agenda and finds in him what suits that agenda. The result is a variety of Nietzscheanisms, none of them able to claim any privileged place as a superior reading of his texts. Correspondingly, the fact that these three thinkers are "all Nietzscheans" implies no common set of methods or views, just a shared affinity for a thinker who opened many doors.

Amidst the diversity, however, there is a shared orientation or concern. Deleuze seeks in Nietzsche new metaphysical concepts, Foucault is looking for a method of going beyond the alleged boundaries of established modes of thought, and Derrida wants to develop styles of thinking the undecidable, that which eludes any decisive conceptualization. In their various ways, each philosopher is intent on thinking what has not yet been—or even what perhaps never can be—caught in the web of our concepts. They are all trying to think what seem to be (or actually are) conceptual impossibilities. Part II will show Levinas and Marion engaging in similar projects, which parallel and confront those of Foucault, Deleuze, and Derrida. This will lead to an explicit understanding of French philosophy since 1960 as directed toward the thinking of the impossible.

[22] Jacques Derrida, *Limited Inc* (Evanston, IL: Northwestern University Press, 1988), 144.

PART II

6

The Turn to Ethics: Levinas and Deleuze

Philosophy on the European continent is often praised for maintaining its connection with the deep human questions of the historical tradition, in contrast to the quibbling technicalities of Anglophone analytic philosophy: existential *angst* versus the existential operator. This would suggest, if nothing else, an ethical orientation for "continental" philosophy. But existentialism's ethical promise fizzled with Sartre's failure to complete *L'Homme*, the "future work" promised in the last sentence of *Being and Nothingness*. This work was to respond to the questions about how to live our existentialist freedom, which, Sartre tells us, "can find their reply only on the ethical plane".[1] Sartre's failure to complete this work—despite the hundreds of pages of drafts and notes now available as his *Notebooks for an Ethics*—suggested that either existentialism could not support a coherent ethics or that there was no longer any point to ethical reflection.

Anti-humanism and ethics

In any case, the young philosophers of the 1960s saw their rejection of humanism as entailing a rejection of ethics. Heidegger's "Letter on Humanism" was more nuanced.[2] It countenances ethics but only if it is rooted in a longing to know "how man, experienced from ek-sistence toward Being, ought to live in a fitting manner". Heidegger agrees that, particularly given the challenge of technology to the "ethical bond", we cannot "disregard our predicament" and should "safeguard and secure the existing bonds even if they hold human beings together ever so tenuously and merely for the present". But he insists that concerns about human solidarity—"ethical" concerns in the standard philosophical sense—must not "release thought from the task of thinking what still remains principally to be thought and, as Being, prior to all beings, is their guarantor and their truth" (p. 255). In other words, ethical issues must

[1] Jean-Paul Sartre, *Being and Nothingness*, tr. Hazel Barnes (New York: Pocket Books, 1966), 798.

[2] Martin Heidegger, "Letter on Humanism", in *Martin Heidegger: Basic Writings*, ed. David Farrell Krell (rev. and expanded edn, New York: Harper Collins, 1993). References will be given in the text.

not distract us from the essential task of thinking being. He drives the point home by reinterpreting Heraclitus' saying, usually translated as "A man's character [*ethos*] is his god [*daimón*]". Heidegger says this translation "thinks in a modern way", presumably because it "deifies" character, the locus of autonomous human flourishing. What Heraclitus really meant, according to Heidegger, is something like, "Man dwells, insofar as he is a man, in the nearness of god [that is, Being]" (p. 256). *Ethos* properly means "the abode of man" and that abode is the place where man thinks being. Accordingly, "that thinking which thinks the truth of Being as the primordial element of man, as one who ek-sists, is in itself the original ethics". But even here Heidegger notes, "this thinking [of Being] is not ethics in the first instance, because it is ontology" (p. 258). Because man is subordinated to being, ethics must be subordinated to ontology.

As we have seen, the French philosophers of the 1960s, fascinated as they were with Heidegger, had little interest in following his ontological path to being. Indeed, they tended to think that, in making man the privileged site for the "revelation" of being, Heidegger was slipping back into humanism. For them, then, ethics itself was just an unfortunate remnant of the humanist folly. Foucault's ironic digression on modern ethics in *The Order of Things* is quirky but characteristic. Apart from "religious moralities" (based on transcendent beings that Foucault would rule out from the start), "the West has known only two ethical forms". The ancient form (but which extended from the Stoics and the Epicureans through the eighteenth century) was "articulated upon the order of the world", from which it deduced "the principle of a code of wisdom or a conception of the city".[3] The modern age, of course, finds no order outside of man to underwrite a morality.[4] Strictly, in fact, modernity "formulates no morality" in the sense that "modern thought has never . . . been able to propose a morality". This, however, is not at all because modern thought "is pure speculation". Quite the contrary, there is no place for the project of developing an ethics because "modern thought, from its inception and in its very density, is a certain mode of action"; "at the level of its existence, in its very dawning, [it] is in itself an action—a perilous action". The point, however, is not the (Marxist) "foolishness" of believing "that all thought 'expresses' the ideology of a class". The point is far more fundamental: modern thought's "knowledge of man . . . is always linked to ethics or politics" in the sense that it always "is advancing towards the region where man's Other must become the Same as himself".[5] Or, to put it less cryptically, modern thought involves man's constant effort to make himself the meaning of the world. Foucault and his generation rejected humanism precisely because it was at root an anthropocentric ethics, which left no room for us to become anything other than more instances of man. The only

[3] Michel Foucault, *The Order of Things*, tr. A. Sheridan (New York: Random House, 1970), 327–8.

[4] In a footnote in *The Order of Things* (p. 343 n. 2) Foucault says that Kant, for whom the law that "the subject . . . applies to himself . . . is the universal law", is the "link" between the ancient and the modern forms of ethics.

[5] Foucault, *The Order of Things*, 328.

available alternatives to the ethical exaltation of humanity seemed to be a falling-back into an ethics based on religious transcendence or a move toward Heidegger's dubious ethics of being. Given the choices, Foucault, Deleuze, and Derrida would understandably see ethics as a non-starter.

Levinas and ethical responsibility

Emmanuel Levinas saw things differently. His *Totality and Infinity*[6] (published in 1961, the same year as Foucault's *History of Madness*) totally concurred with Foucault's rejection of a humanism for which "man's Other must become the Same as himself". But, contrary to the younger generation of philosophers emerging just as his book was published, Levinas saw ethics as of supreme importance and, against Heidegger, insisted on its priority to ontology. Perhaps more strikingly, whereas Heidegger and his French admirers thought phenomenology had passed its use-by date, Levinas says in his Preface: "the presentation and the development of the notions employed owe everything to the phenomenological method" (p. 28).

Levinas's flaunting of a method and a topic both widely regarded as *depassé* no doubt explains the relatively little attention paid his book upon publication. His religious commitment (as a practicing Jew and author of Talmudic commentaries) did not help, nor did his lack of a standard French intellectual pedigree.[7] Born in Lithuania, he lived there and in Ukraine before moving to France when he was 17, and received his philosophical education in Strasbourg. Although Levinas lived in Paris, he had no position in the state educational system but was the director of the École Normale Israélite Orientale. It would be wrong, however, to over-emphasize his outsider status. He had studied with both Husserl and Heidegger, published in 1930 one of the first French books on Husserl (the book that introduced Sartre to phenomenology), was a friend of Merleau-Ponty and of Blanchot, and had published in *Les Temps modernes*. Tempting as it may be, we cannot say that Levinas was the Other of French philosophy in the 1960s. Nonetheless, it was only Derrida—himself born Jewish and outside the French "hexagon"—who took Levinas seriously before the revival of ethics in the 1980s. Even Derrida's detailed attention did not do much to raise Levinas's profile; Descombes's insider account of French philosophy in the 1960s and 1970s does not mention him.

Levinas's ethics is based on an "encounter" with the "Other". By the Other Levinas means another human person, but one encountered in a distinctive way that is the source of ethical responsibility. His approach is phenomenological in the sense that he is trying to describe the lived experience in which another person is encountered as the source of moral responsibility. He is not, for example, deducing this moral responsibility from a

[6] Emmanuel Levinas, *Totality and Infinity: An Essay on Exteriority*, tr. Alphonso Linguis (Pittsburgh, PA: Duquesne University Press, 1969). References will be given in the text.

[7] Also, the book was not published by one of the major Parisian houses but by the Dutch publisher Nijhoff.

priori principles, showing that it is a necessary condition for the possibility of accepted truths, or inferring it from the results of empirical psychology. Also, Levinas insists that his description is not an account of my experience of the Other as a special sort of *object* in my world. Rather, my encounter with the Other is what constitutes me as a subject capable of experiencing (in the ordinary sense) objects. There are numerous thorny questions about how Levinas's descriptions relate to Husserlian phenomenology (at its various stages of development) and to the phenomenological aspects of Heidegger's *Being and Time*. We will pass by these issues but will pay attention to the broader question of how, if at all, Levinas provides descriptive support for his view of ethical responsibility. I will build my discussion around Levinas's phenomenology of "the face" in *Totality and Infinity*.

"The face" is Levinas's term for the Other as I encounter him in the context of ethical responsibility. We, obviously, encounter other people as objects of, for example, sight or touch, but Levinas thinks that there is also always an encounter with them in moral terms. He begins by insisting that this encounter is very different from ordinary visual perception. To the extent that I have access to beings via vision, I dominate (exercise power over) them. "A thing is *given*, offers itself to me" (p. 194). (The idea is similar to that involved in claims, for example, by feminists, that the disinvolved distance of vision is directed toward something that I treat as an object for my manipulation.) Levinas also says that gaining access to a being via sight involves my maintaining "myself within the same" (p. 194), meaning that this sort of experience changes nothing in my fundamental position in the world but merely adds one more thing that I have access to.

In sharp contrast to ordinary vision, "The face is present in its refusal to be contained" (p. 194). This "refusal" counteracts the "given" in visual perception: the "containment" that is refused is the rejection of the experiencing I's domination. (Levinas also speaks of what is refused as my "comprehension" and "encompassing" of the Other.) The Other, precisely as Other, cannot be an object of ordinary sense experience precisely because the experience of the Other is of someone who is not contained in my experience and therefore is not available for my comprehension and domination.

So far Levinas has emphasized what we might call the epistemological distinctiveness of the Other, the fact that my encounter with him is not reducible to ordinary sense experience. But there is also an ontological distinctiveness, which Levinas first expresses by saying that the Other's otherness is not "relative". In Levinas's use, to be relatively other is to be different within a shared genus (a "community of genus" (p. 194)). In this (standard) case, two "different" items belong to different species but remain in the same genus. The Other, however, does not differ from the I by possessing a quality that puts him into a different species within a genus that we share.

In claiming that I and the Other share no genus, Levinas is not, we may suppose, making the absurd claim that there are no terms at all that can be applied to both. Both, for example, are persons and both exist in the space of moral responsibility. Were there literally no common ground at all, there would be no locus for Levinas's description. Levinas's point, I suggest, is instead that the moral relation does not depend on any properties that we share in the world abstracted from moral responsibility. "The face in which [the Other's] epiphany is produced and which appeals to me breaks with the world that can be common to us, whose virtualities are inscribed in our *nature* and developed by our existence" (p. 194).

This "common world", the world of the "same", never exists in isolation from the Other. Indeed, Levinas insists that the relation to the Other is essential for my being a person, not only as a moral agent but also as a reflective, rational being. The world in which each I exists simply in its "interiority", self-contained, with no relation to the "exteriority" introduced by the Other, is just one (essential) dimension of the full and concrete world that also involves my relation to the Other. In this dimension of interiority, I "live off of" (*vivre de*) the objects of my world, objects that I see as existing only so that I can appropriate them for my enjoyment. Levinas offers impressively rich and subtle descriptions of the world of interiority, particularly in what we might call his phenomenology of food, a perceptive description of eating as a paradigm instance of the I's appropriation and assimilation for the sake of enjoyment. But the description of interiority is offered only as a contrast to the concreteness of the world of exteriority that involves the encounter with the Other. And it is essential to keep in mind that, in reality, the I's very existence requires the relation to the Other. The picture of the I freely appropriating objects for its enjoyment must, simply because it includes the I, presuppose a relation to the Other that undermines any thought that the I could concretely exist simply "in myself".

Levinas's claim that the I and the Other have nothing in common is actually a claim about the absolute gap between the aspect of my world that can be described in terms of pure interiority (enjoyment) and my world in the full sense, which includes exteriority (responsibility). The world of interiority is devoid of moral responsibility, whereas the world of exteriority is essentially one of moral responsibility. Levinas expresses this in terms of the "absolute difference" between the I and the Other and of "the incomprehensible nature of the presence of the Other" to the I (p. 195). Levinas thus introduces the central theme—which we have noted earlier in Foucault, Deleuze, and Derrida—of the inconceivable. We will later see how this theme is also developed in Derrida's ethics and in Marion's and Derrida's approach to religion.

"The Other", for Levinas, means a person precisely as existing in (and constituting) the world of exteriority and moral responsibility, and "I" means a person as existing in the world of interiority and enjoyment and at the same time existing in the world of exteriority through an experience of the Other. Levinas's language well conveys the profound difference that moral responsibility makes in our lives. But the dramatic contrast of "I" and "Other" can obscure the obvious truth that Levinas's descriptions of both interiority and exteriority apply to *all* human beings. The referent of "the Other" must be another human being, capable of being described in precisely the same ways that "the I" is described. But Levinas's insight is that our experience of moral responsibility is an experience of other people precisely as putting us in a world radically different from the world of self-contained enjoyment. (This experience also shows that the world of enjoyment is just one dimension of the real world of moral responsibility.) The Other is inconceivable in the sense that the standard concepts of interiority do not apply. It is in this sense that "the Other remains infinitely transcendent, infinitely foreign" to the I (p. 194). In the same vein, Levinas says that the presence of the Other is "infinite" because it "overflows" rather than being "contained in" the boundaries of the non-moral domain of the I.

This language of infinity leads Levinas to his striking comparison with Descartes's ontological argument. Just as Descartes's argument begins from the presence of the idea of an infinite being in the mind of the I, so Levinas's description begins with the presence of the infinite Other in the experience of the I. In both cases, the infinity of the being encountered utterly surpasses (overflows) the finite I, and nonetheless the I is able to have meaningful access to the infinity (to "clearly and distinctly perceive" the existence of God, to "hear the moral call" of the Other). The difference is that, where Descartes's perception is the outcome of deductive argument, "what is produced here is not a reasoning, but the epiphany that occurs as a face" (p. 196).

Levinas's language of absoluteness, transcendence, and infinity is not meant to characterize the Other in theological terms, as a god. The point is rather that encounter with the Other involves "the opening of a new dimension" for the I. Here I must deal with something that goes beyond (transcends) the world in which my own satisfaction is the ultimate goal and standard, that is not contained by the boundaries of this world (is infinite), and that cannot be judged by the standards of this world (is absolute). In other words, the Other (the face) "resists possession, resists my powers" (p. 197). The resistance of the face is not a counter-force, of the same nature as, but of greater strength than, say, "the hardness of the rock" or "the remoteness of a star" (pp. 197–8). Rather, the face "invites me to a relation incommensurable with a power exercised"; it opens a dimension in which, we might say, my power to appropriate and control is no longer relevant. In Levinas's phrase, the face defies "not the feebleness of my powers" but "the power of my power" (*mon pouvoir de pouvoir*) (p. 198, translation modified).

Despite its transcendence (which Levinas sometimes expresses by saying that it is invisible), I do encounter the face as "a sensible appearance" (p. 198). Specifically, I can locate ("see") it and direct my power against it. But there is this essential difference: in ordinary cases (for example, when I move a piece of furniture or plant tomatoes), I am appropriating an object for my own ends, dominating it but also maintaining it for my use. "The 'negation' effected by appropriation and usage remain[s] always partial. The grasp that contests the independence of the thing preserves it 'for me'" (p. 198). I do not, however, encounter the Other as an object for my use, but as something that is not available for my use. To direct my power against him, to try to use him, is to attack the very existence of the Other. It is, in a word, to try to *kill* the Other. As Levinas explains: "To kill is not to dominate but to annihilate." This is the only form that resistance to the Other can take, since any attempt to exercise power over the Other is a negation of what the Other is (a call to a dimension beyond power). Conversely, "the Other is the sole being I can wish to kill" (p. 198)—not, of course, in the biological sense of kill but in the moral sense of *murder.*

Can I in fact kill the Other? In one sense, of course: "It would be pointless to insist on the banality of murder, which reveals the quasi-null resistance of the obstacle." (p. 198). The Other challenges my world of domination, but "the Other who can sovereignly say *no* to me is exposed to the point of the sword or the revolver's bullet . . . and is obliterated because the sword or the bullet has touched the ventricles or the auricles of his heart". The Other can be killed because "in the contexture of the world he is a quasi-nothing" (p. 199).

But murdering the Other does not suppress "the infinity of his transcendence", does not, that is, destroy the face. This infinity, this face, is "stronger than murder" because it "is the primordial *expression* . . . the first word: 'you shall not commit murder'" p. (199). Here Levinas is implicitly making a distinction that I emphasized above between the Other in the sense of other people with whom we live in the world abstracted from ethical responsibility and the Other in the sense of other people as the foci of our ethical responsibility. The distinction is explicit a bit further on, when Levinas distinguishes between the "manifestation of the face" and the ordinary, phenomenal manifestation of a person: "To manifest oneself as a face is to *impose oneself* above and beyond the manifested and purely phenomenal form" (p. 200).

I can murder the Other in the sense that I can kill another person. But doing so will not eliminate the responsibility not to kill that arises from my (moral) encounter with the face. In the encounter with the Other, "infinity presents itself as a face in the ethical resistance that paralyses my powers", even though the face appears with "defenceless eyes . . . in its nudity and destitution". Even if I kill the Other, the appeal of the face remains, "firm and absolute" (pp. 199–200).

Levinas emphasizes the linguistic nature of the call or appeal of the face, which he characterizes as "expression". Here expression is not a matter of conveying information, about, for example, the "interior and hidden world" of the Other. Rather, "in expression a being presents itself" (p. 200) and in a way that "does not leave any logical place for contradiction" (p. 201, translation modified). There are, of course, forms of speech that *represent* things to be in a certain way, and representation always allows, in principle, for a skeptical response: "I don't think so", "So it seems, but I'm not so sure", or just an unbelieving shrug or silence. But "the being that expresses itself imposes itself . . . without my being able to be deaf to that appeal". The "imposition" is not, however, made through a show of the face's might or majesty but "with its destitution and nudity" (p. 200). The face presents its vulnerability as the plea, "Do not kill me", and the I is, by that very fact, responsible for the Other.

The responsibility, Levinas insists, is utterly unavoidable, absolute, and unconditional ("infinite", as he will say). He quotes Rabbi Yochanan (third century AD): "To leave men without food is a fault that no circumstance attenuates; the distinction between voluntary and involuntary does not apply here" (p. 201). A very hard saying: how can I be responsible for what I have no control over? Levinas's subsequent comments suggest that he may not be claiming—as the Rabbi seems to be—that I am obligated to do the impossible. He says that, in the presence of hunger (an expression of the face's vulnerability), the I's responsibility is "measured only 'objectively" and is "irrecusable". But he does not go on to speak of providing food that I am not able to provide. There is no appeal to what I am or have (to my "interiority") that allows me to ignore "the [face's] primordial discourse whose first word is obligation". But what does that discourse oblige? It "obliges the entering into discourse". And Levinas goes on to characterize the obligatory discourse in terms of reason and rationality. It is the "commencement of [the] discourse rationalism prays for, a 'force' that convinces even 'the people who do not wish to listen' [Plato, *Republic*, 327b] and thus founds the true universality of reason" (p. 201).

It seems, then, that the response required by the face is a kind of rational justification of myself before the Other. Of course, if I have food I can provide, there will be no justification for not providing it. But suppose I have no food or have only enough food for my children. Then, that is the justification, the rational response, I am required to give to the hunger of the Other. Levinas's point is not that I am absurdly obliged to give the other what I cannot give or to devote my entire existence, ignoring all other obligations, to trying to alleviate this Other's hunger. But Levinas is still asserting a strong thesis. I can never, on his account, simply ignore the needs of other people. To the extent that I (reasonably) can fulfill these needs, I must do so. If I do not fulfill these needs, I must provide an account (reasons, justification) that shows why I am not able to do so. In no case can I avoid *responding* to the Other. This is the responsibility required by the face.

Here we find the answer to the question, so often raised, of whether Levinas really is dealing with ethical questions. The case for a negative answer is based on the excessiveness of "infinite responsibility". If nothing can mitigate the requirement that I respond to the Other's call, if I must expend all my efforts to feed the Other, even if I have no food; if, even after all exertions on behalf of the Other, I still remain infinitely responsible for him, then I can never fulfill my responsibility and so can never be moral. What then does it matter whether I devote my life to feeding others or do almost nothing for them? In either case I have fallen infinitely short of my obligation. The problem becomes particularly clear when we realize that there is not just one Other to whom I have infinite responsibility but an entire world of such Others. Levinas recognizes this as what he calls the problem of "the third" (the other Other). Any plausible response to this problem reveals what even Levinas suggests may be the "utopian" nature of his view of responsibility. For the only way to take account of multiple Others is to mitigate the "infinity" of the commitment to each and introduce the prioritizations and trade-offs between competing claims that characterize concrete ethical thinking. Levinas's utopian model does not tell us how to do this. Indeed, it does not even provide (as, for example, utilitarian or Kantian accounts do) normative principles that offer general guidance to the concrete tasks of ethics. So in what sense is it a relevant contribution to ethics? At best it would seem to be a murky continental counterpart of the arid "meta-ethical" accounts of the meaning of ethical terms that so occupied analytic philosophers before Rawls.

Levinas's account is undoubtedly meta-ethical. It explains the origin of moral obligation, not, however, by analyzing the meanings of terms but by describing the experience in which, he maintains, we become aware of our moral responsibility. Levinas's intent recalls the analytic project of "refuting the moral skeptic". This project is apparent in the Thrasymachean sentence that opens *Totality and Infinity*: "Everyone will readily agree that it is of the highest importance to know whether we are not duped by morality" (p. 21). Levinas goes on, moreover, to formulate the skeptical case in terms the ancient Greeks would immediately recognize. Human life is overshadowed by "the permanent possibility of war", and "the state of war suspends morality", indeed, "it renders morality derisory". Given the constant threat of war, politics—"the art of foreseeing war and winning it by every means"—must be the paradigm of rationality ("the very exercise of reason"). But, since war is the focus of politics, it follows that "politics"—and hence reason—"is opposed to morality" (p. 21).

The first advantage of Levinas's approach is that it deals with a skepticism that arises from the realities of ethical life itself, not as an abstract philosophical query far removed from human concerns. There is always a temptation to think that the tough-minded practicality of the politician or the general trumps the call of morality. The second advantage is that Levinas's response to ethical skepticism appeals to experience rather than to argument or to linguistic analysis. Argument, as repeated efforts have illustrated, can never refute someone (the "moral fanatic") who is willing to deny the premises needed to produce the moral conclusion. Similarly, linguistic analysis shows only that using certain terms ("good", "ought") commits us to a certain conception of morality—not that using these terms is unavoidable. Levinas tries to eliminate the gap left by such approaches through an appeal to an experience that no one can avoid and that has an unequivocal significance. The first advantage shows that Levinas is dealing with a question of fundamental ethical significance. The second suggests that his approach is at least worth pursuing as an alternative to ineffective responses to the skeptical challenge.

Another feature of Levinas's approach that makes it of great interest is its connection of ethics to other normative domains. Readers are understandably most impressed by the dramatic language of the vulnerability of the face pleading "Don't kill me!" and imposing infinite responsibility. But, as we saw, the operative effect of my encounter with the face is to bring me into the space of moral reasons. The imperative is not in fact to, say, "sell all and give it to the poor" but to justify my behavior toward others with good reasons. Once he has established this ethical point, Levinas's next concern is to show how the encounter with the Other is the source of other sorts of rational obligation. Accordingly, the section following "Ethics and the Face" is "Reason and the Face", which maintains that we can deploy language in inquiries guided by evidence rather than self-interest only because the presence of the Other requires disinterested discussion. If I alone were the judge of what is justified or not, there would be no independent criteria of judgment. "The face is the evidence that makes evidence possible" (p. 204). In the following sections, Levinas offers similar accounts for meaning (signification), objectivity, and reason itself.

Levinas's approach is also particularly interesting because it tries to ground moral responsibility in social relations without making it a matter of community consensus. The source of responsibility is not transcendent to the human situation but, as he puts it, "terrestrial". The relation to the Other is an essential feature of our terrestrial condition, not the (violent) imposition of an external (for example, theological) authority. As a result, "society precedes the apparition of these impersonal structures [of reason]" and "universality reigns as the presence of humanity in the eyes that look at me". In sum: "the pluralism of society [does] not disappear in the elevation to reason, but would be its condition" (p. 208)

But responsibility does not derive from psychological features (desires, choices, emotional orientations) of human beings. The Other's expression is an expression not of his "interiority" but of what is objectively required. As Husserl recognized, "the objectivity of thought consists in being valid for everyone . . . The objective becomes objective only through communication". But in Husserl's account, "the Other who makes this communication possible is first constituted for a monadic thought", for "a cogito that [posits] itself absolutely independently of the Other". This is unacceptable because the "basis of objectivity" cannot be "constituted in a purely subjective process" (p. 210). Here, Levinas suggests, Descartes was in advance of Husserl, since he appealed to God (the divine "Other") as the essential support of his cogito. Levinas's approach is structurally the same, but it avoids the need for an argument connecting the idea of the Other to the existence of the (divine) Other. For the case of a (human) Other, no argument is needed, since I directly encounter the Other. Levinas's account is distinctive because it claims that the human Other presents itself primordially not as a psychological self but as a pure demand for responsibility. Given this, he can ground responsibility in the human community without making it an object of contingent agreement.

Levinas famously says that, for him, in contrast to philosophical tradition since the Greeks, "morality"—rather than metaphysics or ontology—is "first philosophy" (p. 304). This, however, is misleading if we take "morality" in its ordinary sense. What is "first" (fundamental) for Levinas is a responsibility to justify ourselves to others. This responsibility is the source of every sort of normativity—ethical, semantic, logical, and epistemological. The requirement in every case is that I address the Other in a discourse that does not simply express my demands or interests but speaks to shared standards of validity. When the discussion is about how I am responding to other people's needs and rights (to live, to be nourished, to be told the truth), then the normativity is ethical. But, when the discussion is about linguistic meaning, the logical force of an argument, or the evidence for a scientific hypothesis, then the normativity is of other sorts. We may, of course, think that any normativity derived from our relation to others is moral; then all normativity is moral (ethical). But then there is still a need to distinguish ethical responsibility in the narrow sense from semantic, logical, and epistemological responsibility.

Levinas suggests a narrowly ethical construal when he makes the demand of the Other be "Don't kill me!". But the demand could have equally been "Don't affirm the consequent!" or "Don't draw conclusions from non-random samples!" Moreover, as many commentators have noticed, our sheer encounter with the Other does not in fact forbid particular modes of behavior such as murder or affirming the consequent. Rather, it places us in the "space of reasons", where we are required to develop, through discourse with others, specific norms as criteria of justification. As far as Levinas's account goes, the Other's "Don't kill me" has literally the force of "Don't ignore my presence!" or "Don't act as if I don't exist!". It is just this demand for dialogue that cannot be ignored; violating a specific injunction, even "Don't kill me!", may turn out to be justified in a given case.

"Morality is first philosophy", therefore, is really the discovery that ethics, in the broad sense of the normativity associated with the relation to the Other, is itself metaphysics. (And, in fact, just before the famous tag, Levinas says that "the duality of the face to face ... is a situation that ... is metaphysics itself" (p. 304).). What distinguishes Levinas's metaphysics from traditional versions is its rejection of *totality* in favor of *infinity*. "Totality", which Levinas sees as the ruling concept of traditional metaphysical systems, is the "visage of being that shows itself in war" (p. 21)—the war that is the enemy of morality. If reality is at root war, then "individuals are reduced to being bearers of forces that command them unbeknownst to themselves", so that their "meaning ... is derived from the totality" that finally results when the conflict ends. On such a view, "the ultimate meaning alone counts" and "the unicity of each present is incessantly sacrificed to a future appealed to bring forth its objective meaning" (p. 22). Totality dominates any view for which ultimate meaning and truth lie in an eternal objectivity (Plato's Forms, Aquinas's Pure Act, Spinoza's God/Nature, Hegel's Absolute) outside the subjectivity of particular temporal existence.

Levinas explicitly presents his view as "a defense of subjectivity" and of "the particular and the personal", which he characterizes as "unsurpassable". But he insists that his defense will not operate "at the level of [subjectivity's] purely egoist protestation against totality, nor in its anguish before death" (p. 26). In other words, he will not defend the subjectivity of the self in its enjoyment of its own interiority. Rather, he presents subjectivity as involving (at every moment) an essential relationship to the Other before whom it is infinitely responsible. The infinity of this responsibility contrasts with the totality of traditional metaphysics. Both totality and infinity function to connect "the particular and the personal" to something "transcendent" and thereby prevent it from collapsing into the nothingness of its own atomic isolation. But, if we give meaning to a subjectivity that exists as a particular person by connecting it to an eternal transcendent (totality), we surpass its "unsurpassable" particularity. It has no meaning of its own. By instead giving meaning to the subjectivity by relating it to the Other (to which it is here and now infinitely responsible), Levinas's account does not surpass the subject's particularity, but rather shows how this particularity is constituted as unsurpassable.

Levinas, Deleuze, and the Other

Although Deleuze never responded to *Totality and Infinity*,[8] the book would seem to be a serious challenge to his views, and it is well worth reflecting on how this might be so. Giorgio Agamben suggests one tempting approach with his distinction of two "trajectories" of French philosophy: one of immanence, of which Deleuze is a primary example; and one of transcendence, of which Levinas is a primary example.[9] Deleuze rejects all forms of transcendence on the Nietzschean grounds that it always involves a negation of this world in the name of some superior other world. One prototype is the standard interpretation of Platonic Forms as "really real" in contrast to their material "imitations". Another prototype is Hegelian dialectic, in which the synthesis transcends thesis and antithesis, thereby subordinating them to a higher achievement. But the same sort of devaluation is effected by many other standard philosophical moves: by positing universals that transcend particulars, reason that transcends sensibility, or a subject that transcends its experiences. Deleuze sees transcendence as expressed by the abstractions in terms of which philosophers have tried to unify and hence overcome the multiplicity (difference) that is immanent in actual events. "There are no such things as universals, there's nothing transcendent, no Unity, subject (or object), Reason". What there is instead is immanence or, as Deleuze likes to say, "fields of immanence" filled with sheer multiplicities (differences) that cannot be controlled by higher (transcendent) unities. "Unifying, subjectifying, rationalizing" occur, but they are "just processes . . . at work in concrete multiplicities" and "have no special status" in principle over other processes that reverse them. The point is "the production of something new"; unifying, rationalizing, and so on do this sometimes, but "they often amount to an impasse or closing off that prevents" novelty.[10]

We have seen Levinas's emphasis on the transcendence of the Other, as opposed to the immanence (interiority) of the I. But is this in fact an instance of what Deleuze opposes? The Other, after all, does not speak to me from another world. Quite the contrary, the concrete world in which I am a morally responsible subject is constituted by my encounter with the Other. Apart from the Other, there is only the abstraction of the I's life of appropriation and enjoyment. Further, what Deleuze

[8] Deleuze's only mention of Levinas seems to be in a footnote, where he cites his work in a survey of philosophies connected to religious traditions (Gilles Deleuze and Félix Guattari, *What Is Philosophy?*, tr. J. Tomlinson and G. Burchell III (New York: Columbia University Press, 1996), 223 n. 5).

[9] Giorgio Agamben, *Potentialities: Collected Essays in Philosophy*, tr. Daniel Heller-Roazen (Stanford, CA: Stanford University Press, 2000), 239.

[10] Gilles Deleuze, *Negotiations: 1972–1990*, tr. Martin Joughin (New York: Columbia University Press, 1995), 145, 146. For a helpful general discussion of Deleuze on immanence, see James Williams's entry on the term in Adrian Parr (ed.), *The Deleuze Dictionary* (New York: Columbia University Press, 2005), 125–7.

rejects as transcendence corresponds to what Levinas rejects as totality, which locates the meaning of temporal realities in the eternal objectivities such as Plato's Forms or Hegel's Absolute. In Deleuzian language, Levinas is asserting that the Other is immanent to (in the same world as) the I and rejecting the subordination of temporal existents to a transcendent objectivity—both claims that Deleuze accepts. Conversely, Deleuze's immanence correspond not to Levinas's interiority but to his insistence that the I be described with full concreteness (that is, in relation to the Other). Contrary to appearances, we cannot oppose Levinas as a philosopher of transcendence to Deleuze as a philosopher of immanence. Once we sort out what they mean by "transcendence" and "immanence", the apparent conflict disappears.

There is, nonetheless, a deep opposition to Levinas that can be seen in Deleuze's account of the Other in *The Logic of Sense.*[11] The account is developed from a reading of the novel *Friday*, a retelling of Defoe's Robinson Crusoe story by Michel Tournier (Deleuze's boyhood friend). Deleuze presents Tournier's book as a literally "experimental" novel, imagining what a world without the Other would be like and inferring from that "the effects of the presence of Others in our habitual world" (pp. 304–5).

The primary "effect" of the Other is "the organization of a marginal world". According to Deleuze (and Tournier), my sense that, for example, the bar at which I am seated has a back side that I could see if I walked behind it is due to my positing that it is visible to the bartender on the other side. Similarly, "as for the objects behind my back, I sense them coming together and forming a world, precisely because they are visible to, and are seen by, Others" (p. 305). In general, then, the Other helps make my world less frightening by providing a reassuring connection between what I see and what I do not see. Unseen things do not simply "jump out at me" when I turn toward them; their presence has been telegraphed by my sense that the Other is (or could be) perceiving them. Nor is the point purely epistemological. My appropriation of the world also works through the Other: "I desire nothing that cannot be seen, thought, or possessed by a possible Other. That is the basis of my desire. It is always Others who relate my desire to an object" (p. 306).

When the Other is removed, as in Tournier's story, my experience loses its softening around the edges; there is no longer a reassuring bridge between what I see and what I don't see: "My vision of the island is reduced to that of my own eyes, and what I do not see of it is to me a total unknown. Everywhere I am not total darkness reigns" (p. 306).[12] The result, as Deleuze makes vivid, is frightening: "A harsh and black world, without potentialities or virtualities: the category of the possible has collapsed. Instead of relatively harmonious forms surging forth . . . and back . . . [there is] only a groundless abyss, rebellious and devouring" (p. 306). There are no more soothing transitions ("the sweetness of contiguities" (p. 307)), no way of anticipating what I will encounter at the next turn.

[11] Gilles Deleuze, *The Logic of Sense*, tr. M. Lester and C. Stivale (New York: Columbia University Press, 1990), 301–31. References will be given in the text.

[12] Citing Michel Tournier, *Friday*, tr. Norman Denny (New York: Pantheon, 1985), 55.

By comparing my world with the Other to my world without the Other, "we are in a position to say what the Other is" (p. 307). The first thing to say, according to Deleuze, is that, contrary to most philosophers (including Sartre), the Other is not present as a particular object or subject. "The Other is neither an object in the field of my perception nor a subject who perceives me". Rather, the Other "is a structure of the perceptual field", essential for the field's functioning. Particular subjects (which may also be objects), "real characters", may "actualize" the structure within a given field (p. 307). But the structure itself is not reducible to these characters.

Precisely what is this structure? It is, first of all, "the structure of the possible". This is not, however, a mere abstract possibility, "designating something which does not exist". A frightening possibility, for example, is "expressed" by a "frightened countenance" (indeed, a face), and "the expressed possible world certainly exists", although "it does not exist (actually) outside of that which expresses it". The possibility exists as expressed in the Other's face or, especially, speech. In fact, "language is the reality of the possible as such" (p. 307). In sum, then, "the Other, as structure, is *the expression of a possible world*; it is the expressed, grasped as not yet existing outside of that which expresses it" (p. 308).[13]

The Other structures the perceptual field according to a set of categories, including even the subject–object distinction and the temporality of the world in which subject and object exist (pp. 310–11). But, Deleuze asks, what happens when the Other disappears? At first, the "structure continues to survive and function". But, according to Tournier, eventually the structure disappears, and even when another person (Friday) shows up, Robinson "will no longer apprehend him as an Other" (p. 309). Initially, Robinson experiences "the loss of Others as a fundamental disorder", but in time he discovers that this loss is a great opportunity, the opening to his "adventure" (p. 309). It turns out that "the Other was the trouble" (p. 311). It is, in fact, Friday—the non-Other, as Tournier presents him—who leads Robinson into a new world, one not weighted down by the structures imposed by the Other, and "open[s] up a possibility of salvation" (p. 315). Deleuze is dramatic but unspecific in saying what this salvation involves. He speaks of "liberat[ing] pure elements which are ordinarily held prisoner" (p. 319), of a "dehumanized Robinson", now capable of "standing erect" without the weight of the Other's "recumbent organization" (pp. 312–13), of Robinson's "conquest of the Great Health" (p. 315). What is clear is that the new world is a sharp break with the structures imposed by the Other (in Tournier's story, this is brought about by an explosion Friday unintentionally causes) and that, in particular, Robinson escapes from the category of the subject and lives without taking any account of the Other. There is no place for an ethics of interpersonal responsibility.[14]

[13] Although Deleuze does not say so explicitly, his point is presumably that the possibility expressed by the Other exists *for me* only in this expression. For the Other, this possibility is, surely, actual.

[14] As Peter Hallward puts it, "Nothing is more foreign to Deleuze than an unconditional concern for the other as other" (*Out of this World: Deleuze and the Philosophy of Creation* (London: Verso, 2006), 92).

There is a surprising amount of agreement between Deleuze's and Levinas's "phenomenologies" of the Other. They agree on the key claims that my position as a subject in a world of objects is constituted by the Other and that this constitution is effected through linguistic expression. Also, in placing me in this world, the Other in both cases sets requirements on how I can conduct myself in it. Deleuze expresses these requirements in terms of ontological structure, whereas Levinas does so in terms of moral responsibility. But there is good reason to think that these emphases correspond to two compatible dimensions of the Other's world that both philosophers would accept. Levinas would hardly deny that the subject–object world has an ontological structure (of, for example, space, time, and causality) in addition to the ethical structure he insists on. And Deleuze certainly sees the constitution of the world as fraught with ethical responsibility to the Other. From what is Robinson being liberated if not this responsibility? Certainly not the causal laws of motion. If the subject–object world lacks ethical responsibility, there is no sense to his rejection of this world. Also recall Deleuze's claim that, when the Other is present, my desire is always related to him.

The disagreement lies in Deleuze's claim that it is both possible and desirable that responsibility to the Other be eliminated from the world. What he denies is the "infinity" (unavoidability) of my responsibility to the Other. This is a Nietzschean twist on moral skepticism, in which the skeptic does not deny the de facto presence of responsibility to the Other but maintains that this is merely a contingent fact that we should, moreover, try to overcome. Here we see the convergence of Deleuze's metaphysics with Foucault's genealogy.

The appeal to genealogy seems necessary if Deleuze is to make a case against Levinas. Simply on the level of phenomenological description, Deleuze has no way of denying that our world includes moral responsibility to Others. How can he show that a world without the Other is even possible? We might think that his turning to Tournier's novelistic "experiment" is a version of Husserlian imaginative variation, revealing possibilities that are implicit in the experience being described. But imaginative variation can uncover only possibilities based on the categories of the world being described. I can "see" that a sphere can be indefinitely increased in size because that is a truth underwritten by the categories of ordinary spatial perception. Nothing in my experience of the world can support the possibility that the structure imposed by the Other is eliminable. (I can imagine a world from which all others have vanished, but, as Deleuze himself emphasizes, this is not the same as eliminating the corresponding categorical structures.) Tournier's novel is not an experiment but science fiction; like most fictional accounts of time travel, it "imagines" what is conceptually impossible.

On the other hand, if Deleuze appeals (through Nietzsche or Foucault) to the historical genealogy of ethical responsibility, Levinas cannot cut off that appeal by simply reiterating the phenomenologically perceived necessity of responsibility to the Other. When there is a plausible opposing account that suggests a contingent origin for responsibility, then we must remain open to the possibility that our a priori description is flawed. (Here a parallel would be a mathematician who denied the consistency of well-developed systems of non-Euclidean geometry on the basis of the intuitive "necessity" of the Euclidean system.) Nor does there seem to be any likelihood of refuting the genealogical account on its own historical terms. How could we show simply from *historical* evidence that morality is not a historical contingency?

Deleuze and Levinas disagree regarding the alleged infinite (ineradicable) responsibility to the Other. Their phenomenological descriptions cannot settle the matter: Deleuze has no way of establishing even the possibility of a world without the Other, much less the preferability of such a world. Levinas has no way of responding to a genealogical undermining of the apparent necessity of responsibility. But genealogy is not decisive. An appeal to Nietzsche or Foucault may raise doubts about Levinas's account, but could never refute it. The problem is not that an argument from genealogy amounts to the genetic fallacy of negatively evaluating something because of its "base" origin. An argument from dubious origins is entirely in place when, as is often done for morality, a practice is defended precisely because of its "noble" origin (the will of God, the requirements of human nature). But Levinas does not argue from the origin of ethical responsibility. To do so would be to invoke the nature of the Other (for example, his interiority) as the reason why we must heed his call. Levinas merely points to the patent authority of the Other's "Do not kill me"; there is no "account" of the Other that grounds this authority. Even the most debunking historical account of how ethical responsibility originated would be consistent with its *also* having, independently of this origin, its intrinsic authority.

The stalemate between Deleuze and Levinas indicates, I suggest, that their conflicting accounts of the Other begin from opposing pre-philosophical evaluations of ethical responsibility. We saw in Chapter 5 how Nietzsche's critique of values was based on his conviction that they derive from evaluations that are themselves base or noble. Just as that conviction precedes and informs his genealogical critique, so Deleuze's conviction opposing responsibility to the Other precedes his account of the Other. But the same is true of Levinas. At the most, his phenomenology of the Other can show that the Other's call is authoritative in terms of the subject–object framework it constitutes. Phenomenological description does not have the resources to show that there are no coherent or even preferable alternatives to the framework in which it occurs. When Levinas claims this, he can only be appealing to a pre-philosophical conviction that he brings to his account of the Other. Phenomenological description is not sufficient to establish his ethical position.

7

The Turn to Ethics: Derrida, Levinas, and Foucault

Derrida and Levinas on justice

Unlike Deleuze and like Foucault, Derrida took an explicitly ethical turn in the 1980s. Previously, there had been debates about whether his thought (specifically the technique of deconstructive reading, so widely applied—or at least mimicked) had ethical and political implications. Some saw Derrida's ambivalence toward the events of May 1968 as a sign of disengagement. We have already noted (in Chapter 1) his muted comments in "The Ends of Man", delivered in October 1968. Looking back in 1991, he said:

> I was not what is called a "soixante-huitard"... Even though I participated at that time in demonstrations and organized the first general meeting at the École Normale, I was on my guard, even worried in the face of a certain cult of spontaneity, a fusionist, anti-unionist euphoria, in the face of the enthusiasm of a finally "freed" speech, of restored "transparence", and so forth. I never believed in those things.[1]

But hesitations and nuance before the "events" were more likely to be a sign of serious ethical engagement than the reverse. The real issue concerns the implications, if any, of Derrida's ideas for ethical issues, and, at least, we can say that in his early work—in contrast, say, to Foucault—these were not clear.

But by the 1980s Derrida was directly applying deconstructive analysis to ethical notions such as justice, hospitality, and friendship, and his views seem importantly similar to those of Levinas, whom he explicitly cites. Many of the pertinent issues arise in a discussion of Derrida (and Levinas) by Richard Rorty, Simon Critchley, and Derrida himself.[2] Rorty begins with a rough distinction between "philosophers... whose work fulfills primarily public purposes, and those whose work fulfills primarily

[1] Jacques Derrida, *Points... : Interviews, 1974–1994* (Palo Alto, CA: Stanford University Press, 1995), 347.

[2] Chantal Mouffe (ed.), *Deconstruction and Pragmatism* (London: Routledge, 1996), 16. Further references to essays by Critchley, Derrida, and Rorty in this work will be given in the text.

private purposes" (p. 16). He cites Mill, Dewey, and Rawls as public philosophers and Nietzsche, Heidegger, and Derrida as private philosophers. The work of public philosophers has direct applications to the discussion of political problems (capital punishment, education, distributive justice), whereas that of private philosophers "produc[es] private satisfactions to people who are deeply involved with philosophy (and therefore, necessarily, with metaphysics) but not as politically consequential, except in a very indirect and long-term way" (p. 16). Rorty's favorite Derridean texts are those, like the novelistic "Envois" section of *The Post Card* and the autobiographical *Circonfession*, that are particularly "vivid and forceful forms of private self-creation". But he regards even Derrida's "more 'strictly philosophical'" writings, such as those on Husserl, as "attempts to work out his private relationships to the figures who have meant most to him" (p. 17).

Rorty classifies as "private" books such as *The Politics of Friendship* and *The Gift of Death*, which many see as explicitly ethical and political. His reason is that they express "the specifically Levinasian strains in [Derrida's] thought". He goes on to say, in a passage particularly interesting for our purposes: "I am unable to connect Levinas's pathos of the infinite with ethics or politics." This is because Rorty sees "ethics and politics . . . as a matter of reaching accommodation between competing interests, and as something to be deliberated about in banal, familiar terms—terms which do not need philosophical dissection and do not have philosophical presuppositions" (p. 17).

Critchley agrees that Derrida's later thought is ethical in precisely Levinas's sense of ethics: "Derridian deconstruction can and indeed should be understood as an ethical demand, provided one understands ethics in the particular and novel sense given to that word in the work of Emmanuel Levinas" (p. 32). But, he claims, this is precisely why "deconstruction . . . qualif[ies] as public by Rorty's own criteria" (p. 34). His argument turns on the audacious claim that Levinas's ethics is in practice equivalent to Rorty's own liberalism. Adding to this Critchley's claim that Derrida's ethics is Levinasian yields the conclusion that Derrida's ethics is as politically relevant as Rorty's liberalism.

Critchley illustrates the ethical tie between Derrida and Levinas through an analysis of Derrida's striking assertion "Deconstruction is justice".[3] This is based on Derrida's distinction between law and justice. Law is the set of rules we establish to ensure justice, understood vaguely as fair treatment for everyone. In fact, however, applying any set of laws will result in injustice for some cases. This is because the concepts in terms of which laws are formulated will sometimes fall short of the implicit ideal of justice. A rule that is just for a wide range of instances will be unjust for some particular instances. Therefore, we can deconstruct any system of laws, showing how it is eventually inconsistent with its own goal of justice. But, if law is deconstructable, then justice—in light of which law is deconstructed—must be undeconstructable, "the undecon-

[3] Jacques Derrida, "Force of Law: The 'Mystical Foundation of Authority'", in D. Cornell, M. Rosenfeld, and D. G. Carlson (eds.), *Deconstruction and the Possibility of Justice* (Cambridge, MA: Harvard University Press, 1992), 14–15.

structable condition of the possibility for deconstruction" (p. 34). Because deconstruction has justice as its condition of possibility, Derrida concludes that "nothing is more just than what I today call deconstruction" (p. 34).[4]

What exactly is justice for Derrida? Critchley points out that, although Derrida sometimes talks of it as an experience of "the mystical" or "the impossible", he most often says that "justice is an 'experience' of the undecidable" (p. 34) (the same term he uses of textual readings). It is, Critchley notes, precisely to explain his notion of undecidability that Derrida evokes Levinas. "An undecidable experience of justice does not arise in some intellectual intuition or theoretical deduction, rather, it always arises in relation to . . . the singularity of the other" (p. 34). Here Derrida explicitly cites Levinas's definition of justice in *Totality and Infinity* as "the relation with the Other".[5] Critchley explicates: "Justice arises in the particular and non-subsumptive relation to the other, as a response to suffering that demands an infinite responsibility" (p. 34). On Critchley's reading, the experience of the Other (and hence of justice) is "undecidable" because the singularity of the Other "exceeds my cognitive powers" (p. 35) so that decisions about justice cannot be adequately justified. They have, Derrida says, the aspect of a Kierkegaardian leap or what Kierkegaard also calls "the madness of the decision".

Derrida's undecidability is a more radical version of Levinas's unconceivability of the Other. Levinas's Other, as we saw in Chapter 6, is inconceivable in terms of the concepts of interiority, but can, nonetheless be understood through a phenomenological description of our encounter with him. Derrida's Other is inconceivable *tout court*, and, in particular, is not accessible to phenomenological description.

The undecidability of justice "must lie outside the public realm", but our experience of it leads to public decisions and actions. Accordingly, Derrida's (and Levinas's) ethical notion of justice "seems to be essentially connected to the possibility of political reformation, transformation and progress", and Derrida cites as examples such paradigmatic liberal achievements as "the Declaration of the Rights of Man and the abolition of slavery" (p. 35). Indeed, Derrida has no qualms about an unequivocal endorsement of the classical liberal ideal of emancipation: "Nothing seems to me less outdated than the classical emancipatory ideal" (cited p. 35).

At this point, Critchley claims to have shown that Derrida's "experience of justice" is equivalent to or based on Levinas's "experience of the Other", and that their common ethical position has consequences for concrete ethico-political action. Why is this ethical position basically the same as Rorty's? Because, says Critchley, Rorty's definition of liberalism (which expresses his fundamental ethical stance) is the same as Levinas's definition of ethics as a relation to the Other. Rorty's definition of liberalism

[4] Citing, Derrida, "Force of Law", 21.

[5] Emmanuel Levinas, *Totality and Infinity: An Essay on Exteriority*, tr. Alphonso Linguis (Pittsburgh, PA: Duquesne University Press, 1969), 62–3. Critchley notes that, in his preface to the German translation of *Totality and Infinity*, Levinas says that in that book justice serves as a synonym for the ethical (p. 34).

is that "cruelty is the worst thing there is", and that this rejection of cruelty is "the only social bond we need" (p. 33). Implicit in this formulation are an ethical and a methodological point: ethically, the only principle we need to guide our relations with others is the injunction not to hurt them; methodologically, this principle itself is basic and needs no support—philosophical or otherwise—from further considerations. But Levinas too holds that harm to the Other is the unique ethical demand, and he holds that we are bound by this demand simply because, before the face of the Other, we directly experience its undeniability. Critchley allows that Rorty would be uneasy with the hints of foundationalism in Levinas's use of phenomenological description, but submits that their positions on ethics are "essentially doing the same work" (p. 33). Assuming that Rorty's liberalism, like that of Mill, Dewey, and Rawls, has strong relevance to the public sphere, it follows that Levinas's ethics does too. And, since Derrida's ethics is essentially Levinasian, Derrida's ethics, contrary to Rorty's claim, is likewise relevant.

In his reply to Critchley, Rorty countenances no reconciliation with Levinas (nor with the Levinasian aspects of Derrida's ethics). Confronted with talk of ethics as an infinite responsibility to the Other or of justice as an experience of the unexperiencable, he says little more than that he does not see the point of such locutions. He agrees that deciding ethical questions can be difficult, but thinks it is "pointless hype to dramatize our difficulties in knowing what to do by labeling our goal 'indescribable', 'unexperiencable', 'unintelligible', or 'infinitely distant'" (p. 42). We might have expected something more positive from Rorty, whose tendency in reading continental authors is to happily translate their obscure jargon into good pragmatic sense whenever he can and ignore it when he cannot. In particular, it might seem that Rorty might have at least resonated to Levinas's turn to ethics as a healthy move away from 1960s anti-humanist radicalism of Deleuze and Foucault. No doubt one counter-wind to such a move is the religious overtones in Levinas, which would certainly have put off an atheist like Rorty. But, even apart from the whiff of religion, there is (contrary to Critchley's—no doubt somewhat ironic—suggestion) little to attract a pragmatic liberal like Rorty to his ethics.

To begin with, Critchley is stretching things when he suggests that my relation to the Other enjoins against making other people suffer. As we have seen, the drama of "Don't kill me" is merely an emphatic expression of the requirement that I never simply disregard the Other; that, to the extent that I do not respond to the Other's needs, I must provide a justification for not doing so. For all the Levinasian encounter with the Other shows, I may be able to justify my ill-treatment of certain people on the grounds that it is necessary for a higher moral good. The encounter presents the Other as no more than someone who deserves the respect of an explanation. It provides no basis for preferring one sort of ethical explanation over another. I must always acknowledge that the Other's suffering is a matter of my concern and that I must alleviate it to the extent that it is morally proper for me to do so. But Levinasian ethics provides no account at all of what is morally proper, for it does not yield any guidance about what sort of human world moral behavior is meant to produce. It provides, in other words, no first-order norms, but only the meta-norm that I must justify what I do in terms of first-order norms.

This normative thinness derives from the *infinity* of responsibility that Levinas insists on. An infinite responsibility is one to which I must always attend and can never entirely fulfill. It concerns something that I always owe to everyone. There is a dramatic *frission* in the thought that morality makes me assume an unbearable burden, that my entire existence must be devoted to the Sisyphean task of, say, freeing everyone from pain, making everyone happy or free, or whatever else might be the *telos* of ethical life. We can be fascinated and excited by the prospect of so heroically tragic a task. But a bit of reflection makes it clear that there can be no moral responsibility of this sort. "Ought" does imply "can", and there is no way that I can be morally obliged to (judged at fault if I do not) bring about a result that I cannot bring about. Infinite responsibility concerns not the results I must bring about for others but the attitude I must maintain toward others no matter what. Morality may, in fact, require me to inflict or permit an immense amount of suffering on others. What Levinas's Other demands is that, however much suffering I must inflict or allow, I must also maintain a sense of the moral importance of the Other's needs and the necessity of having a good moral reason for in any way making the Other suffer. But it does not and cannot demand that, in a given situation, I improve (or even try to improve) the lot of any particular other.

We can also put the point in terms of what Rawls and others have called conceptions of the human good. What Levinas shows by his description of the encounter with the Other is that I owe every other person moral respect, which implies that I must strive to achieve the human good for everyone. But my infinite responsibility for the Other is not based on any particular conception of the human good. This is why Critchley cannot assimilate Levinas to Rortyan liberalism. The liberal commitment is not just to moral respect for everyone but to a particular conception of the human good that all moral behavior must try to achieve. Moral respect requires constant recognition of the Other's needs but, lacking a conception of the human good to specify these needs, it requires no specific action on the Other's behalf. Since Rorty's liberal claim that cruelty is the worst thing we can do is (part of) a specific conception of the human good, Critchley is wrong to claim that Levinas's ethics is equivalent to Rorty's.

This normative thinness of Levinas's ethics is why it is not relevant to the public realm of ethico-political discussion. This realm presupposes participants who are already committed to moral responsibility—and indeed to shared or at least overlapping (in Rawls's sense) conceptions of the human good. The question of whether we are morally responsible for one another (for the Other) does not arise in the public domain, which therefore has no need of Levinas's account. Such an account could in principle be relevant for moral skeptics, for, that is, individuals who have doubts about the reality of moral responsibility and therefore—to the extent these doubts are not purely hyperbol-ical—might withdraw from public ethico-religious discussions. But only the most unusual of moral skeptics will overcome their doubts through the study of a complex philosophical treatment of moral responsibility. Falling in love, having children, nursing a sick friend, or even hearing the right preacher—is more likely to do the trick.

This irrelevance of Levinas's account is due to its meta-normative character—the fact that it does not propose norms that can be used for deciding ethico-political questions but instead develops an account of why there are any norms at all. As Diane Perpich puts it, Levinas's ethics is about "normativity without norms".[6] In the ordinary analytic parlance, it is meta-ethical. And no worse for that. Many philosophical discussions question assumptions that are essential for carrying on everyday life. (Is it possible to know anything? Are there minds other than my own? Are human actions free?) We learn a great deal from reflecting on such questions, but we can hardly expect that finding answers to them would be a concern *within* domains of thought and action that already assume such answers.

The relevant criticism of Levinas is not that he discusses meta-normative rather than normative issues but that he so often gives the impression—through his highly charged dramatic language—that he is proposing ethical norms. Caught up in his drama of a vulnerable face pleading "Do not murder me!" and imposing an infinite responsibility, we at first readily assume that Levinas is proposing a startlingly new normative principle. He seems to be saying that I may never harm another in any way, or perhaps that I am responsible for others to the extent that I should give up everything to relieve their misery. Levinas sounds like Peter Singer on transcendental steroids. Even after we realize that Levinas cannot be meaning anything quite so extreme, it remains unclear how to mitigate the view, and, when efforts in that direction prove unconvincing, the very question of what Levinas means by ethics—or even whether he is doing ethics—becomes the interpretative focus. So Diane Perpich, one of his most perspicuous recent readers, begins her discussion with the chapter "But Is it *Ethics*?" (p. 1). After several more chapters, she rightly concludes that Levinas deals with normativity and not norms, but notes that, "despite the fact that Levinas's commentators regularly want to divorce his work from so-called normative ethics, almost no one actually adheres to the terms of such a divorce" (p. 125).

In any case, the meta-ethical nature of Levinas's treatment takes it out of the public domain of ethico-political discussion about how to make people's life better. The intense language may serve to motivate some of us better to focus on our generic responsibility to others, and Levinas's descriptions of the encounter with the Other may occasionally help remove doubts about the reality of ethical responsibility. But, for the most part, Levinas's achievement is theoretical, not practical.

Finally, how does Derrida fit in the picture? We can start with Critchley's claim that Derrida's "deconstruction is ethical in the peculiarly Levinasian sense". To support this Critchley puts forward, as a paradigm example, Derrida's twice citing Levinas at crucial

[6] Diane Perpich, *The Ethics of Emmanuel Levinas* (Stanford, CA: Stanford University Press, 2008), 126. Further references will be given in the text.

points in his discussion of justice. In the first passage, Derrida has characterized justice as "infinite" and "incalculable", outstripping the law's "calculable . . . system of regulated and coded prescriptions". He then says, "I would be tempted, up to a certain point, to compare the concept of justice . . . to Levinas's", which Levinas defines in *Totality and Infinity* as "relation to the Other". Derrida is particularly struck by the "infinity" and the "heteronymy" (asymmetry) of the relation to the Other, both of which evoke his own idea of justice as beyond the grasp of the order of our thought. But Derrida quickly backs away from the comparison: "since Levinas's difficult discourse would give rise to other difficult questions, I cannot be content to borrow conceptual moves without risking confusions or analogies. And so I will move no further in this direction" (*Force of Law*, p. 22). The second mention of Levinas is just as tentative. Derrida is explaining his view that the deliberative assertions of the law, governed by the rational rules for true discourse, presuppose the "madness" of the precipitate decision that he calls "justice". As an aside, he says that he would understand Levinas's statement "Truth presupposes justice"[7] in terms of this explanation. But, he cautions, Levinas is speaking "in a whole other language and following an entirely different discursive problem" (*Force of Law*, p. 27). Derrida may well agree with Levinas's account of our infinite responsibility to the Other, but these guarded and deliberately undeveloped comparisons do not support the conclusion that his deconstructive view of justice is equivalent to or even presupposes Levinas's views.

The thought that the two views are closely connected if not the same is tempting only because they both posit, at a key point, an essential unintelligibility. For Levinas, moral responsibility derives from an experience of the Other that cannot be conceptually explicated (at least in terms of anything outside the experience) or turned into a rational justification. For Derrida, justice is likewise an experience that goes beyond what we can conceptualize or make reasonable. But, as we have seen, for Levinas the inconceivability is merely relative to the concepts of interiority, whereas for Derrida it is absolute. Moreover, even if there are truths that are beyond our understanding, it does not follow that they are the same truth. In the dark, all cows are not actually black, they just all *look* black. The fact that conceptual–rational understanding cannot discriminate two truths does not show that they are the same truth, unless we make such understanding a necessary condition of truth. But then we have rejected the idea that there are truths beyond such understanding.

There is also good reason to think that Levinas's infinite responsibility and Derrida's justice operate in different ethical domains and so cannot come to the same thing. Levinas's experience of the Other provides an account of the source of normativity that, however, has no consequences for discussions about specific norms. But Derrida explicitly presents his experience of justice as the source of a decision that has consequences for our acceptance or rejection of specific norms. For him, "justice is what

[7] Levinas, *Totality and Infinity*, 61–2.

gives us the impulse, the drive, the movement to improve the law",[8] to improve, that is, our current system of norms. Derridian justice, unlike Levinasian responsibility (and despite its absolute inconceivability), is meant to have consequences for what norms we accept.

There is, however, something to Rorty's claim that these consequences are not particularly impressive. Once again, high rhetoric suggests more than it delivers. What, for example, does the dramatic "deconstruction is justice" amount to? Well, first of all, it is not quite that deconstruction *is* justice. Rather, our "experience" of justice gives us the "impulse" to deconstruct the law for the sake of "improving" it. What this means in practice is that we will always find in any system of laws features that do not accord with our (not entirely articulable) sense of what justice requires. Starting from this sense, we can "deconstruct" the given legal system; that is, we can point out ways in which it falls short of what we think justice requires and present them as "contradictions" in the system. We may, for example, think that something is going wrong when spending unlimited amounts of money lobbying legislators can be defended as an exercise of the constitutional right to free speech. It may be true that our present system of constitutional law does not have the resources to express what has gone wrong here; perhaps the system as currently formulated does require the protection of unrestricted lobbying as free speech. But, like Rorty, I see no value (and some risks) in characterizing our sense that something is wrong as an experience of the "infinite" or the "undecidable". Such language suggests a mystical, transcendent authority that our hard-to-articulate instincts or intuitions do not deserve. As Rorty says, "granted that there are limit situations in which neither familiar practices nor familiar language offers anything very useful, it is no help to characterize what is going on in such situations as self contradiction". It is sufficient—and less misleading—to "think of justice as muddling through—the way judges do when deciding hard cases" (p. 42). Less flippantly, we can think of justice as the process of seeking reformulations of the law that fit better with our intuitions of what it should be. Rorty's point, in any case, is to give our intuitions about justice room to develop without suggesting that they put us in contact with some source of ineffable truth and are not just our halting, fallible sense that something is wrong.

Foucault and ethics

Foucault's last writings lack the high-voltage ethical drama of Levinas and Derrida, but they offer an approach that is more robustly ethical and a distinct alternative to Rorty's common-sense liberalism.

Foucault's work always had an ethical impetus in his outrage over "intolerable" contemporary institutions or practices. His histories were designed to trace the

[8] Jacques Derrida, response in "Villanova Roundtable", in John Caputo (ed.), *Deconstruction in a Nutshell: A Conversation with Jacques Derrida* (New York: Fordham University Press, 1997), 16.

genealogical origins of, for example, the treatment of insanity as "mental illness", the punishment of criminals by imprisonment, the movement to "liberate" sexual behavior through self-understanding. As members of an enlightened modern society, we see no scientifically or ethically acceptable alternatives to these approaches to madness, crime, and sexuality. But Foucault's histories set out to show how they arose from intellectually and morally dubious conceptions that are by no means inevitable. The idea is to provide historical tools for those opposing an intolerable aspect of modern social life.

In every case, Foucault's ethical objection to modern practices seems to have been broadly existentialist: they make people be something they have not chosen for themselves. But he rejected any comprehensive philosophical account (for example, of the "nature of man") supporting this moral stance and simply began from his intense pre-philosophical conviction that the practices were morally intolerable. The issue of an ethics in any philosophical sense was not a meaningful option as Foucault analysed the intertwined structures of knowledge and power underlying modern social practices.

This, however, began to change when Foucault's historical study of modern sexuality made explicit the central role of the subject or self in the network of social constraints. It was, in particular, now apparent that constraints on our behavior were not only externally imposed (by, for example, confinement in an asylum or a prison); they were also internalized as our own view of our self-identity (for example, my "liberating" acceptance of my sexual identity). As a result, the first volume of Foucault's history of sexuality (intended as an introductory overview of four further projected volumes on children, women, perverts, and couples) highlighted the role of the individual subject (self) for the understanding of modern sexuality.

Extending his studies to the self led, however, to a corresponding extension of the historical scope of Foucault's studies. Although he had been previously able to restrict himself to the broadly modern period (with brief looks at the Renaissance), he now decided that he could not understand the modern self without relating it to the medieval Christian view of the self. This Foucault undertook in a study of medieval sexuality (*Les Avoux de la chair*), but, before it was properly finished, he decided that he could understand the medieval stance only by contrasting it with the ancient Greek and Roman history that had preceded it. This led to two volumes on Greek and Roman sexuality, published in 1984. Since this was the year of Foucault's death, the volume on medieval sexuality, in accord with Foucault's dictate of "no posthumous publications", has not appeared.

The two books on ancient sexuality appeared as the second and third volumes of Foucault's history of sexuality, even though they did not carry out any part of the history of modern sexuality projected by the introductory first volume. It is not just that the move to Greece and Rome broadened Foucault's historical scope; it also led to a new conception of his topic. His original project, previewed in volume I, was to tell in detail the story of how individual subjects internalized the normalizing structures of society's power–knowledge. But Foucault found in the ancients the possibility of a meaningful self-construction of the self. This meant not just internalizing external norms or resisting them through counter-power. Rather, it meant the possibility of forging, even if in the interstices left by social constraints, an autonomous self-identity, a project that could, even in a traditional sense, be called ethical.

Readers of Foucault's previous histories might well wonder how his picture of individuals formed by the social power–knowledge nexus can allow room for any project of ethical self-formation. I suggest that the answer lies in his (implicit) move from a focus on *marginalization* to a focus on *problematization*.[9] Marginalization occurs when the constraints of the power–knowledge network are so strong as to threaten a group of individuals with total loss of identity, allowing them no meaningful place in the society (the mad, the criminal, the sexually "perverse"). Here there is a choice only between submitting to normalization (and losing self-identity) and asserting self-identity entirely through opposition to the constraining society. All of Foucault's earlier histories (except for *The Order of Things*, which has at best very indirect social significance) concern marginalized groups.

"Problematization", by contrast, is Foucault's term for a set of fundamental issues and choices confronting "mainline" (non-marginalized) members of a society. Talk of problematization assumes a preliminary definition of a person in terms of social constraints, but in this case (as opposed to marginalization) the constraints allow room for creative self-development in accord with self-chosen goals and standards. Why the difference from marginalization? Because here the individuals in question are not, in virtue of objective features over which they have no control, subject to an almost total constriction of their choices (for example, the mad, women, certain racial minorities). As opposed to the marginalized, those whose lives are merely problematized have a "social essence" compatible with a significant range of freedom. In the history of ancient sexuality, problematization implicitly replaces marginalization as the focus of the discussion. Although Foucault's ethical emphasis is on an individual's construction of a self (an identity), he does recognize the role of ethical codes (rules of behavior), the force of which will vary depending on the manner in which a given individual is "subjected" to it (see below). Although Foucault says little about ethical codes, it is reasonable to suppose that he would see them as general frameworks required for life within a given social structure but not necessarily the central concern of ethical life, which is instead the construction of a self.

This construction involves four elements (which Foucault calls the four "modes of subjectification") that characterize an individual's relations to an ethical code.[10] The

[9] See "Polemics, Politics, and Problematizations" (interview with Paul Rabinow, 1984), in *Essential Works of Foucault 1954–1984*, ed. Paul Rabinow, vol. i, ed. Paul Rabinow (New York: New Press, 1997), 11–119.

[10] See Michel Foucault, *The Use of Pleasure* (History of Sexuality, vol. 2), tr. Robert Hurley (New York: Vintage, 1990), intro, ch. 3.

first mode is *ethical substance*: the various aspects of life relevant to ethical behavior (for example, in the case of sexual ethics, desires, pleasures, actions, virtues, etc.) Second, *the mode of subjection* (to be distinguished from subjectification) is the sense in which an individual is subject to the ethical code (some possibilities are the rigid following of highly specified rules, inspiration by highly general principles, dialectical reasoning to reconcile principles in tension with one another). Third, the *forms of elaboration* are specific kinds of activity that lead to an acceptance of the ethical code (for example, rigorous training through negative reinforcement, prolonged meditation on paradigm instances found in sacred texts, imitation of admired mentors). Finally, the *telos* (end) is the ultimate goal posited as the purpose of morality (for example, social stability, individual enlightenment, control of the passions, eternal happiness).

Like moral codes themselves, the modes of subjectification that relate individuals to their societies' codes are not the free creation of individuals. But, in contrast to the code, a given mode of subjectification allows a significant range of choice for some individuals. A particular mode will typically offer alternatives (e.g., celibate vs married life) for its implementation and any alternative will be underdetermined as to its specific form (e.g., active vs contemplative religious orders). This allows for individual choice in self-formation, based, for example, on personal standards of aesthetic value, corresponding to what Foucault calls an *aesthetics of existence* (of which more below).

Based on the schema of the four modes of subjectification, Foucault offers case studies of the ancients' problematizations of sexual ethics.[11] These studies are essentially archaeological, looking at the underlying conceptual structures of the ethical thought of the ancient world—first that of the fourth-century Greeks, second that of the Latin and Greek world around the time of Christ. A constant benchmark is the contrast with Christian ethics, which in fact Foucault sees as emerging in the later ancient period from non-Christian sources. The ethical substance of ancient sexual behavior comprises desires, acts, and pleasures (*ta aphrodisia*) viewed as natural goods, though subject to some dangers and concerns (primarily because of their ties to our lower, animal nature and their exceptional intensity). By contrast, Christians, according to Foucault, see sex as in itself intrinsically evil. As a result, the ancients' mode of subjection to the ethical code regarding sexual behavior is careful use (*chresis*) of pleasures, in contrast to the Christians' denial (austerity), effected either through complete celibacy or through restriction of sexuality to monogamous marriage, directed to procreation.

As to the forms of elaboration, the ancients emphasize self-mastery (*enkratia*), achieved through training (*askesis*) in self-control. We achieve conformity to the sexual code through exercises designed to make reason the master of our desires and feelings. By contrast, for Christians this internal battle between reason and passion is replaced by a struggle between the self's desire to maintain ultimate control of itself and the imperative for it to yield to God, in whom alone it can find its true identity and happiness. As a result,

[11] Foucault, *The Use of Pleasure*, pt I, chs 1–4.

the telos radically changes from the ancient to the Christian world. For the ancients, the telos is moderation (*sophrysune*), achieved by the proper use of pleasures to attain the ideal of human freedom in both its negative and its positive forms (freedom from domination by passions, freedom for rational mastery of self and others). For the Christians the telos is total subjection of self to God—the negative freedom of denial of self for the sake of a positive freedom achieved only by living entirely in and through God.

What is the point of Foucault's excursions into the ancient history of sexual ethics? The point is not, as in his previous histories, a genealogy of our current practices that will show their contingent, dubious origins and provide ammunition for attacks on their privileged position. The ancient world is too far removed from ours for such a history to sustain sufficient connection to contemporary concerns; it cannot be what Foucault called a "history of the present". But Foucault thinks he can find in the ancient world a model for an ethics of self-creation that will be relatively independent of the power–knowledge structures of our society. This is by no means a matter of "going back to the Greeks" and reviving their way of ethical life. Apart from the historical impossibility of doing any such thing, there are many central features of their ethics that we would not want to emulate (for example, their focus on the value—literally phallocentric—of virility, their disdain for women, their acceptance of slavery).[12]

But Foucault does think we can profitably adapt the ancients' general notion of an ethics based on an *aesthetics of existence*. An aesthetics of existence is a *techne*, a practical method of ethical formation devoted not (like Christianity) to redeeming the self (saving it from Hell and for Heaven) but to creating a beautiful life on this Earth (p. 260). Such an aesthetics derives from an individual's distinctive taste, so that the ethical formation it guides allows for an existence that avoids the full force of social power structures by finding a location within the interstices of these structures where the individual as such can flourish. As we have noted, such a project of self-formation is not available to the marginalized people on whom society imposes an identity. For them the only choices are submission or resistance. But for those with sufficient status in a society, there are resources for creative self-formation within the social fabric.

An aesthetics of existence has, as Foucault sees it, a significant advantage because it makes ethics an essentially private enterprise, rather than the imposition of public (universally binding) rules for how we should live. He acknowledges that we need a minimal universal ethical code to maintain a stable social context for our lives. But this is little except the core injunctions that humans have endorsed for millennia. The remainder of ethical life is a matter for private choice, with in particular no role for public moralities derived from allegedly scientific sources such as sociobiology or psychoanalysis. This privatization provides an alternative to the normalizing characteristic of modern society, since it replaces universal ("scientifically" underwritten) standards of moral

[12] Michel Foucault, "On the Genealogy of Ethics: An Overview of Work in Progress" (interview with Hubert Dreyfus and Paul Rabinow), in *Essential Works of Foucault*, i. 256–7. Further references will be given in the text.

perfection with personalized ideals of a "beautiful life" (p. 254). This allows a separate space in which ethics can be practiced in relative independence of "the great political and social and economic structures" (p. 261). This does not mean, however, that an aesthetics of existence cannot include a concern—lacking in ancient Greece—for the marginalized of one's society. Activism on their behalf can be, as it was for Foucault, an integral part of creating a beautiful life.

Foucault's ethics obviously has little to do with the traditional efforts of philosophers to formulate the norms of ethical codes or with the meta-normative concerns of Levinas. Nothing he says rejects these projects, but he finds the ethical center of gravity elsewhere, in the private sphere of aesthetic self-formation. A natural objection is that such a self-centered project should hardly be called ethical. It is, however, ethical in its concern with the fundamental values that guide an individual's life. The worry, presumably, is that, since these values concern *self*-formation, they lack the directedness to others characteristic of ethics. But to this Foucault would have two responses. First, there is a moral code that constrains self-formative behavior that would harm others. Second, given that there is no harm to others, it would seem that perfecting oneself is an essential aspect of a good human life. It might be suggested that the perfection in question is tied only to individual preferences (taste) and so lacks the universal quality of ethical goods. But to this Foucault can plausibly reply that, on his view, it is a universal human good that each individual engage in a project of aesthetic self-creation. This, indeed, is Foucault's ethical reason for supporting the struggles of marginalized people.

Another question is whether Foucault's turn to ethics reverses his earlier rejection of philosophy as a study of the subject. It is true that his histories of ancient sexuality work along not just his previous two axes of knowledge (archaeology) and power (genealogy). They add an axis of the individual subject, which "constitutes" itself in the context of the first two axes. But, of course, merely bringing into the discussion the individuals who are the subjects of knowledge and power hardly requires philosophical assumptions about subjectivity. Some, however, have suggested that Foucault's ethical turn requires him to appeal to a transcendental subject (ego). Béatrice Han, for example, says: "Foucault reactivates the perspective of a constitutive subjectivity and understands the constitution of the self by means of the atemporal structure of recognition",[13] a position that would put him firmly back into the philosophy of the subject.

But why does Han insist that Foucault makes such a surprising move? Simply because Foucault presents the subject as forming itself by a process of reflection and action, as, for example, when he says that thought (that whereby the subject gives itself a specific meaning) is "freedom in relation to what one does, the motion by which one detaches oneself from it, establishes it as an object, and reflects on it as a problem".[14]

[13] Béatrice Han, *Foucault's Critical Project: Between the Transcendental and the Historical*, tr. Edward Pile (Stanford, CA: Stanford University Press, 2002), 187. Further references will be given in the text.

[14] Paul Rabinow (ed.), *The Foucault Reader* (New York: Pantheon, 1985), 388; cited by Han, *Foucault's Critical Project*, 165.

On Han's reading, such passages imply that Foucault's subject is "autonomous" (p. 172), even, she suggests, in the radical sense of Sartrean existentialist humanism (p. 169). She goes so far as to claim that Foucault's

> insistence on the importance of problematization and recognition as *voluntary* and *reflective* activities leads Foucault to envisage the relationship to the body in a purely unilateral manner, as an action of the self on the self, where the body only appears as material for transformation while consciousness seems to be paradoxically reinstalled in the sovereign position that genealogy had criticized. (p. 165)

But I think that Han is overinterpreting. "Freedom" and "reflection" need not be read as the technical terms of idealist philosophy but may refer to everyday features of human life (the metaphysical equivalent to Freud's famous reminder that sometimes a cigar is just a cigar). In their everyday sense, freedom and reflection do not imply Kantian (or Sartrean) autonomy. They may, for example, represent the small spark of subjectivity in a context heavily constrained by the social system of power-knowledge. In his books on ancient sexuality, Foucault of course often uses Platonic vocabulary, which smacks of strong autonomy. Moreover, since the power-knowledge constraints of ancient Greece and Rome are no longer relevant to us, he has little to say about them. He is simply looking for modes of thinking about the self (for example, in terms of an aesthetics of existence) that might suggest strategies in our struggle with modern disciplinary society. None of this provides grounds for concluding that Foucault has lapsed into transcendentalism. (But it does raise once again the question of how far he actually is from Sartre's ethical stance in *Existentialism Is a Humanism*.)

Foucault's account of ethical subjectification does recall Levinas's account of how the encounter with the Other constitutes the I as a subject. But Foucault's "subject" already exists at the center of a world of objects prior to the encounter with the Other. In contrast to Levinas's subject, Foucault's is not constituted *tout court* by the encounter with ethical demands. It is merely constituted as an ethical subject; that is, it develops (partly by its own decisions) distinctive modes of being "subject to" the ethical code. This is an event that occurs within the world of subjects and objects, not one that constitutes this world. Foucault's ethics does not provide necessary conditions for anything other than ethical life itself.

More generally, Foucault's ethics is not a contribution to philosophy in the sense that has defined the discipline since at least Kant and Hegel: a body of theoretical knowledge about fundamental human questions. He had no such theoretical conclusions to offer us, just ethical and political commitments to the kind of life he wanted to live. This was a life of continual free self-transformation, unhindered by unnecessary conceptual and social constraints. His intellectual enterprise was the critique of disciplines and practices that restrict our freedom to transform ourselves. He did not object to those who continued to build new theoretical structures, and, in some cases, such as Deleuze, he seemed to endorse their results. But he was not really a philosopher in the modern sense. Of course, Foucault's books, like other classics of intellectual history, exhibit enormous philosophical talent and are often of great interest to philosophers. Moreover, as his final work makes clear, although he did not pursue philosophical truth, he did aspire to lead, in the ancient sense, a philosophical life.

Ethics and anti-humanism again

There was no "ethical turn" in the work of Levinas or in the later work of Derrida and Foucault, if we use "ethics" in the standard philosophical sense of a theory (or applications of a theory) about ethical norms. Our French philosophers operate either above (Levinas and Derrida) or below (Foucault) the normative level. Foucault, ironically, comes the closest to offering a "guide to life", but his account of ethical subjectification and the aesthetics of existence does not operate in normative space. Levinas's "ethics" are explicitly prior to the specific normative content of an ethical code and even to the principles (for example, utilitarian, deontological) that could directly guide the formation of such a code. Derrida's account of justice is similarly removed from normative considerations.

The reason for this continuing aversion to ethics seems rooted in the pervasive anti-humanism of these thinkers. They are deeply convinced that there is no philosophical (or other theoretical) account of human nature (or even—in something like an existentialist sense—the human situation) that provides a basis for philosophical conclusions about the ethical code that should guide our lives. Nor is there any philosophical account of human beings' relation to someone or something else (a divine person, Heidegger's being, or even, as we saw with Levinas, other people) that provides such a basis.

But why the aversion to humanism? It helps to think their anti-humanism with their anti-Hegelianism. The attraction of Hegel was his promise of some sort of meaning to history. But the ultimate decision against him was that he could fulfill this promise only with a totalizing story—an account that claimed to comprehend everything, including responses to every possible objection (which were always subsumed as earlier stages of the dialectic). To these philosophers, thinking in the wake of the disasters of fascism, Nazism, and Soviet Communism, totalization was the open road to totalitarianism. Their history told them that to (claim to) understand all was not to forgive all but to control all. It was precisely claims to a comprehensive understanding of what the world meant that led to the horrors of totalitarianism.

But, we may think, is not the humanism of the West precisely the opposing force to the totalitarianisms of the East? Only if you do think that the complacencies of advanced capitalism do not exert their own less dramatic (but perhaps even more effective) control over our lives. Souls are destroyed as much when co-opted by commodity-driven materialism as when persecuted by totalitarian ideology. Here, of course, the European experience is quite different from the American. The young French philosophers, born of parents with vivid memories of one war and into the world of another war, saw the bourgeois greed and stupidity around them as also responsible for the horrors of the century. Humanisms (scientific, religious, or existential) were simply comprehensive accounts justifying as inevitable the vicious inanity of bourgeois life. Totalitarianism with a human mask—or, perhaps, Hegelianism without the philosophical depth and rigor.[15] Put summarily: ethics requires humanism, which is a practical equivalent of Hegelianism; so rejecting Hegel means rejecting ethics.

Rejecting ethics does not, however, mean that these philosophers reject morality in the mundane sense of the term. In fact, their opposition to standard normative ethics is precisely in the name of an intensely moral opposition to constraints on human freedom. What they fear is philosophical ethics, ethics grounded in comprehensive philosophical views. Why, then, not accept Rorty's pragmatism, which likewise opts for a democratic morality free of philosophical support? Because Rorty's view is merely an uncritical acceptance of the moral common sense of his class. Our philosophers do not want philosophical foundations of philosophy, but, unlike Rorty, they distrust a morality that is not constantly challenged by philosophical reflection. The role of philosophy is precisely to keep us intellectually off balance and alert so that we never slip into a dogmatic moral doze. Philosophy establishes no moral conclusions, but its vibrant intellectual imagination opens us to new possibilities that challenge not our basic moral convictions but our understanding of how they might apply to a complex world. Each of our philosophers has a different way of doing this. Foucault applies his philosophical intelligence to post-Kantian "critiques" of alleged practical necessities, Deleuze constructs constantly new versions of his ontology of novelty, Derrida probes the endless complexities of traditional philosophical concepts, and Levinas keeps us ever alert to the incomprehensibility of the Other. In all these varied ways, they combine moral commitment with a constant sense of its dangers and limitations.

[15] Levinas, of course, would have different but parallel religious grounds for uneasiness with secular humanisms.

8

Phenomenology, Religion, and Incomprehensibility: Derrida and Marion

Like anglophone analytic philosophy, French philosophy in the twentieth century long had a strongly secular and often anti-religious slant. Bergson was the last major philosopher sympathetic to religious belief, and his defense of religion in his last book, *Two Sources of Morality and Religion*, was one reason for his rapid eclipse on the French scene. Similarly, Gabriel Marcel's religiously oriented existentialism, although developed in the 1920s, was swamped by Sartre's atheistic formulation over a decade later. Subsequently, Paul Ricœur's work on phenomenology and hermeneutics received strikingly little attention from the dominant existential phenomenologists, at least in part because of his explicit religious commitment and interests. And, as we have seen, Levinas, whose work had obvious connections to his Judaism, did not receive a full hearing until some twenty years after he had published *Totality and Infinity* in 1961.

This anti-religious attitude did not derive from any formidable philosophical case against religious belief. Since the Revolution, religion in France (for the most part, the Catholic Church) had largely identified itself with reactionary political positions for which most intellectuals had no sympathy, and religion did not present itself as an option to be taken seriously. Sartre in his autobiography tells how, at age 11, to pass the time while waiting for some friends, he began thinking about God and quite suddenly saw intuitively that no such being existed—a conviction he maintained for the rest of his life.[1] There were some, for example, Merleau-Ponty and Althusser, who were believers in their youth, but sloughed off religion as they came to intellectual and political maturity. Prior to the 1960s, there had been important Catholic philosophers—Marcel, Emmanuel Mounier (founder of the "personalist" movement), and Thomists such as Jacques Maritain and Étienne Gilson. But their influence was limited and was not sustained through the latter half of the century. As the generation of Foucault, Deleuze, and Derrida came of age, religious philosophy was barely a blip on the horizon.

[1] Jean-Paul Sartre, *The Words*, tr. Bernard Frechtman (New York: George Braziller, 1981), 250–1.

That began to change in the 1980s with the work of Jean-Louis Courtine and, especially, Jean-Luc Marion, who developed phenomenology in ways open to religious belief and thought. (Their work also brought to the fore earlier work by Michel Henry.) We will focus on Marion, particularly on his debate with Derrida about phenomenology and religion. To appreciate this debate, we need to begin by connecting the question of religious experience to Husserl's project of phenomenological description.

The phenomenological background

There are good reasons in the nature of religious belief for seeking its basis in experience, particularly in the phenomenologist's sense of the immediacy of lived experience (*le vécu*). Like such experience, the religious experience of believers is personal, concrete, and compelling. But comparing religious experience with the descriptions of Husserl, the founder of phenomenology, reveals some interesting differences. For Husserl (as for Descartes, whose project Husserl sees himself as continuing in a more radical way), immediate experience is privileged as the fundamental locus of four epistemic elements: knowledge, truth, clarity, and certainty. Knowledge and truth are obvious pairs, since knowledge implies truth; similarly, clarity is the primary sign of certainty. But religious experience seems to split this fourfold phenomenological field, since it typically claims truth and certainty but speaks of faith rather than knowledge and mystery rather than clarity. So the question is whether we can make phenomenological sense of an experience that involves faith and mystery but nonetheless attains truth and certainty. Or does attaining truth and certainty require, respectively, knowledge and clarity? If so, a phenomenological approach would exclude religious experience.

We can best approach these questions in terms of Husserl's central phenomenological notions of intention and fulfillment. Consider a case of ordinary sense perception—for example, seeing that a stick of butter is yellow. Husserl points out that this experience has two aspects: a meaning or significance (intention) in terms of which I understand (for example, the butter as yellow) and a content that, to a greater or lesser extent, fulfills ("conforms to") this understanding (the butter is in fact yellow). So, in the successful case, when the content "fulfills" the intention, I know (or have strong evidence that) the butter is yellow. In other cases, the fulfillment may be weaker, so that I could rightly say only "The butter is probably yellow" or "The butter seems to be yellow; or even, if fulfillment is very weak or non-existent, "there is no reason to say the butter is yellow" or "the butter is not yellow".

Given this intention/fulfillment distinction, we can readily understand in its terms the four elements of experience noted above. They are all a matter of the degree of fulfillment of the intention in the experience. If, for example, there is sufficient fulfillment, I will know that the butter is yellow (and what I know will be true); and, given sufficient fulfillment, the closer the fulfillment comes to completion, the clearer and more certain my knowledge is. In Husserl's terminology, that which fulfills the intention is that which is *given* in (or by) the experience. The given is that which we know (have certainty about) when our intention is fulfilled.

In the case of sense perception, the fulfillment of intentions is always incomplete, which is why sensory knowledge is never totally certain and always subject to revision. In formal disciplines like logic and mathematics, where the intuitions are intellectual rather than sensory, complete fulfillment—and so certain knowledge—seems to be possible. Husserl at least sometimes suggests that philosophy, using phenomenological descriptions, can also achieve certainty.

In these Husserlian terms, a religious experience would have to be an experience in which the meaning intended and fulfilled is God. But here there seems to be a contradiction. In experience, an intention is either completely fulfilled or incompletely fulfilled. Since religion requires certainty about God, it would seem that the intention must be fulfilled completely. But religion also holds that God is mysterious, that is, his reality cannot be caught by the meanings specified by our concepts. If so, it would seem that, in an experience of God, my intention cannot be completely fulfilled; otherwise, I would have a complete understanding of God. It seems, then, that an experience of God cannot maintain both the certainty and the mystery about God that religion requires.

At this point, we might invoke the tradition of negative theology, which approaches God by denying the applicability of our concepts to him. Might not the inadequacy of our concepts show up precisely in an experience of their lack of fulfillment in the presence of God? Such an approach is suggested by Derrida's critique of Husserl and the metaphysics presence, where he argues that fundamental metaphysical and epistemological concepts are incapable of fulfillment. They correspond to intentions that, when pushed to the limit, are "impossible" because there is always a *difference* between our experience and what these concepts intend. To express this "fundamental" level of difference Derrida introduces his notorious neologism, *différance*. Might not the experience of God be an experience of Derridian *différance*?

Derrida, *différance*, and God

Long before Marion was on the scene, Derrida, in his 1967 essay "*Différance*",[2] broached the idea that his "philosophy" of *différance* might be a version of negative theology. "The detours, locutions, and syntax in which I will often have to take recourse will resemble those of negative theology, occasionally to the point of being indistinguishable from negative theology" (p. 6). Although Derrida briskly rejects this suggestion, it will be helpful for understanding Derrida's position in his debate with Marion to look more closely at just why the suggestion presents itself.

[2] Jacques Derrida, "Différance", in *Margins of Philosophy*, tr. Alan Bass (Chicago: University of Chicago Press, 1982), 1–27. References will be given in the text.

Derrida introduces *différance* as part of his critique of the metaphysics of presence, a critique that, as we shall see, underlies Marion's religious phenomenology. The main elements of the critique can be formulated in terms of the limitations of both philosophical language and philosophical concepts.

Nowadays, at least, serious philosophy is generally carried out in written language. Such language has obvious limitations: taken in itself, we can never eliminate unclarities that are due to ambiguities, ignorance of context, carelessness of expression, and so on. These limitations are often treated as non-essential, since they could in principle be eliminated if we had a direct access to the author (and the author's period), which would (it is claimed) allow us to resolve each unclarity. Derrida, however, argues that even if, for example, we were contemporaries of Plato, speaking directly with him, there would still be unresolvable unclarities simply because of the limitations of language in general (spoken or written).

Many philosophers would accept this argument, noting that the communicative use of language always involves a gap (for example, between speaker and hearer) that can never be entirely bridged. But this, some claim, is still non-essential, since I can always have recourse to the "inner speech" of thought, which will present, with total clarity, my thought to myself. But to this Derrida responds that the very fact that I am using a language to express my thoughts introduces the possibility of misunderstanding: the language is not my creation (there is no "private language") but a socially produced structure the meaning of which may escape me (even regarding the claims I am making to myself).

Some philosophers would grant even this but claim that it merely shows that language itself is an imperfect vehicle of thought. Total clarity, they would claim, is found only in my immediate awareness of my own (prelinguistic) thoughts. But the French philosophers of the 1960s (like most recent analytic philosophers) would respond that thought is essentially linguistic so that there can be no prelinguistic thought and therefore no total clarity (or certainty). Because of this, according to Derrida, philosophy can never be more than a "kind of writing", subject to the limitations of this allegedly "derivative" medium, and so not capable of achieving the clarity (and therefore certainty) aimed for by traditional philosophy.

We can also put the point in terms of concepts (or terms) and their application to the things we experience. Language is based on distinctions, contrasts between the meanings of concepts. The philosophical demand for clarity insists on absolutely sharp distinctions, so we can always say whether or not a term applies to a subject. This is typically presented as a matter of logic, based on the principle of excluded middle: any given subject is either A or not A and not both. But in many actual cases, this requirement is not met: "Is that sky grey or not?" "It's kind of in between—both grey and not grey." (Or, "Are you happy?" "I'm happy-sad.") Such cases do not refute the logical principle of excluded middle; rather, they exhibit the inadequacy of a given conceptual scheme (or vocabulary). Presumably, there is a continuum of color on which grey gradually shades into non-grey, and, if we have a more refined vocabulary, we can eliminate the apparent contradictions. Indeed, we typically save ourselves from non-contradiction by saying that the sky is grey in one sense and not grey in another, etc. But such locutions are really promissory notes on a more refined vocabulary that will be able to specify the needed senses. According to Derrida, such promissory notes can never be fully redeemed. At some point, all of our concepts fail to catch the content of our experiences.

Derrida introduces the neologism *différance* as a summary of his critique of the metaphysics of presence and as an alternative to the vocabulary of this metaphysics. *Différance* is intended to "express" and "explain" the limitations of both words and concepts, so Derrida insists that it is, strictly, "neither a concept nor a word". Insofar as we can speak of it as having a "meaning", it combines in a single noun the two distinct but related senses of the French verb *différer*, which, unlike its English counterpart, means both "differ" and "defer". The "misspelling" introduced by the "a" differentiates this new term from the French *différence*, which, like our "difference", signals only differing. *Différance* thus involves an ambiguity that fails to distinguish between being different and being put off (what we might think of as conceptual and temporal "species" of one genus). Another key ambiguity arises from the orthographically inappropriate *a*, which on the one hand suggests (in French) the active present participle *différant* but on the other hand suggests more passive (or middle) forms that end in *–ance* (e.g, *mouvance*). Because of its negativity and ambiguity, *différance* steers us away from thoughts of clear and distinct presences.

Derrida goes on to deploy *différance* as a kind of "counter-principle" to the classical terms of the metaphysics of presence. He suggests that we think of *différance* as "the playing movement that 'produces'—by means of something that is not simply an activity" the differences of our experience (p. 11). He hastens to add that this does not mean that *différance* is a metaphysical cause, a subject or a substance, existing fully present and self-contained prior to the effects it produces. It is, rather, "the non-full, non-simple, structured and differentiating origin of differences"—although, of course, this means that "the name 'origin' no longer suits it" (p. 11) and that the differences are not effects in the standard sense of the term. Nonetheless, Derrida says he will speak of *différance* as "the movement according to which language . . . or any system of referral in general, is constituted 'historically' as a weave of differences" (p. 12) and allow himself to say that *différance* "produces" or even "creates" differences. But he notes that he utilizes concepts such as *constitution, production, creation*, and even *history* "only for their strategic convenience and in order to undertake their deconstruction at the currently most decisive point" (p. 12). In any case, we must keep in mind that standard oppositions such as static/genetic and structural/historical "have not the least pertinence to *différance*", which is precisely what "makes the thinking of it uneasy and uncomfortable" (p. 12).

This brief excursion into the linguistic and conceptual tangles of Derrida's introduction of *différance* shows how he has constructed the term as an ultimate vehicle of indetermination. Its fundamental "denotation" is ambiguous between differing and deferring, its connotations are ambiguous between active and passive, verb and noun, any characterization of the "reality" to which it refers is either through negation (we are continually told what *différance* is not) or terms in scarequotes (which means that the terms do not "really" apply), with a promissory note to deconstruct the quoted terms at a later date.

The profound negativity of *différance* immediately suggests that, like the terms of negative theology, it is being used to speak of what cannot be positively characterized. Indeed, since the uncharacterizabilty is at the most basic, why should we not take *différance* as Derrida's way of referring to God? And, if this is so, what separates his discourse from that of negative theology? The reason is that "negative theology" is not in the end really negative (which is why, as we shall see, Marion eventually prefers to call it "mystical theology"). Negative theology, Derrida says, is "always concerned with disengaging a supraessentiality beyond the finite categories of essence and existence, that is, of presence, and always hastening to recall that God is refused the predicate of existence only in order to acknowledge his superior, inconceivable, and ineffable mode of being". By contrast, in Derrida's work "there is no question of such a development", because *différance* is "irreducible to any ontological or theological—onto-theological—reappropriation" (p. 6, translation modified).

This reappropriation corresponds to what has traditionally been called the third (and final) stage of negative theology, the way of *pre-eminence*. Derrida has no problem with the first two stages—that of naive affirmations about the inconceivable via our concepts, followed by the negations of these affirmations as inadequate. But, as he sees it, the third stage returns to affirmation, the only difference being that it is hyper-affirmation, affirmation to the highest degree. Derrida's talk of *différance* is a sophisticated development of the second stage, but stopping there will hardly satisfy religious people, who will see it as equivalent to atheism or, at best, agnosticism (and Derrida himself says that he understandably passes as an atheist). Returning to the language of Husserl, Derrida's talk of *différance* is a way of driving home the point that all positive concepts fail to be fulfilled when applied to the experience of the incomprehensible. As long as our positive delineations of God remain unfulfilled, all we can say is what he is not, or even, perhaps, that he is not.

Marion vs Derrida

Jean-Luc Marion agrees that religious experience cannot involve a lack of intentional fulfillment. But, he maintains, it is an experience in which the fulfillment *exceeds* the intention, where the intention is "saturated" by "an overflow of givenness". To the charge, formulated above, that there is a contradiction in the very idea of a religious experience that it is both certain and mysterious, Marion responds that it is an experience in which God is given as certainly exceeding (saturating) the intentions (meanings) that we bring to the experience.

One particularly helpful development of Marion's line of thought came out of a conference where he and Derrida debated the issue. Marion's opening paper presents negative theology as a major challenge to Derridian deconstruction and connects it to his phenomenology of religious experience.[3]

Marion on negative theology

Marion begins by discussing Derrida's critique of negative theology, focusing on his "fundamental and unified argument" that negative theology "persist[s] in making affirmations about God—while denying that it does so—in particular the affirmation of existence—and thereby . . . fail[s] to think God outside of presence and to free itself from the 'metaphysics of presence'" (p. 23). Marion entirely agrees with Derrida's rejection of the metaphysics of presence. In particular, he rejects any idea of God as a maximal being that could be understood in concepts applicable to other beings and so be present to our experience or understanding. Derrida's objection will have force if he can show that negative theology "does not annul [ne nie pas] the essence, Being, or truth of God, but denies [les denier] them so as to better re-establish them, in something like a hyperbole" (p. 23, brackets in quoted text). Putting the point in Christian theology's own terms, Derrida is asking "to what extent does [negative theology's] negation not just re-establish in the *via eminentiae* what the apophasis [denial] seemed to have disqualified?". If negative theology cannot but fall back into an affirmation of God in terms of our concepts, then it is "reducible" to the metaphysics of presence and so "subject to deconstruction" (p. 23).

Marion takes this challenge seriously, but he points out that the issue is not merely one of defending negative theology from deconstruction. The case of negative theology is not just a matter of deconstructing another approach that claims to have vindicated the metaphysics of presence (like traditional metaphysical systems from Platonism to Hegelianism). Negative theology claims to avoid, not vindicate, the metaphysics of presence but still in some sense achieve a connection with divine reality. It claims "to deconstruct God [by denying all affirmations about him] and nevertheless to reach him"; or, put another, more paradoxical, way, "it claims to put us in the presence of God in the very degree to which it denies all presence" (p. 22). Accordingly, negative theology is not just another object of deconstruction but its rival—"its first serious rival, perhaps the only one possible" (p. 22), because it claims to employ deconstructive methods to achieve what deconstruction itself cannot achieve. Unless Derrida can deconstruct ("as radically as possible") this claim, its rival will marginalize deconstruction, refuting its insistence that "there is no access to God, outside presence and without being" (p. 22).

Derrida's effort to deconstruct negative theology is based on his assumption that theology can speak of God only in the two modes of "metaphysical predication:

[3] The entire discussion is presented in John D. Caputo and Michael J. Scanlon (eds.), *God, the Gift, and Postmodernism* (Bloomington, IN: Indiana University Press, 1999.) References will be given in the text.

affirmation and negation". If it speaks of God only negatively, then it collapses into atheism (denying even his existence). But if it speaks of God affirmatively, it willy nilly speaks of God "within the horizon of essence, thus of being", thereby falling back into the metaphysics of presence and so "beneath the sword of deconstruction" (p. 33). But why assume that theology has available only metaphysical affirmation or metaphysical negation (where these correspond to knowing something by applying our concepts to it—conceptual knowing)? Perhaps there is a "third way", a way of making positive claims about God that does not treat him metaphysically, that is, does not make him just a being among beings, an object of conceptual knowledge. Certainly, theologians have, historically, claimed to be seeking such a third way. They speak in particular of "a kataphatic nomination of God", by which they mean the knowledge of God without any conceptual knowledge of him. Marion takes "the biblical thesis, 'No one has seen God' (John 1: 18)" to mean that "a God that could be conceptually comprehended would no longer bear the title 'God'" (p. 34), so that knowledge of God must be non-conceptual knowledge. He reads in terms of this distinction the historically repeated assertion by theologians from the Greek and Latin fathers through Aquinas and Bernard that (to use Augustine's formulation) "God, the highest . . . is known better than knowing" (p. 35, citing *De Ordine*, II, 16, 44).

Negative theology, then, depends on the claim that we can have non-conceptual knowledge of God, knowing that is not knowing in the ordinary sense. But is such knowledge itself conceivable? "On what conditions would the renunciation of comprehension remain an authentic form of knowledge and not just a failure of knowledge?" (p. 36). Marion proposes the following line of reasoning, starting from a "formal definition" of God by the Anselmian formula (given earlier by Augustine and Boethius) "that than which nothing greater [better] can be thought" (p. 37). We can always conceive that there is something greater than anything that we can comprehend (it is conceivable that there is something inconceivably greater than it). So, if we could comprehend God, then he would not be that than which a greater cannot be conceived. So it follows that "incomprehensibility therefore belongs to the formal definition of God" (p. 36). It further follows that any knowledge of God has to be knowledge without comprehension, which is to say, non-conceptual knowledge.

From this Marion concludes that the theological "naming" of God is in fact a "de-nomination" of God. The name "that than which nothing greater can be thought" is "given as having no name, as not giving the essence" (p. 37). In other words, the formal definition of God "names" him only in the sense of asserting that he is beyond any name that would express his essence (that is, the concepts in terms of which we must comprehend him). The theological name of God refers to him only as one that has no name in the ordinary sense of a conceptual characterization.[4] Naming God in this sense does not amount to making him present in the manner of the metaphysics of presence

[4] One naturally wonders if Marion's point could make use of Kripke's notion of a name as rigid designator rather than a definite description.

(as something we can comprehend). Instead of a metaphysics of presence we have a "pragmatic theology of absence" (where "pragmatic" refers to an access without understanding, via community practices). In sum: "no ground, no essence, no presence" (p. 37).

Marion thinks that the above discussion shows the conceptual viability of negative theology (theology of absence) against Derrida's attempted deconstruction. But, he admits, this establishes only its "formal possibility", and says nothing about whether there is any way that we could in fact encounter the God of absence. To answer this question, we need to make sense of an experience of such a God. To do this, Marion turns to the phenomenology of religious experience, insisting, however, that this phenomenology will have nothing to say about whether such an experience actually occurs, only about whether it is phenomenologically possible. "Phenomenology is to make decisions only about the type of phenomenality that would render this phenomenon thinkable" (p. 39).

The saturated phenomenon

Here Marion returns to his idea of the "saturated phenomenon" as a way of avoiding the fatal dichotomy of a fulfilled intention (which would make God comprehensible) and an unfulfilled intention (which would make him non-existent). The terms of this dichotomy correspond to the naive affirmation (in terms of our concepts) of God that negative theology rejects and to the mere rejection of this affirmation (without an encounter with God as absent). The crucial step, of course, is to make sense of a third relation between intention and fulfillment, in which the fulfillment "exceeds" the intention.

Husserl's phenomenology begins from "the inescapable duality of appearing and what appears [*l'apparâitre et l'apparaissant*]", a duality variously expressed by "the pairs signification/fulfillment, intention/intuition, or noesis/noema" (p. 39). Husserl himself (like Kant) allows two possible relations between these terms. Either (1) "the intention finds itself confirmed [fulfilled], at least partially, by the intuition" so that the intuition provides evidence of the truth of the intention; or (2) "the intention can exceed all intuitive fulfillment", so that "the phenomenon does not deliver objective knowledge" because of the lack of fulfillment. If these are the only two possibilities, then there is no room for non-conceptual knowledge of God. But Marion claims there is a third possibility: (3) "the intention (the concept or the signification) can never reach adequation with the intuition (fulfillment)" but not because of any lack in the intuition; rather, because the intuition (fulfillment) "exceeds what the concept can receive, expose, and comprehend" (p. 39). This possibility is what Marion calls the *saturated phenomenon*.

This third possibility is like the second in that "no predication or naming any longer appears possible"; that is, no such predication or naming is supported by the evidence provided by the intuitive content of the experience. But in the third case the reason for this lack of evidence is reversed. It is not that "the giving intuition would be lacking" (would fall short of the content of the concept) but that "the excess of intuition overcomes, submerges, exceeds—in short, saturates—the measure of each and every concept". In this third case, "what is given disqualifies every concept" (p. 40). There is a "shortcoming" but it is "a shortcoming that results from a lack of utterable signification, not of intuition".

This third case allows for an experience in which "God remains incomprehensible, not imperceptible—without adequate concept, not without giving intuition". The names whereby we would understand God are not eliminated ("the infinite proliferation of names does indeed suggest that they are still there"), but the very fact that there are so many names "flags as insufficient the concepts they put in play and thereby does justice to what constantly subverts them". We are dealing with an experience that "registers the ineradicable insufficiency of the concept in general" (p. 40).

Marion acknowledges a "final objection" to this third possibility: "how, without resorting to a meaningless and even mad paradox, can the excess of giving intuition in the case of God be considered plausible, when the evidence attests that precisely and *par excellence* God is never given intuitively?" (p. 40). As he notes, this is not strictly an objection to the *formal possibility* he has suggested. It does not ask whether it is possible to have an experience of God as exceeding all our concepts but whether it could ever be *plausible* to conclude that such an experience has occurred. The point is that, if such an experience occurred, it would provide evidence that God is *not* given intuitively, since by stipulation we are considering an experience in which the concept of God is not fulfilled by the intuition. Marion may be right that it is possible to experience God (for God to be given intuitively) without the corresponding concept (intention) being fulfilled. But, if the intention is not fulfilled, all the evidence provided by the experience supports the conclusion that the object has not been experienced. By what right, then, could we reasonably conclude from the experience that it was an experience of God? The claim, though possible, is implausible.

Marion's response is that the objection works only on the assumption that any experience must be of something given as an object (as fulfilling or falling short of our conceptual intentions). As his formulation of the third possibility shows, "it is by no means self-evident that every phenomenon must be submitted to the conditions of possibility for experiencing an object and cannot sometimes contradict them" (p. 41). If the content of the intuition exceeds that of our concepts, then there will, of course, be no object presented; that is, there will be nothing that either fulfills or falls short of fulfilling our concepts. But this will be evidence that nothing has been experienced only if we can exclude the possibility that the experience in question is one of excessive givenness. But this is precisely what we cannot exclude in the case of an experience of God. Given the incomprehensibility that follows from the formal definition of God, excessive givenness is "a requirement proper to the phenomenality of God"; there is no other way that he could be experienced.

Marion further suggests that there may well be indications in our experience that it involves an excess of fulfillment. Citing a comment by St John Chrysostom (in *On the*

Incomprehensible Nature of God) about the "holy terror" that came on him while writing about the divine incomprehensibility, he says: "the excess of intuition is accomplished in the form of stupor, or even of the terror that the incomprehensibility resulting from excess imposes on us." He also suggests that "it could also be that the excess of intuition is marked—strangely enough—by our obsession with evoking, discussing, and even denying that of which we all admit to having no concept". If we were not fascinated by an intuitive experience of divine excess, "how could the question of [an incomprehensible] God dwell within us so deeply?" (p. 41).

The gift and the given

Marion's discussion of the incomprehensible connects with Derrida's treatment of the gift. The link is conceptual impossibility. To say that God is incomprehensible is to say that He cannot be understood in terms of our concepts. This does not mean that God is self-contradictory, like a square circle. A square circle is adequately understood as falling under both the concept *square* and the concept *circle*, which is precisely why it is self-contradictory. The conceptual impossibility of God is a matter not of self-contradiction but of the inadequacy of the concepts that allow us to make judgments of contradiction or non-contradiction.

Derrida maintains (and Marion agrees) that the gift (like other ethical and religious notions such as justice and friendship) is a conceptual impossibility. His argument, put briefly, is that, although a gift is not an object of economic exchange, our efforts to conceive of the practical situations in which gifts are given always reduce it to such an object. Giving a gift frees me (at least for the time being) from having to do anything more for the receiver, while the receiver is obliged (at some point) to return a corresponding gift. So, although giving is not supposed to have anything to do with the economic notions of owing or being owed, the practice, when we think it through concretely, winds up being understood in terms of owing and being owed. To heighten the tension, it is the receiver who winds up owing the giver. Whether or not we agree with Derrida's "deconstruction" of the gift, the point here is that for Derrida the gift is an example of the incomprehensible (conceptually impossible) in at least roughly the same sense as God is incomprehensible for Marion (and Marion and Derrida agree that both God and the gift are incomprehensible). Accordingly, Derrida's claim that the gift, precisely as incomprehensible, cannot be given phenomenologically is a direct challenge to Marion.[5]

This is particularly so because Marion maintains that there is an intimate tie between the ethical–religious gift and the phenomenological notion of the given or givenness. He regards phenomenology as the "science of the given". Husserl ("to some extent") thought that to be given was to be describable as an object experienced by a subject. Heidegger, rejecting the ultimacy of the subject–object distinction, held ("in the

[5] See Chapter 10 for some criticism of Derrida's discussion of the gift.

main") that the given should be described as a being in the world of Dasein. According to Marion, he and other recent thinkers (including Levinas) have been interested in "some very strange phenomena" (p. 57) that cannot be described as either objects or beings—because they are incomprehensible. Among these phenomena he includes Levinas's Other, Derrida's *différance*, and, of course, the incomprehensible God of religious experience. In his terminology, Husserl's objects appear as the result of a transcendental reduction, Heidegger's beings as the result of an existential reduction, and incomprehensible phenomena as the result of a reduction to (sheer) givenness.

Marion insists that we must start from whatever it is that is given to us, not exclude certain phenomena on the grounds that it is (a priori) impossible to experience them. (But, as we have seen, he has provided an argument for the possibility of such experiences.) Moreover, he maintains that the phenomena of religious experience "seem given par excellence"; they are "more given, or given to a larger and higher degree than others". In accord with his earlier comment that religious experience is "pragmatic", he cites communal religious practices such as the Eucharist and other sacraments and the preaching of the Word of the Gospel, which we encounter as "saturated phenomena" (p. 57).

Derrida rejects Marion's connection of the gift with givenness; that is, he denies that it (or any conceptual impossibility) is available for phenomenological description: "the event called gift is totally heterogeneous to theoretical identification, to phenomenological identification" (p. 59). He adds, however, that this does not mean that there is utterly no access to the gift: "the gift as such cannot be known, but it can be thought of." It may be that "thinking . . . is not the right word", but in any case "there is something in excess of knowledge". Derrida also seems sympathetic to Marion's "pragmatic" move: "a gift is something you do without knowing what you do" (p. 60).

Why, nonetheless, does Derrida deny that the conceptual impossibility, the gift, which can be "thought" or "practiced", can be experienced? In his discussion with Marion, he puts the point in a variety of ways, of which two seem especially salient. First, he says that a description of a phenomenon must be a description of it "as such"—just as it appears. (This presumably does not require a description that excludes all vagueness or ambiguity: if the phenomenon is vague or ambiguous, we must be able to describe it with just the vagueness and ambiguity it has.) But, Derrida maintains, when we are dealing with conceptual impossibilities, there is no place for the "as such" (p. 65), since we do not have concepts that can delineate just what is given.

Marion agrees with this last point. "There is no 'as such' in a structure which is by definition open, not closed"—a structure that, for example, cannot have a cause and cannot be repeated, since causality or repetition requires a conceptual context to specify the laws of causality of the criteria of repetition. He admits that "it is not so easy to reach a place which you can describe as free of any 'as such' " (p. 65), but still maintain that such a description is possible.

A bit later, in response to Marion's directly asking him why there cannot be a phenomenological description of the gift, Derrida puts his point in terms of the "principle of all principles" that Husserl formulated as the basis of all phenomenological description. This is the principle that the only way to justify a claim is by appealing to the evidence of intuition. According to Derrida, "the principle of all principles ... implies finally ... the fullness of the intuition, the presence of something". He himself is interested in the excess associated with the gift and other conceptual possibilities but "it is not an excess of intuition, of phenomenality, of fullness, of more than fullness" (p. 71).

Marion does not respond to this formulation, probably because he has a bit earlier tried to finesse the entire issue of "fidelity" to Husserl and phenomenology: "As to the question of whether what I am doing, or what Derrida is doing, is within phenomenology or beyond, it does not seem to me very important." He then cites "a famous sentence of Heidegger, 'We are not interested in phenomenology, but in the things that phenomenology is interested in'". He maintains that he is "still faithful to phenomenology" but is willing to let future students of phenomenology decide the question (p. 68). What is important is whether experience of the divine (the conceptually impossible) is possible and whether he is right that we can describe this experience.

The experience of the impossible

Derrida agrees with the first claim: "What I am interested in ... is precisely this experience of the impossible. This is not simply an impossible experience. What happens in the experience of *the* impossible, which would not be simply a non-experience. That is what I try to do" (p. 72). He also says that he is willing to try to talk about the truth of conceptual impossibilities such as the gift. This could not be "an ontological–phenomenological concept of truth, as revelation or unveiling or adequation". But, he says, "I am looking for another possible experience of truth, through the event of the gift, with all these conditions of impossibility" (p. 72). But he remains adamant about the impossibility of *describing* an experience of impossibility.

Marion accepts Derrida's suggestion that the question is "to think impossibility, *the* impossible as such". He poses this question in the context of the history of modern philosophy (from Kant on), which he presents as a "transcendental enterprise" that takes for granted and starts from "the I, ego, subjectivity" with the goal of establishing the "limits of possibility". Regarding any claim to religious revelation, the transcendental attitude is that it must be conceptually possible: "religion within the limits of reason alone". Specifically, any claim to a religious experience would have to be an experience of what is conceptually possible. Marion sees Derrida and himself as reversing this stance, beginning with the undeniable fact of the experience of the conceptually impossible and asking what is required to think this. "The question is, how is it possible to remain rational and to have a discourse dealing with the impossible?" (p. 74). (Derrida agrees with this point. He says he wants to approach the experience of the impossible as "a rationalist, a phenomenologist" [Marion interjects, "You are!"], "a man of the Enlightenment, and so forth and so on".)

Marion admits that "we have to take seriously the fact that we cannot have an experience of the impossible in the same way that we have an experience of the possible". With regard to impossibility, he proposes to speak of "counter-experience", which he characterizes as "of bedazzlement, of astonishment or *Bewunderung*". A counter-experience is not of "an object or a being" but of "an event that we cannot comprehend but nevertheless we have to see". He maintains, moreover, that this is "the correct and consistent kind of experience appropriate to every decisive experience in our life—death, birth, love, poverty, illness, joy, pleasure, and so on". Of all these things, he says, "we see them but we know our inability to see them in a clear manner; and nevertheless, these impossible and unintelligible evidences play the most important role for us" (p. 75).

We began with a debate between Marion and Derrida on the phenomenology of religious experience, but it should now be clear that this apparently regional discussion in fact concerns the very nature of the philosophical enterprise as a discourse about the conceptually impossible. In these (essentially metaphilosophical) terms, the question concerns the nature of our experience of the conceptually impossible and of the kind of philosophical discourse that expresses it. Both Derrida and Marion agree that the impossible is not a presence; not, that is, something that we can directly grasp and locate exactly in our conceptual network. Marion, however, holds that, nonetheless, the impossible is *given* to our experience—not conceptually (that is, as fulfilling the intentions with which we come to experience) but as saturating and overflowing these intentions, exceeding them with its incomprehensibility.

Religion and the impossible

Despite the wider significance of the debate between Derrida and Marion, we should end by returning to the original question about religious experience. According to Marion, the language that best expresses and responds to the experience of the incomprehensible is the religious language of praise and worship, as, for example, in the Catholic liturgy. This is language that recognizes and celebrates the incomprehensible's having revealed itself to us, having indeed become human and lived among us. The conceptual absence that is due to the incomprehensibility of God is replaced by an overwhelming non-conceptual givenness.

According to Derrida, however, the incomprehensible is "*neither* present nor *given*".[6] It is, instead, encountered *only* as a promise or a hope, as that which is always to come but never actually comes. This is what Derrida calls his "messianic" view of the inconceivable, in contrast to the "messianistic" view that the coming has been or will some day be realized. There is no given to replace the conceptual absence of the incomprehensible, just the traces of an always disappearing *différance*. In the debate with Marion, Derrida refers not to *différance* but to *khora* (the "receptacle" of Plato's *Timaeus*), an avatar of *différance* in Derrida's later writings. *Khora*, like *différance*, is

[6] John D. Caputo, "Apostles of the Impossible: On God and the Gift in Derrida and Marion", in Caputo and Scanlon (eds.), *God, the Gift, and Postmodernism*, 199. Caputo's discussion is an invaluable reflection on the debate between Derrida and Marion.

prior to any historical place or time, a "place which remains irreducible to historicization, humanization" and hence to the "anthropo-theologization of revelation" (p. 76). The difference between Derrida and Marion can be summed up in terms of their respective relations to the classical tradition of negative or (as Marion prefers) mystical theology. Both accept the traditional initial steps of putting forward naive affirmations about God and then showing how this must be negated. Marion thinks that there is a coherent way of moving to the traditional third stage of "eminent" discourse about the incomprehensible that does not fall back into the conceptualizations of the metaphysics of presence but still expresses what is given in our experience of the incomprehensible. Derrida, however, maintains that the third stage is not possible, that we can talk of the incomprehensible only in terms of its indefinitely postponed arrival, never in terms of its actual givenness to us. Derrida denies, while Marion affirms, the possibility of a historical giving (revelation) of the incomprehensible. We might say that Derrida goes as far as a religion of the Annunciation (Mary's assent to the promise of a child: "be it done to me according to thy word") but not so far as a religion of the Nativity (a declaration that the promise has been fulfilled: "unto us a child is born").

Derrida suggests that this difference has serious practical implications, that our experience of the incomprehensible as *khora* could "translate . . . into what we could call ethics or politics" (p. 77). Because *khora* "has nothing to do with . . . revelation", which occurs in historical time, it is "an absolutely universal place, so to speak", and, as such, is "also the condition for a universal politics" (p. 77) that would allow a discourse beyond the particular claims of revelation made by Christians, Jews, and Muslims. It would thus provide "a place where a new discourse and a new politics could become possible" (p. 76). Although he does not put it this way, Derrida seems here to play once again the "man of the Enlightenment", who shows the way to moving beyond the conflicts of religious denominations; not, like Voltaire and company, to a unity of understanding but to a unity of hope rising from a shared experience of incomprehensibility.

But we should not misunderstand the effect of this "Enlightenment" move. The reason that identifying incomprehensibility with *khora* opens the way for a universal politics is that it *undermines* the claims to special religious revelation. It "has nothing to do with . . . revelation", and, if revelation does not come from our experience of the incomprehensible, how could it provide us with anything except an idol (a being we can *understand*) to worship? Just as Voltaire thought we could achieve tolerance by showing the arbitrariness of the doctrines of warring sects, so Derrida's "absolutely universal place", where, presumably, all mankind could live together in peace, requires our giving up our claims to have a privileged access to religious truth. Without such claims, how is anyone seriously Christian, Jew, or Muslim? For all their mutual sympathy, Derrida and Marion express, in postmodern terms, the traditional modern distinction between secular enlightenment and the claims of revealed religion.

Whatever we may think of the significance of the debate between Derrida and Marion for the specific issue of religion, there remains the global question of whether or how it is possible to experience or think about what we cannot conceive, what is incomprehensible to us. This, I will argue, has emerged from our account as the central issue of French philosophy since 1960, and we shall confront it more fully in Chapter 10. First, however, we need to look at Alain Badiou's very different approach to the incomprehensible, an approach that puts him (along with Gilles Deleuze) in fundamental opposition to Derrida and Marion.

9

Ontology, Ethics, and Incomprehensibility: Alain Badiou

Badiou is unmoved by declarations of the death of philosophy. Contrary to Derrida and Marion, he is practicing, not deconstructing, the grand ontological style in philosophy, and he has no inclination to worship at the shrine of incomprehensibility. He does not, however, use Hegelian rational analysis and argument or Sartrean phenomenological description, to cite the two most prominent systematizers in his philosophical past. Rather, like Deleuze, he employs his remarkable intellectual imagination to construct a vision of how things in general are and how they hang together. The result is an impressive ontology, based on a sophisticated deployment of formal set theory. As we shall see, this ontology challenges Derrida's and Marion's enshrinement of the incomprehensible as the inescapable limit of philosophical thought and offers a forthrightly atheistic philosophical vision. Further, contrary to Foucault, Levinas, and Derrida, Badiou claims that his ontology provides the basis for a full-blooded ethics that is, however, not a revival of humanism.

Being

Badiou's ontology starts[1] from a fundamental division between the static structure of *being* and the (potentially) dynamic action of *events*, between, that is, the natural and the historical. His overall vision has no place for any antecedent purpose or meaning of the universe (and in that sense is atheistic) and no place for realities other than those of nature and history (and in that sense is materialistic). On the other hand, and in contrast to most of his contemporaries, he insists on objective truth and on the central role of the subject. However, he locates truth and subjectivity in the domain of events, not in the ontological realm of being.

[1] My discussion of Badiou's ontology centers on his *Being and Event*, tr. Oliver Feltham (London: Continuum, 2006). References will be given in the text. For a helpful commentary, see Christopher Norris, *Badiou's* Being and Event (London: Continuum, 2009). I do not take account of the second volume (published in French in 2006), *Logic of Worlds (Being and Event 2)*, tr. Alberto Toscano (London: Continnum, 2009). The best guide to Badiou's work as a whole is Peter Hallward, *Badiou: A Subject to Truth* (Minneapolis, MN: University of Minnesota Press, 2003).

As Badiou sees it, a being is always presented in a particular situation; that is, in a specific structured context. The structure of this context determines the manner in which the being is presented as a unified whole (as one being). In Badiou's terminology, the situation determines how the being will be "counted as one". Since presentation involves counting as one, it follows that a being is presented as a sheer multiplicity that becomes a set of "elements" through the presentation. Accordingly, Badiou will say that a being is what is presented as a consistent (unified) multiplicity. (Prior to presentation, what we have is a non-unified—"inconsistent"—multiplicity.) In standard cases, a multiplicity is "counted as one" in virtue of a property that all of its elements share: belonging to a human body, being members of a certain club, being chemical constituents of a piece of gold. Different situations correspond to different ways of characterizing multiplicities. For example, in a situation defined by the context of political action, multiplicities will be characterized by the political groups or causes they support; in a situation defined by the context of chemical analysis, by their molecular or atomic constituents; in a situation defined by the context of literary criticism, by the linguistic elements that make them up. What about the case of an irreducible individual, not presented as made up of components? Then we can speak of a multiplicity that contains only one element—the individual itself. (In set theory, this corresponds to the "singleton set".)

The inquiry traditionally called ontology (or fundamental metaphysics) is concerned not with what can be said of something as a certain kind of being (an atom, a tree, a lyric poem) but what can be said of it simply as a being (being qua being). Badiou holds that being qua being, being precisely insofar as it is being, has a mathematical structure that is accurately described by the set theory developed by Cantor and other nineteenth- and twentieth-century mathematicians. This makes perfect sense given his understanding of reality as a matter of the presentation of multiplicities. Since beings are multiplicities, that is, collections of elements that belong to the multiplicity, a being simply as such will have to be merely the formal structure of collections (sets) formed from elements, with no account being taken of the non-formal properties (what Badiou calls "presentative predicates") of the sets or the elements. The study of being in this sense is the study of "the presentation of presentation itself".[2] This is, of course, precisely the subject of the mathematical theory of sets.

We may wonder how there could be a purely formal treatment of multiplicities, since they would seem to be made up of entities (their elements) that are particular kinds of things—rocks, trees, planets, numbers, and so on. But, Badiou will insist, precisely as a being and nothing else, a given multiplicity will be made up of nothing but other multiplicities; the elements of a multiplicity will be multiplicities. Ontology, therefore, concerns nothing but sets: nested series of sets containing other sets. This means that ontology, in the traditional sense of the study of being as being, is not the province of philosophy but of mathematics. However, as we have seen,

[2] "Politics and Philosophy: An Interview with Alain Badiou" (with Peter Hallward), appendix to *Ethics: An Essay on the Understanding of Evil*, tr. Peter Hallward (London: Verso, 2001), 127.

philosophy does have the role of showing how and why set theory is applicable to an understanding of being as being. That is, it presents the vision of reality as the presentation of multiplicities, from which it follows that ontology is given by set theory. But this vision itself is not provided by set theory.

Let us now turn to a more detailed discussion of Badiou's ontology, based on a fairly close reading of a few key sections of *Being and Event*.

Badiou begins with the oldest of philosophical puzzles: the one and the many. His formulation is in terms of two aspects of our experience of being: on the one hand, a being is presented as multiple (having various attributes, perspectives, and so on); on the other hand, what is presented is one thing—a being. As Badiou puts it: "what *presents* itself is essentially multiple; *what* presents itself is essentially one" (p. 23). The presentation of the being is multiple but the being is one. More precisely, in Badiou's terminology, the presentation is of an "inconsistent" (ununified) multiplicity, whereas the being is a "consistent" (unified) multiplicity. (Note how these formulations are neutral among specific forms of presentation or experience, which may be sensory, intellectual, affective, and so on). This experience, however, leads directly to the puzzle, formulated, for example, in Plato's *Parmenides*: (*a*) If being is one, then (by contraposition) what is not one is not being; therefore, since the multiple is not one, it is not being and so is not. But if there is no multiple, then there is no presentation of being, so that we have no way of encountering (and hence knowing) being. (*b*) Conversely, if there is a presentation of being, then the multiple necessarily is (since the presentation is multiple), which means that being need not be one (since there is something that is not one). But this makes no sense, since a given presentation is the specific multiple that it is only because it presents this specific being (that is, "what it presents can be counted as one" (p. 23)). From (*a*) it follows that, if being is one, then it cannot be presented to us, whereas from (*b*) it follows that, if being can be presented to us, then it need not be one. Both conclusions contradict our experience of being presented with a being that is essentially one.

Some may think the puzzle—whether in this formulation or in the many others that have been put forward—turns entirely on details of its logic or even grammar; for example, can we rightly move from "this is not being" to "this is not" or from "this is multiple" to "the multiple is". Badiou, however, thinks that the puzzle has deeper roots, roots in the ontological assumptions that underlie it. In particular, he suggests that the puzzle, in one form or another, will continue to arise as long as we work from the assumption that "the one is"; that is, that the basis of all thought and reality must be something that is essentially self-identical (one with itself). Contrary to this, he decides to make (and to make sense of) the assertion: the one is not; that is, to build an ontology that is not grounded on self-identical being. This does not mean, he hastens to tell us, that unity (Oneness) will have no place in his ontology. In some sense, "There is Oneness" (as Lacan insisted in formulating the principle of what he calls the "symbolic"). But Badiou will try to show how this does not require us to say that "there is a being of the one" (that the one has being). This idea, of course, is not easy to formulate.

We might, for example, try to distinguish between "there is——" and "the——is (a being)". But even saying "there is one" itself "concedes a point of being to the one" (p. 24).

Badiou proposes instead a distinction between *presentation* and *operation*. When there is a presentation of being, being is presented (indeed, presents itself) as one, but the one that it is is "an operational result" of the presentation. Via the presentation, being "is-counted-as-one". In itself (that is, apart from its presentation), being is not one, nor is it even multiple (since "the multiple is solely the regime of presentation" (p. 24)). (Or, as Badiou also puts it, it is an inconsistent rather than a consistent multiplicity.)

Badiou goes on to introduce the term *situation* (noting that we need to neutralize any Sartrean connotations it may have for us). He first says that a situation "is any presented multiplicity", although he also says (in the next sentence) that it is a place ("the place of taking-place") and (in a note) that it is "a space of structured multiple presentation"). The latter characterizations fit better with his further discussions, and we should identify the situation not with the presented multiplicity but with the structure in terms of which a multiplicity is presented as one (the structure determining how the being thereby presented is "counted-as-one"). Specifically, he says that, "when anything is counted as one in a situation, all this means is that it belongs to the situation in the mode particular to the effects of the situation's structure" (p. 24). Summing up Badiou's view here: when we encounter something as a being (when being is presented or presents itself), this occurs in a situation that is structured in a way that determines how the being is presented and, in particular, the sense in which the being is to be counted as one thing.

Given the above account, Badiou asks: "What form would a discourse on being-qua being-take . . . ?" (p. 25). On this account "there is nothing apart from situations"; that is, being is presented only in or through situations. Therefore, if there is such a thing as ontology (a discourse on being qua being), ontology must be a situation. But thinking of ontology this way leads to difficulties. (1) Since a situation is a presentation, it would follow that ontology would be a presentation of being qua being, whereas "it seems rather that 'being' is included in what any presentation presents" and "one cannot see how it could be presented *qua being*" (p. 25). (2) Also, if ontology is a situation, it must involve the count-as-one structure that unifies what it presents, in this case, being as such (being qua being). But if, as Badiou is assuming, being is not one, how can the situation present it as counting-as-one? We seem led back to the ancient paradoxes of being and the one. Indeed, is not this precisely the result of our having concluded, above, that being is neither one nor multiple?

In the face of such difficulties, it is tempting to give up the claim that ontology is a situation and assert that "only an experience situated beyond all structure will afford us an access to the veiling of being's presence" (p. 26). This, in fact, is the "Great Temptation", given in to by historical ontologies such as Plato's of the Idea of the Good, which is beyond being, and medieval negative theologies (see pp. 26–7). Such ontologies are what Badiou calls "ontologies of presence", where presence is "the exact contrary of presentation" (p. 27), since the presence they seek reveals being as beyond all structure and, therefore, beyond rational discourse and knowledge. Contrary to such ontologies, Badiou will develop an ontology based on the presentation of being that places it "within the positive regime of predication, and even of formalization", with results that are "fully transmissible within knowledge" (p. 27). In Badiou's ontology "being is said solely as that which cannot be supposed on the basis of any presence or experience" and is presented through a mathematical method of "deductive invention" (p. 27).

Badiou's approach is "subtractive", since it makes being not available through presence or experience. This, however, is quite opposed to "the Heideggerian thesis of a withdrawal of being". For Heidegger, being's withdrawal from presence makes it accessible to us only through a "poetic 'overturning'" of ordinary human language. For Badiou, by contrast, the separation of being from presence means that, "repealing every poem", being "is constrained to be sayable, for humanity, within ... the most rigid of all conceivable laws, the law of demonstrative and formalizable inference" (p. 27). Badiou's project, then, is to employ the formal resources of logic and mathematics (specifically, set theory) to resolve the paradoxes that arise when we take ontology as a situation and so to develop a rational, human discourse about being.

Badiou's solution to the paradoxes of ontology is to have "the ontological situation be the *presentation of presentation*" (p. 27). This, he says, solves paradox (1): that being is presented in every situation and so cannot be distinctively presented in just one situation. For, if the ontological situation is the presentation of presentation, "then it is quite possible that what is at stake in such a situation is being qua being, insofar as no access to being is offered to us except presentation" (p. 27). The idea seems to be that, if being is presented in every presentation, this may be precisely because what being is just as being is presentation itself. If so, a presentation of being will be a presentation of being as being.

This does not, however, resolve paradox (2): that being cannot be presented because it cannot be counted-as-one (since being is not one). Badiou approaches a resolution by noting that, as we have been understanding presentation, the only predicate that applies to it is "multiple". Therefore, "if the one is not reciprocal with being, the multiple, however, is reciprocal with multiplicity" (p. 28). From this, Badiou draws the conclusion that the ontological situation, if it is possible, must (as a presentation of presentation) be "the situation of the pure multiple, of the multiple 'in-itself'". More precisely, this means that "ontology can be solely the theory of inconsistent multiplicities as such", where "as such" means that the ontological situation presents the multiple simply as the multiple (p. 28).

Now the obvious problem is this: how can the multiple be presented without, contrary to its very nature, being presented as one? In all other cases, the law of presentation is precisely a way of counting what is presented as one. But for the multiple itself to be presented, it must "be inscribed in the very law itself that the one *is not*" (p. 28). In other words, not only must what is presented be nothing other than multiple (that is, the multiple can be made up of only further multiples, not ones), but also the multiple must be presented simply as multiple, not as one. Summing up these conditions, Badiou says that there are two "prerequisites for any possible ontology":

1. The multiple from which ontology makes up its situation is composed solely of multiplicities. . . .
2. The count-as-one [for the ontological situation] is no more than the system of conditions through which the multiple can be recognized as multiple. (p. 29)

Badiou acknowledges that the "second requirement is extreme". The count-as-one (the law of presentation) for the ontological situation "must stipulate that everything it legislates on is multiplicities of multiplicities" (condition 1) and, further, "it must prohibit anything 'other' than the pure multiple . . . from occurring within the presentation that it structures" (condition 2) (p. 29). The second condition is "extreme" because it means that the law of presentation cannot take the form of a criterion or a definition for pure multiplicity, since this would make the multiple as multiple be one—it would be a unity instantiating its definition and, as Badiou puts it, "being would be lost again" (that is, reduced to the one, contrary to the basic assumption of Badiou's ontology). Accordingly, the law of the ontological situation cannot be explicit; it can only be implicit.

We know, however, how to specify a law without explicitly stating a definition expressing it: by formulating a system of axioms. An axiomatic presentation begins with non-defined terms for which it prescribes rules of manipulation (rules for "composing" more complex terms from the undefined terms). These axioms implicitly exclude treatment of the terms that would violate the implicit rule we want to apply to our terms, but we never encounter "an explicit definition of what an axiom system counts as one" (p. 30).

Finally, Badiou puts all of this in terms of his distinction between consistent and inconsistent multiplicity. Inconsistent multiplicity is "pure" multiplicity, multiplicity prior to its presentation, via a count-as-one law, as *a* multiplicity. This latter—multiplicity presented and so counted-as-one—is "impure" or "consistent" multiplicity. Being qua being is inconsistent multiplicity. The law that allows us to count it as one cannot be explicitly formulated (on pain of logical contradiction), but it can be implicitly formulated by the deployment of an axiom system. "The effect of the axiom system is that of making the [inconsistent multiplicity] consistent" (p. 30). In ordinary (non-ontological) situations, any multiplicity will be presented as consistent. But in the ontological situation any multiplicity "must no longer possess any other consistency than that of their pure multiplicity, that is, their mode of inconsistency within situations" (p. 30). Accordingly, their "primitive consistency is *prohibited* by the axiom system" (since such consistency is "ontologically inconsistent"). Correspondingly, "their inconsistency . . . is *authorized* as ontologically consistent" (p. 30). In this precise sense, we can say that the application of the axiom system forms "consistency into inconsistency" and "inconsistency into consistency" (where contradiction is avoided by the distinction of ontological vs non-ontological consistency and inconsistency).

Being and set theory

Although Cantor, in his pioneering work, spoke of sets in terms of intuitions and objects, later formulations by Frege and Russell rightly used a purely formal language that referred only to the extensions of properties or concepts. This approach has two sorts of advantages. First, we can "rigorously specify the notion of a property by reducing it . . . to the notion of a predicate in a first-order logical calculus" (p. 39). This allows us to avoid numerous problems arising from the vagaries of ordinary language. Second, we can exchange Cantor's fuzzy talk of intuition totalizing its objects for a precise thesis specifying that, for any property expressible as a predicate in our formal language, there is a set that has as its elements exactly those things to which the predicate (and hence property) applies. Given this thesis (the axiom of comprehension), we have a language (axiomatic set theory) that gives us total mastery over the multiple; that is, every multiple corresponds to a precise specification of the criteria that define its members.

Unfortunately, the axiom of comprehension is false because it leads to contradiction. As Russell first showed, the failure can be derived from the most banal of properties, one possessed by almost every set: the property of not being a member of itself (so, for example, the set of all giraffes is not a giraffe, the set of all whole numbers is not a whole number, and so on). On the other hand, there are relatively few cases of sets that are members of themselves (perhaps most obviously, the set of all sets). Given the axiom, we can assert that there is a set of exactly all those sets that are not members of themselves. The contradiction (Russell's paradox) arises from the simple question: is this set (the set of all sets that are not members of themselves) a member of itself? Logic requires that it either is or is not a member of itself. But a bit of reflection shows that neither alternative is viable. (*a*) If the set (Badiou calls it *p*) is a member of itself, then it must meet the criterion for being a member of the set; namely, it must not be a member of itself. So, if *p* is a member of itself, it is not a member of itself. Similarly, (*b*) if *p* is not a member of itself, then it does not meet the criterion for membership; that is, it must not *not* be a member of itself, which is to say that it is a member of itself. So, if *p* is not a member of itself, it is a member of itself. Putting (*a*) and (*b*) together, we see that the very idea of the set is self-contradictory; there can be no such set.

Badiou notes that most logicians think the paradoxical set *p* is "too large" to be counted as a set, meaning that *p* exhibits "an excess of being-multiple over the very language from which it was to be inferred" (p. 41). Cantor goes further, saying that the reason some multiplicities cannot be "totalized" is that they are "absolutely infinite" (not merely mathematically "transfinite") and relates them to God as a being, beyond language, that unites all multiplicities into one. As Cantor sees it, mathematical inconsistency points us toward a God who is beyond the requirement of consistency.

But Cantor can also be read—dropping his insistence on a unity beyond consistency—as realizing that "the absolute point of being of the multiple is not its consistency . . . but its inconsistency". This inconsistency corresponds to a "multiple-deployment that no unity gathers together" (p. 42). Such is the standpoint of mathematical ontology, which accepts the consequences of the paradox without trying to escape to a unity of being beyond thought and language. In other words, mathematical ontology accepts that "paradoxical multiplicity . . . quite simply *is not*" and takes it as "the point of non-being from whence it can be established that there is *a* presentation of being" (p. 42). Here Badiou speaks of a "decision" that separates the ontology of presence from the ontology of presentation: the decision to "declare that beyond the multiple . . . the one is" versus the decision to declare that, beyond the multiple, there is nothing ("pure non-being"), that, in other words, "the one is not" (p. 42). Badiou makes the latter decision and maintains that set theory provides the most effective way of developing it.

To support this claim, he shows how axiomatic set theory can be developed to avoid the paradoxes and how other set theoretical notions, from the null set (a set with no members) to Cohen's sophisticated theory of forcing, can explicate various aspects of his ontology. Also, Badiou is able to develop his ontology simultaneously in terms of his philosophical language of multiples-presented-in-a-situation and in terms of the mathematical language of set theory. The first allows us to see connections with the ontological tradition from Plato through Heidegger; the second provides a formally rigorous mode of expression that helps clarify some of the obscurities of the non-formal philosophical language. Both languages have their uses, but Badiou makes it clear that ontology strictly speaking (the account of being as being) is entirely determined by the axioms of set theory.

As just one example of Badiou's use of set theory, let us look at his treatment of a central problem for his ontology. This arises from the truth of what Badiou calls "Leibniz's thesis": "what is not *a* being is not a *being*"; that is, we encounter (are presented with) being only as a unity (*a* being of a certain sort). This poses an obvious difficulty for Badiou's ontology, which holds that the presentation of a being is a matter of different elements, previously merely dispersed, being "counted-as-one" and thereby grouped together into a set. For Badiou must say that "there is" such a merely dispersed group of elements (this is what he calls an "inconsistent multiplicity"). But what is the force of this "there is", given that all we are ever presented with is a being (a consistent multiplicity); that is, elements that are members of a set in virtue of a rule for counting them as one?

Of course, once we have an initial set presented, there is no problem understanding how further sets could be presented. If we already have a set *I*, then we can form the set that contains *I*: {I}, then the set that contains I and {I}: {I, {I}}, and so forth. What we need is an initial set. It would seem that this is no help, since we still need some way of understanding how there could be dispersed elements of this set prior to their inclusion in the set (since to be is to be included in a set). To avoid the problem, we would have to start with a set that had no members, since for such a set there would be no question of "dispersed members" existing independently of their inclusion in a set. But here set theory provides the solution, since it allows for a set with no members (the *null set*, designated ϕ). If, as set theory does, we postulate the existence of such a set, if, that is, we postulate $(\exists\phi)[\sim(\exists\alpha)(\alpha\epsilon\phi)]$ ("there exists a set such that no set is an element of it"), then we have the initial set we need to avoid the inconsistency of having to start from the dispersed elements of a set not yet formed. Badiou's earlier discussion of this issue in traditional philosophical terms gets bogged down in a complex and obscure argument about the existence of the void. The ease with which the set-theoretical approach resolves the issue illustrates its power as an instrument of ontological clarification.

Event

Although philosophy has nothing to add to set theory as an account of being qua being, it does have something to say about beings that are specified in more particular ways. Even here, however, it does not have the first word. According to Badiou, beings fall into four fundamental domains: science, politics, art, and love. Roughly, these correspond to the natural world (including mathematics), the social world, the aesthetic world, and the world of personal existence. In different periods there are different intellectual enterprises that deal with each of these domains, but philosophy is not one of them.

Rather, philosophy is concerned with providing a framework for thinking about all of these domains together as a coherent whole. Plato, for example, offers a vision of science as knowledge of Forms, politics as defined by the ideal state, love as directed to the Form of the beautiful, and art (that is, poetry) marginalized as a danger to the other three domains. Modern philosophy from Descartes on involved various modes of conceptualizing the science, politics, art, and love of our age in terms of subjectivity and objective truth. Badiou, in opposition to his "postmodernist" predecessors, maintains that it is still possible to carry out such a conceptualization. Showing how this is possible is the heart of his philosophical enterprise.

Badiou's account of the modern situation is based on his philosophy of the event—the complement to the ontology of being. An "event", in his parlance, is not just any one of the occurrences that make up the passing of time. Rather, it is an occurrence that introduces radical novelty into existence, an occurrence that is literally unintelligible in terms of the conceptual structures that define the situation from which it emerges. An event is eventually recognized as a revolution in one or more of the four domains of existence.

Some of Badiou's main examples of events are political: the French Revolution, the Russian Revolution of 1917, the student revolt in France in 1968. But there are also artistic examples (Schönberg's invention of atonal music, the development of abstract painting in the twentieth century, Samuel Beckett's introduction of his version of minimalist literature) and scientific examples (the quantum revolution in physics, Gödel's proof of the incompleteness of formal systems). Badiou has given special attention, in his book on St Paul,[3] to the fundamental Christian event of Christ's resurrection. Even though he rejects Paul's theological standpoint, he is willing to describe the event that transforms his life—and that of other revolutionaries—as being due to grace (although he qualifies it as "laicized grace").

It is crucial to realize that an event is not just a matter of an instantaneous occurrence. It is this—an explosion out of a situation that cannot contain it—but its meaning and power emerge only through a prolonged process that involves both subjectivity and objective truth (the two elements Badiou thinks he can save from the attacks of postmodernism).

Subjectively, an event takes on meaning and efficacy only to the extent that individuals commit themselves to it, making it a focus of their lives. They are taken up in the event—as Paul was by his vision of the risen Christ or Robespierre by the revolt of the French people or Badiou himself by the student outrage of 1968. In other modes, mathematicians or poets are taken up by the power of new forms of proof or of new ways of writing poetry. And two lovers are swept into the startling event of what they have come to mean for one another. Badiou speaks of the *fidelity* whereby individuals remain committed to the event as a focus of their lives. Initially, of course, there is just sheer fidelity to the event, which is named but not understood: "Christ has risen", "The revolution has begun", although the elements of my situation give me no way of understanding how or what this could be, or even say that such a thing is impossible ("Miracles just don't happen", "The state's power is invincible").

Nonetheless, I live out my fidelity in a series of encounters with elements of my situation that I insist on appropriating to (making sense of in terms of) the event. So, for example, an eighteenth-century Parisian revolutionary may have been able to understand the riots of rural peasants as expressions of the revolution but could see the interest without commitment of his noble friends as nothing other than fundamental opposition to it. From this series of encounters there gradually emerges a new understanding of the situation—indeed, a new situation—that was previously impossible.

The above account assumes, of course, that it is possible, in the given case, to effect an understanding of the event. (Drawing a term from Cohen's work on set theory, Badiou will speak of "forcing" an understanding.) The effort, for all my fidelity, may fail, and this requires us to balance the subjectivity of commitment with the objectivity of truth. In particular, the event belongs to what Badiou calls the realm of the *generic*, meaning that it has significance for everyone without restriction. We have, for example, Paul's insistence that "there is neither Jew nor Gentile, man nor woman, slave nor freeman" as far as the salvific force of Christ's resurrection is concerned, and the French Revolution's insistence on universal rights. The ultimate goal of a given subject's fidelity to an event is to establish its universal validity—validity for all subjects—and in this sense its objective truth. Accordingly, for Badiou there is an

[3] Alain Badiou, *Saint Paul: The Foundation of Universalism*, tr. Ray Brassier (Stanford, CA: Stanford University Press, 2003).

essential tie between being a subject and having a commitment to objective truth. In this way, the standard dichotomy between subjectivity and objectivity dissolves, and, at the same time, the postmodernist rejection of both is overcome.

In *Being and Event*, Badiou introduces his notion of an event by turning from being as being to what is *not* being as being. He says that he will follow Heidegger to the extent of holding that the "place" of what is not being (as being) is the non-natural; that is, the historical ("the abnormal, the unstable, the anti-natural" (p. 174)). In terms of his basic notion of multiplicity, the normal is what is *both presented and represented*, whereas a singular (as opposed to a normal) multiplicity is *only presented*. A multiplicity is presented when it "belongs to the situation"; it is represented when it is "included in" the situation (p. 174). The difference between belonging and being included is the difference (in set-theoretical terms) between being an element and being a subset.

This last distinction is perhaps the most useful for getting a sense of what Badiou is talking about. Recall that what is presented in a situation is a multiplicity—a grouping together of entities. The multiplicity is a set and each entity is an element of it. To take Badiou's own example, think of a social situation in which a "family of people" is a presented multiplicity (for example, they live in the same house, take part in common activities, and so on). In other words, they appear in the social world as a unit. To say that the family is also a represented multiplicity is to say that each one of its members (elements) has a discernible status within the society (for example, a legally recognized standing, such as citizen, resident alien, or tourist with a visa). This means that each family member belongs to some other multiplicity that is presented in the situation (the multiplicity of citizens, resident aliens, and so on). In such a case, the set of family members (the elements of the multiplicity) will also be a subset of some other multiplicity. To take the simplest case, if every family member is a citizen, then the family is a subset of the set of citizens. (Or, to take a more complex case, if half the family are citizens and the other half resident aliens, then the family is a subset of the set of those who are either citizens or resident aliens). The point is that we can "place" all the members of the family within the society in ways that go beyond their merely being members of the family. They all have some independent status in the society. This is what it means to say that the family is not only presented but also represented.

In developing his account of events, Badiou is interested in the case in which the individual family members have no status in the society apart from their family membership; for example, when the members are all illegal immigrants (*sans-papiers*). Here the point is that illegal immigrants have no status in the society as such; they do not fit into any category recognized by the laws that define the members of the society.[4] There is, in other words, no other group (multiplicity) to which the family members belong other than the family itself. This means that the family is a singular (abnormal) multiplicity: an element of the society but not a subset of it; that is, the

[4] For simplicity, I am assuming that, apart from recognizing the fact that there are families containing illegal residents, the laws do not recognize such "illegals" in any other way (e.g., as employees or taxpayers).

family is present(ed) in the society, but there is no way of understanding (in terms of the society's legal structure) what its members are (putting them in other groups that would represent them as something other than members of the family).

What, we may ask, does any of this have to do with what Badiou has called events? The family of illegal immigrants has entered the society by means that have no place in the society as a legal structure. Strictly speaking, it makes no sense (in terms of the laws that define the society) that there could be such a family. This corresponds precisely to Badiou's idea of an event as an occurrence that is unintelligible, incomprehensible. The existence of the family is an occurrence in the situation (in this case, the society). The society (as a system of laws) can understand that this occurrence exists—is presented in the society—but it has no way of understanding what sort of occurrence it is (that is, no way of understanding how the family members fit into the society as a whole).

The intrusion of the family into the society can be thought of only as an "outlaw" occurrence, something that properly should not exist. Strictly speaking, such an anomalous occurrence is not an event because an event requires subjects who commit themselves to its importance and devote themselves to developing ways of transforming the situation so that it can be understood. But the anomalous occurrence is what Badiou calls an "evental site" (p. 175), a point from which an event can originate. He also says that such an occurrence is "on the edge of the void" and "foundational" (p. 175). It is "on the edge of the void" in the sense that it is minimally intelligible in its situation: "the minimal effect of structure which can be conceived; it . . . belongs to the situation, whilst what belongs to it in turn does not" (p. 175). In other words, the anomalous occurrence is as close as possible to the "void" of unintelligibility without being totally beyond understanding. There is a definite "surface" of comprehension, but any penetration into what lies beneath this surface has no conceptual content in the situation.

The evental site is foundational, first, in the sense that its "conceptual content" (that in virtue of which it is "counted as one") does not derive from anything else presented in the situation. (In other words, as we have seen, its members are not a subset of any other multiplicity.) Accordingly, it is irreducible to anything else and is, therefore, fundamental. On the other hand, the evental site can, as an irreducible multiplicity, "enter into consistent combinations; it can, in turn, *belong* to multiples counted-as-one in the situation". In set-theoretical terms, the event (more precisely, the evental site) can be understood as a set that has only members that are not subsets of any other sets in the domain we are considering (the intersection of the event with any other set is the null set). This is the formal equivalent to the event's not being reducible to anything else.

To return to Badiou's example, the family of illegal immigrants is recognized as a family and so can be grouped with other families. Because of this, the evental site can be the starting point (foundation) for new ways of conceiving the multiplicities with which it is associated. Such new conceptions will result, however, only if there are conceptual innovations that allow us to think of illegal aliens (the members of these families) in ways that were not possible in our original situation. For example, we might come to change our idea of whether "illegal" is a proper designation for people who make an essential contribution to our economy—so giving up the idea their "illegal" status requires that they be jailed or deported. Such new conceptions will allow the formulation of new truths about these families, truths expressing what simply made no sense prior to our commitment to the evental site.

I began this chapter by suggesting that Badiou stands against Derrida and Marion on the topic of incomprehensibility Having now seen his account of being and the event, we are in a position to formulate this opposition more precisely. All three philosophers agree on what we have seen emerge as the main thrust of recent French philosophy: the need to respond to the incomprehensible, to that which cannot be understood in terms of our conceptual framework. Derrida and Marion regard incomprehensibility as a limit that we can never overcome and for which we must find non-conceptual alternatives of expression. But Badiou (like Deleuze) sees any particular incomprehensibility as a challenge to create new concepts that will be capable of understanding it. Each new conceptualization encounters new incomprehensibilites that it is unable to master, but that merely calls for another conceptualization, and so on. We might say that, for Derrida and Marion, the conceptually impossible is an absolute obstacle before which conceptual thinking is stopped and which calls for non-conceptual thinking, whereas for Badiou the conceptually impossible is always relative to a particular set of concepts and can be thought by creating a new set. This is why the thought of Derrida and Marion is open to the mystery of religion, while that of Badiou is fundamentally anti-religious (assuming, of course, that religion derives from an experience of absolute incomprehensibility).

The event and ethics

Badiou is uneasy with the idea of an ethics because of its association with humanism, which he, like the philosophers of the generation before, regards with disdain. He invokes the pantheon of 1960s anti-humanists—Foucault, Althusser, and Lacan—to support the rejection of "the idea of a natural or spiritual identity of Man, and with it . . . the very foundation of an 'ethical' doctrine in today's sense of the word".[5] Here humanism means the assumption that there is a human essence that provides a basis for "consensual law-making concerning human beings in general, their needs, their lives, their deaths" and, correspondingly a "universal demarcation of evil" as "what is incompatible with the human essence" (p. 6).

Badiou particularly objects to an ethics based on the idea of universal "human rights", an idea that had become very popular in the 1980s as part of the reaction against the anti-humanisms of the 1960s.[6] Such an ethics, he says, is centered on human suffering, with human rights being primarily injunctions against the horrors of murder,

[5] Badiou, *Ethics: An Essay on the Understanding of Evil*, 6. Further references will be given in the text.

[6] Luc Ferry and Alain Renaut were among the most prominent figures in this revival of humanism. See, e.g., their *French Philosophy of the Sixties: An Essay on Antihumanism*, tr. Mary H. S. Cattani (Amherst, MA: University of Massachusetts Press, 1990).

torture, humiliation, and so on. (Recall Rorty's assertion that cruelty is the worst thing we do.) Badiou's case against the ethics of rights is that it in effect defines man in terms of victimhood (susceptibility to suffering). Ethically, we are all either victims or those who are called to save the victims. Badiou's first objection to such an ethics is that it reduces humanity to little more than an animal species, "mortal and predatory". "If the torturers and bureaucrats of the dungeons and the camps are able to treat their victims like animals destined for the slaughterhouse . . . it is because the victims have indeed become such animals" through the indignities they have suffered (p. 11). The understandably rare cases of those who remain human in these circumstances are of precisely those who assert their identity as other than victims. These resistants show that they are "immortal", not in the sense that they will not die but in that they are not essentially "beings-for-death". The problem with the humanistic ethics of rights is that it treats those it would save as nothing more than beings-for-death, whose only fulfillment is release from their suffering. This is why the noble benefactors (for example, white Europeans) so often feel an implicit contempt for those they save.

Badiou further argues that an overwhelming emphasis on eradicating evils leads to social and political conservatism. "If our only agenda is an ethical engagement against an Evil we recognize a priori, how are we to envisage any transformation of the way things are?" (pp. 13–14). The implicit view of human-rights ethics is that the only problem is the failure of many people to enjoy the "benefits" of existing (capitalist) society. It is taken for granted that the goal of ethics is achieved once everyone has sufficient material resources to avoid suffering. This amounts to accepting the capitalist conception of the human good. This ignores what Badiou regards as the fundamental ethical goal of "affirmative invention": "To forbid [Man] to imagine the Good, to devote his collective powers to it, to work towards the realization of unknown possibilities, to think what might be in terms that break radically with what is, is quite simply to forbid him humanity as such" (p. 14). This is the voice of an unrepentant *soixante-huitard*, rejecting the disillusionment of so many of his former comrades, who now regard all revolutionary movements as "utopian" and see them as doomed to turn into a "totalitarian nightmare" (p. 13).[7] Badiou's ethics is his effort to preserve the essential spirit of *les événements de mai* (in which he played an important role), while freeing it from its admittedly naive endorsement of totalitarian regimes.

Badiou just as strongly rejects the anti-humanistic ethics of Levinas's encounter with the Other. He regards Levinas's ethics as the replacement of Greek rationalism with Jewish religion. For the Greeks, "adequate action presumes an initial theoretical mastery of experience, which ensures that the action is in conformity with the rationality of being" (p. 19). The encounter with the Other undermines this mastery in favor of our subordination to the Other, who imposes an unquestionable Law. Despite Levinas's protests to the contrary, Badiou claims that this ultimate appeal to

[7] Here Badiou particularly cites André Glucksman's *The Master Thinkers*, one of the founding texts of the "new philosophers" (mostly 1960s radicals turned centrist liberals) of the 1970s.

authority over reason means that his ethics is essentially religious. Levinas's "ethics requires that the Other be in some sense *carried by a principle of alterity* which transcends mere finite experience". He "calls this principle the 'Altogether-Other', and it is quite obviously the ethical name for God" (p. 22, emphasis in original).

Badiou recognizes that Levinas claims to base his ethics on broadly phenomenological descriptions, not religious faith. But he denies that phenomenology alone can sustain the radical alterity of the Other that Levinas requires. Lacan's psychoanalytic account of the "mirror-stage", presenting "a 'mimetic' conception that locates original access to the other in my own redoubled image", is at least an equally plausible reading of the phenomenological data. Phenomenology cannot decide disputes about the proper way of thinking about what the phenomena present. "As always, the pure analysis of phenomenal appearing cannot decide between divergent orientations of thought" (p. 21).[8] Levinas's preferred orientation is expressed in his implicitly religious axiom (replacing reason with divine authority) for interpreting our experience of the Other. Badiou, as we have seen, has no problem with thinking on the basis of axioms. But he proposes his own axiom: "There is no God", which he takes as equivalent to his ontological claim "the One is not" (p. 25), and uses it, along with the rest of his ontology, to develop a non-humanistic and non-religious approach to ethics.[9]

Badiou starts with a line of thought derived from his critique of humanistic ethics. Since there is no universal human nature, no "abstract subject" that can take on a priori the role of ethical agent, the human animal must become an ethical subject by something that happens in some particular circumstances. Unless something happens, the animal simply remains in its routine world, driven by the biological needs of its species. "We must suppose, then, that whatever convokes someone to the composition of a subject is something extra, something that happens in situations as something that they and the usual way of behaving in them cannot account for" (p. 41). It is natural to think of this "something" as what Badiou's ontology speaks of as an *event*. Ontologically, an event cannot be conceptualized in terms of the situation from which it arises, and this corresponds to the break with the "routine world" through which the human animal becomes an ethical subject. In particular, we become ethical subjects by committing ourselves (pledging fidelity) to the event, thereby undertaking to create (and live) the conceptual resources through which we will eventually understand it. "To be faithful to any event is to move within the situation that this event has supplemented by thinking . . . the situation 'according to' the event". Badiou emphasizes that "all thought is a practice, a putting to the test" (p. 41), so that to think according to the event is to live according to it. Further, since the event makes no sense in terms of the concepts and practices of the current situation, it "compels the subject to

[8] A conclusion in accord with our discussion of Levinas and Deleuze in Chapter 6.

[9] Why does Badiou maintain the term "ethics", with its alternatively humanistic and religious associations? Because he wants to associate himself with "those who, after Aristotle, have used the word in a reasonable way" and "make up a long and honourable lineage" (p. 42).

invent a new way of being and acting in the situation" (p. 42). Badiou sees ethical events emerging in all four of the dimensions of human life: science, politics, art, and love.

Although Badiou rejects what he sees as the religious approach to ethics in Levinas and Marion, it is interesting to note that, in his own way, he includes a key notion of each. Like Levinas, he sees the ethical event as constituting the subject: "The subject . . . in no way pre-exists the process. He is absolutely nonexistent in the situation 'before' the event" (p. 43). Like Marion, he uses the category of "excess" to describe his ethical experience. For example, "lovers as such enter into the composition of *one* loving subject, who *exceeds* them both" (p. 43, emphasis in original); likewise, the revolutionary enters into a revolutionary group (say, a party) that exceeds him, and the work of art exceeds the artist. Of course, Badiou's accounts of constitution and excess take very different directions from Levinas's and Marion's. Badiou's constitution results from the individual's decision not from the Other's command, and his excess is a matter of being part of something greater, not of being dazzled by the incomprehensible. But his agreement that ethical experience is both constitutive and excessive remains significant.

Badiou's emphasis on the subject's *fidelity* to the event suggests a subjective commitment à la existentialism, and it is undeniable that the fidelity itself is subjective, at least in the sense of originating from a subject. But Badiou maintains that this fidelity leads to a "truth-process" that produces a new *objective truth*, not a subjective construction. This objective truth is discovered in the situation from which the event arises. It transforms our conception of the situation (for example, after "the musical event known by the name of 'Schoenberg' " (p. 42), we know a great deal more about what is possible in writing music; after Einstein, we know the new direction that must be taken by physics). This transformation is a break, not a development of what was already established in the situation: "the event . . . meant nothing according to the prevailing language and established knowledge of the situation" (p. 43). But it is also an "immanent break"; the new "truth proceeds in the situation, and nowhere else—there is no heaven of truths" (pp. 42–3).

Nonetheless, the truth arising from the truth-process is objective, both in the sense, noted above, that it is generic (meant for everyone, not just an individual or sub-group) and in the sense that the one faithful to the event pursues it disinterestedly. This disinterest is not, however, a lack of passion but rather a passion that is entirely directed toward ("poured out into", Badiou says, 50) the future development of the event, with no connection to "my interests as a mortal and predatory animal" (49). Badiou even goes so far as to say that the truths resulting from the truth-process "shall endure eternally" (70). But his view remains quite different from standard sorts of metaphysical realism. The truths are not "already there" (in some epistemic heaven) prior to the truth-process undertaken by the subject in response to the event. They are the outcome, not the literal discovery, of the truth-process. Moreover, according to Badiou, "eternal truths", having originated in a situation for which they were incomprehensible, return (in the manner of Plato's philosopher going back to the cave) to the situation where they "force" revisions in the body of previously established knowledge. This revised body of knowledge in turn becomes the established knowledge of a new situation, and this knowledge (which Badiou calls "opinion" in contrast to the eternal truths) may well be later challenged by a new event. Even though Badiou insists that such a challenge would have no effect on the eternal truths themselves, he would have to admit that it would require changes in the "established knowledge" (opinions) of the subjects in the situation. It is not easy to see how Badiou can reconcile his claim that the eternal truths never change with his earlier claim that they do not exist in some Platonic "heaven". But, even if his position is consistent, it is quite different from what many have in mind when they speak of "objective truth".

Badiou's critique of human-rights ethics plausibly objected to an ethics dominated by the injunction to avoid obvious evils such as human suffering. That, however, does not mean that there are no such evils or that ethics can avoid taking account of them. How do we know that the truth-process following from a given event will not lead to horrific evils rather than eternal truths? Consider (as Badiou does) the stereotypical but inevitable example of Hitler and the Nazis. How does the event of the Nazi electoral victory of 1933 differ from that, say, of the establishment of the French Revolutionary Republic in 1792? Badiou agrees that there is no "formal difference" between two such cases. Each meets the nominal definition of a new upsurge that is incomprehensible through the concepts of the present situation alone but is supported by people pledging their fidelity to the truth-process they hope will eventually invent the concepts that will transform our understanding and lead to new truths. Why should we judge one evil and the other not?

To answer this question, Badiou sketches a "theory of Evil", which traces the roots of evil in three dimensions: terror, betrayal, and disaster, corresponding, respectively, to the event, our fidelity to it, and the truth produced by this fidelity. Terror results from mistaking a "simulacrum" of an event for a genuine event. A genuine event calls for fidelity from everyone and generates a truth-process leading to universal truths. A terroristic simulacrum, like Nazism, addresses itself to a particular group of individuals (for example, the German people, the Aryan race) and excludes others (for example, the Jews) and is therefore not generic. This of itself shows that Nazism was "radically incapable of any truth whatsoever" and so that it did not correspond to a genuine event. Badiou notes that even the Nazis' hatred of the Jews mimics fidelity to an event, since such fidelity always encounters enemies whom it must oppose vigorously: "the ethics of truth is always more or less militant, combative" (p. 75). But those faithful to an event always regard their enemies as potential allies. "For however hostile to a truth he might be, in the ethic of truths every 'some-one' is always represented as capable of becoming the Immortal [Badiou's term for those faithful to the event] that he is" (p. 76). The call to fidelity includes everyone, even those most opposed to the event.

Betrayal arises out of a crisis. "When you have lost the thread, when you no longer feel 'caught up' in the process, when the event itself has become obscure", you face a "pure choice between the 'Keep going!' [*Continuez!*] proposed by the ethic of truth" and a return to the thinking and living of the situation before the event (to "the logic of the 'perseverence in being' of the mere mortal that I am" (p. 78). Those who abandon the event, of course, convince themselves their previous fidelity was to an illusion: "the former revolutionaries are obliged to declare that they used to be lost in error and madness . . . a former lover no longer understands why he loved that woman" (p. 79). This is betrayal, "an Evil", Badiou says, "from which there is no return" (p. 80).

Disaster, the third form of Evil, is the identification of "a truth with total power" (p. 71). As we have seen, a new truth returns to and transforms the situation out of which its event arose. This "changes the regime of opinions", with the result that "formerly obvious judgements are no longer defensible, that others become necessary, that the means of communication change". Badiou calls "this reorganization of opinions the *power* [*puissance*] of truths" (p. 80). Here we need to make explicit Badiou's distinction between "the language of the situation" and "the language of the subject". The language of the situation corresponds to "the pragmatic possibility of naming the elements that compose [the situation], and thus of exchanging opinions about them" (p. 81). Such language is essential for us to pursue our interests in the pre-ethical world (below good and evil, we might say), the world in which we exist as "predatory animals". The language of the subject (subject-language) is, by contrast, the language through which we formulate the truths of the event to which we have pledged fidelity. The formulation of these truths is motivated not by pragmatic interests but by the disinterested passion for the event. But throughout the truth-process, we continue (as always) to live in the situation, which is why the truth transforms this situation. "The power of a truth, directed at opinions, forces the pragmatic namings (the language of the objective situation) to bend and change upon contact with the subject-language" (pp. 82–3)). So, for example, the language of Christianity transformed the meanings of Roman terms such as *imperium, caritas*, and *lex*—to say nothing of *deus* and *caelum*.

It might seem possible and proper to replace entirely the language of the situation with the subject-language. It is, after all, the truth, not mere opinion. Why not, then, apply "the *total* power of a truth" in order to "name and evaluate all the elements of the objective situation from the perspective of the truth process" and thereby "name the whole of the real, and thus to change the world" (p. 83)? Badiou, however, says this would be a *disaster*. The reason is that the subject that produces the truth is, for all its fidelity to the event, also and always a human animal with pragmatic interests in the objective situation. "The Immortal exists only in and by the mortal animal" (p. 84) and "truths make their singular penetration [*percée*] only through the fabric of opinions" (pp. 84–5). For all its limitations and stupidities, the world of the situation is our world: "There is no History other than our own; there is no true world to come" (p. 85). To eliminate our world is to eliminate us, the human animals who are the foundation of the truth-process. It follows that "truth does not have total power" and "that the subject-language, the production of a truth-process, does not have the power to name all the elements of the situation" (p. 85). At least one element or another of the situation must remain "unnameable" in the subject-language (p. 86). (Badiou cites Gödel's Theorem as in effect establishing the unnameability of non-contradiction in formal mathematics.) If we ignore this unnameability, we bring on the disaster of trying to live the truth without a basis in the real world of our situation. This is what happened to the Chinese Cultural Revolution in 1967, when the Red Guards aimed for "the complete suppression of self-interest". Badiou also cites the examples of Nietzsche's project of "exploding Christian nihilism and generalizing the great Dionysian 'yes' to Life", of the nineteenth-century positivists' effort to put "scientific statements" in place of "opinions and beliefs about all things", and of "the German Romantics [who] worshipped a universe entirely transformed by an absolutized poetics" (p. 84).

Badiou's response to the problem of evil seems to bring him closer to the humanistic ethics he so firmly rejects at the outset. He distinguishes between a genuine event and a simulacrum by appealing, in a Kantian manner, to the universalizability of the call for fidelity to an event. The self-betrayal of the ethical subject who makes a "pure choice" to reject fidelity and convinces himself that the truth is an illusion evokes Sartrean freedom and bad faith. The disaster of rejecting the world of our human interests is in effect a concession to Rorty's pragmatic liberalism. Finally, although Badiou successfully rejects the strong normativity of standard consequentialist and deontological ethics, he does not seem so far from popular ethics of self-fulfillment. Such convergences raise questions about the distinctiveness and ultimate consistency of Badiou's ethics (as do our earlier questions about the objectivity of ethical truths). But the fact remains that Badiou is the first major French philosopher since Bergson to propose a full-blooded account of the ethical life.

10

Conclusion: Thinking the Impossible

The preceding chapters have shown a distinctive unity to French philosophy since 1960: a fundamental concern with thinking what is conceptually impossible. In one sense, of course, philosophy has always been about thinking what at least seems to be impossible. How can there be change? How can we be free in a world of scientific laws? How can a mind move a body? How can evil exist in a world created by God? How can we know anything outside of our own minds? How can there be something rather than nothing? Philosophy gets going just at the point when thought encounters contradictions and, rather than lazily accepting or turning away from them, sets out to put things right.

Thinking is typically a matter of using concepts to order things—to describe, distinguish, classify, relate them. Concepts themselves raise many philosophical questions—it is not easy to fit together consistently everything we want to say about them—and any particular concept of concepts is likely to be rejected by a good number of philosophers. But, if we define them nominally as whatever it is that we typically use for thinking about the world, philosophy cannot avoid coming to terms with concepts. Often enough, philosophical thought is itself a matter of using concepts to make sense of things. But philosophy, open to questioning anything, has also often challenged the value of conceptual thinking and tried either to trace its limits (à la Kant) or even to replace it with non-conceptual experience or (if this is not a contradiction) non-conceptual thinking. But even philosophers who challenge concepts will, if they want to remain philosophers, have to formulate and defend their views in conceptual terms. Philosophy without concepts is both empty and blind, even if it is legitimately pointing to limits or alternatives to conceptual thinking. It must at least *conceive* how such limits or alternatives are possible. It is entirely possible to give up doing this; then you may be writing poems, praising God, or even just living life—but you are not philosophizing.

But if all philosophy is in a way a matter of thinking the impossible, the French project is still distinctive in comparison with analytic philosophy.[1] A good first pass at

[1] The project of thinking the impossible is also a key feature of much European philosophy from Hegel through Heidegger. The project takes various forms, often quite different from that of the French thinkers we

how what the French do differs from what analytic philosophers do is to say that the analysts typically act as if there is nothing that cannot be understood conceptually. They may tacitly or even explicitly acknowledge that there are things that cannot be conceived. (For example, many say this of qualitative sensations, and Colin McGinn says it of the mind–body relation.) But the general assumption is that the domain of the conceptually impossible marks the boundary of philosophy, which is precisely in the business of trying to conceive what seems inconceivable. By contrast, our French philosophers are particularly fascinated by what is not conceivable—or at least by what is not conceivable in any standard way.

This last qualification ("in any standard way") points to the fundamental division we have encountered between *absolute skeptics* about conceivability (Levinas,[2] Derrida, and Marion), who hold that there are ineliminable conceptual impossibilities (which cannot be thought by any concepts), and *relative skeptics* (Foucault, Deleuze, and Badiou), who claim only that there are conceptual impossibilities for any given set of concepts (but that new concepts can be developed to eliminate the impossibilities). My "in any standard way" signals the latter position, which allows that there are conceptual impossibilities relative to any particular conceptual framework (which may, in fact, be the only framework available in a given historical context) but maintains that it is always possible for us to develop new concepts that will allow us to think such impossibilities.

This division can be understood by reference to the Hegelianism that all our philosophers were, in their various ways, trying to avoid or overcome. Hegel's mature philosophy insisted on two things. (1) The processes of conceptual thought typically lead to contradiction. (2) Further conceptual thought is capable of eliminating any given contradiction and, properly pursued, will lead to a final conceptualization that is free of contradiction. (2) implies that, as Hyppolite emphasized, Hegel opposed any claim that philosophy had to rest on ineffable truths, somehow intuitively known but incapable of consistent conceptual formulation. But (1) implies that, at any stage prior to the final stage (of Absolute knowledge), thought would also encounter conceptual impossibilities. These could be removed by broadening our thought to a wider context, but each wider context would generate its own contradictions that would be removed only at the next stage.

By denying (2), Levinas, Derrida, and Marion challenge Hegel's rejection of the ineffable and avoid the totalization of his system by insisting on experiences of the inconceivable that can never be integrated into a consistent conceptual whole. Deleuze, Foucault, and Badiou are closer to Hegel on this point. Like Hegel, they

have discussed, but all sharply different from standard analytic philosophy. My discussion concerns only the contrast between analytic philosophy and recent French philosophy. It is also worth noting that in recent years analytic philosophy has become a considerable force on the French scene through the work of thinkers such as of Jacques Bouveresse, François Recanati, and Pascal Engel, to mention just a few.

[2] As I will emphasize below, Levinas belongs among the absolute skeptics only in his views about God, not in his ethical views.

reject any absolutely irreducible ineffability, while allowing that the concepts we have at any given time may not be adequate to our experience, so that understanding will require developing new concepts. They differ from Hegel in rejecting the central claims of his dialectic: that the concepts eliminating contradiction develop inevitably from the intrinsic logic of the mind's reflection, and that this inevitable process ends with complete conceptual understanding.

Analytic philosophers' commitment to conceptual understanding immediately divides them from the absolute skeptics about conceivability. Analytic philosophers are like the relative skeptics in their efforts to develop concepts that enable us to understand what common sense (or even science) may not be able to conceive. But their project is to achieve this on the basis of already available concepts, without, like Deleuze, creating radically new concepts.

When analytic philosophers set out to dissolve an apparent impossibility (say, the seeming contradiction between free actions and deterministic scientific laws), the concepts they start from are almost always those used in our ordinary, everyday thinking. These are concepts expressing the "obvious truths"—which any sensible person would have to accept—that operate as the standard by which analytic philosophers ultimately evaluate any conclusions they put forward. Such concepts and the truths they express are what current analytic philosophers often call "intuitions". By this term, they do not refer, as some of the great philosophical dead have, to a special (perhaps infallible) insight peculiar to the philosophical mind. They mean only the "entirely obvious" (even if individually fallible and revisable) truths that no one competent to judge sincerely denies.

Analytic philosophers recognize, of course, the need to clarify and refine these concepts by introducing further distinctions needed to eliminate seeming contradictions, and they begin from a large body of such distinctions introduced by their philosophical predecessors. They even recognize that the process of eliminating contradictions may require the radical revision or rejection of some of the intuitively obvious concepts and truths from which they began. But the ultimate standard by which they judge philosophical discourse is its overall adequacy to these obvious, essentially undeniable truths. This is strikingly apparent in the pervasive use of counterexamples. Let an analytic philosopher venture any general assertion (say, "Everyone desires pleasure", "Knowledge requires certainty", "Everything has a cause") and colleagues immediately begin a search for cases for which the generalization is obviously (intuitively) false. The response to the counterexample is to modify the generalization to allow for it (to respect the intuition), to show that the example does not obviously contradict the generalization (to deflect the intuition), or to show that the counterexample is not intuitively grounded. In all cases, intuition, our sense of what is obviously true, rules.

By contrast, recent French philosophers see their work as taking us beyond pre-philosophically "obvious truths" and into the realm of the inconceivable. Drawing on material encountered in earlier chapters, I will discuss three main aspects of this project of thinking the impossible. First, there is the effort to show how concepts or texts collapse into incoherence (or undecidability) upon close analysis. Here Derrida's deconstruction offers the primary examples, and I will reflect on his deconstructions of the concepts of gift and of law and on his deconstructive readings of Nietzsche in *Spurs*. Second, there is the project of thinking what is claimed to be radically inconceivable—whether by ordinary concepts, revisions of ordinary concepts, or even entirely new concepts. Here I will discuss Derrida's introduction of *différance* and Marion's treatment of the incomprehensibility of God. Finally, there is the project of developing new concepts that will enable us to think what has not been thinkable through the concepts of "obvious truths" and traditional philosophical concepts derived from them. This is the motivation behind Deleuze's metaphysical innovations, of which I will discuss his novel conception of *repetition*.

I will argue that all of these examples involve serious difficulties. Derrida's deconstructions fail because they lack the logical rigor that his own standards of success require. His treatment of *différance* (and Marion's of the divine incomprehensibility) cut themselves off from the basic pre-philosophical concerns that lead us to philosophy in the first place. Even Deleuze's (apparently less radical) project of conceptual innovation falls into a crippling obscurity. I pay special attention to this obscurity, since it is so often the sore point for would-be readers of recent French philosophy.

Derrida's deconstructions

Derrida's analysis of the gift[3] begins by noting that the idea of a gift is of something that is "aneconomic"—outside the circle of economic exchange, which is governed by the principle of something for something. When I give a gift, it cannot be with the intention of receiving something back in return. That would undermine the generosity of the gift: "if there is a gift, the given of the gift . . . must not come back to the giving. . . . It must not circulate, it must not be exchanged" (p. 7).

But, Derrida maintains, it is not possible for a gift to avoid the economic circle, and so it is impossible. Putting it formally: the conditions of possibility for the gift are "simultaneously the conditions of the impossibility of the gift" (p. 12). It cannot "take place except on the condition of not taking place" (p. 35). The problem is that, as soon as either party recognizes the gift as a gift, that recognition turns the gift into an economic exchange. If the giver recognizes the giving, "the simple intention to give, insofar as it carries the intentional meaning of the gift, suffices to make a return payment to oneself". For example, the satisfaction of having given is my reward for having given the gift. Similarly, if the recipient realizes that I am giving a gift, this recognition "gives back, in the place, let us say, of the thing itself, a symbolic equivalent" (p. 13); namely, the recipient's gratitude, which, once again, is the reward to the giver.

[3] Jacques Derrida, *Given Time I: Counterfeit Money*, tr. Peggy Kamuf (Chicago: University of Chicago Press, 1992). References will be given in the text.

This line of thought is attractive as a psychological account of what often goes on in gift giving. Frequently, we give not so much for the sake of the recipient but for the sake of our own feeling of satisfaction at having given. As Caputo says in discussing Derrida on the gift: "If the agent expends all its energies on the other without return, that is after all what the agent *wants*, and that is how the agent gets her kicks. If you don't believe that, try blocking the way of someone who is working for the other. These people are impossible."[4] But this psychological point about how people often behave is not sufficient to make the conceptual point that the logic of giving a gift involves a self-contradiction.

In order to establish a contradiction in the very notion of a gift, Derrida must first assume that for me to give a gift my motive must be entirely aneconomic; that is, exclude any consideration of my own self-interest (for example, expectation of a gift in return or at least of the recipient's gratitude). But this is far too strong an assumption. If I have no motive except gaining something for myself, then my "giving" is just a means of getting what I want and so not really a gift. But in actual life, gifts often involve a mixture of altruistic and self-interested motives. I may give my wife a present both because I selflessly love her and want to make her happy *and* because I will enjoy her response. At the most, a genuine gift requires only a predominance of the altruistic motive. We even, contrary to Derrrida, have practices of *exchanging* gifts, which explicitly accept the appropriateness of giving a gift as essentially tied to receiving one.

Further, even if we grant Derrida's assumption that total purity of motive is necessary for a gift, there is no reason for his further assumption that such purity is not possible. I may have just bought a bag of candy and, as I walk out of the store into a beautiful day I feel a surge of sheer happiness and spontaneously give a piece of candy to a passing stranger, with no thought of anything I might get in return. It may even be impossible to avoid feeling happy as a result of the gift I have given or to avoid thinking about the possibility that I will receive some return from it. But this does not mean that the happiness or the possible return were motives for giving the gift. And, even if human psychology were such as to exclude our giving gifts, it would not follow that there could not be non-human agents capable of doing so.

It might be claimed that Derrida is talking about the gift in an ideally perfect sense, a gift that would require not only no selfish motives but also no *awareness* of any possible return from the giving.[5] Such a view seems implied by Derrida's claim that the recipient's "simple recognition [of the gift as such] suffices to annul the gift" (p. 13). Here the idea seems to be that, if the recipient acknowledges receiving a gift, the giver will be aware of this, and this awareness alone will undermine the generosity essential

[4] John Caputo (ed.), *Deconstruction in a Nutshell: A Conversation with Jacques Derrida* (New York: Fordham University Press, 1997), 148. Cf. also: "She's the sort of woman who lives for others—you can always tell the others by their hunted expression" (C. S. Lewis, *The Screwtape Letters* (New York: HarperCollins, 2000), 145).

[5] Penelope Deutscher suggests an account along these lines in her *How to Read Derrida* (London: Granta Books, 2005), 77–9.

to the gift. This ideal replaces a volitional condition on a gift (the giver must not intend to receive anything in return for the gift) with an epistemic condition (no awareness of a possible return for the gift). But such a replacement is not an idealization but an arbitrary transformation of the idea of a gift; generosity is a matter of not wanting a reward, not of not knowing that I might get a reward.

Derrida is no doubt making some perceptive claims about giving, but his claims of inconsistency are not established. He seems to be noticing, in the tradition of La Rochefoucauld's "Our virtues are often vices in disguise", a common phenomenon of selfish "gifts" and then forcing all giving into this model. But he does not establish that the very logic of a gift makes it be selfish in a way that destroys its nature as a gift.

As we saw in Chapter 7, Derrida claims that justice is not deconstructible, whereas the laws whereby we try to achieve justice are. This is because laws always fall short of the ideal of justice and so can be deconstructed (shown to contradict their ideal), whereas justice always remains the standard for this deconstruction and so cannot itself be deconstructed. In this sense, however, "deconstruction" does not show the inapplicability or inconsistency of a system of laws. It merely shows that, since even the best crafted generalization may not do "justice" to every instance it covers, applications of generalizations may not be entirely satisfactory. This is a far cry from saying that legal systems are logically inconsistent or not applicable to actual cases.

But, interestingly, Derrida also maintains that justice itself can be deconstructed in the sense of showing that it is conceptually impossible.[6] He offers two versions of what he says is essentially the same aporia. I will follow the first, which he calls the "épohkè of the rule".

He begins from the fact that a judge's decision, whether just or unjust, must be made freely. But, at the same time, a just decision ("this decision of the just") "must follow a law or a prescription, a rule" (p. 23). On the other hand, if "the act simply consists of applying a rule" in a mechanical way, "of enacting a program or effecting a calculation", then "it would be wrong to say that the decision is just". This is because, to be just a decision "must not only follow a rule of law . . . but must also assume it, approve it, confirm its value, by a reinstituting act of interpretation, as if ultimately nothing previously existed of the law, as if the judge himself invented the law in every case". This means, Derrida says, that, "for a decision to be just and responsible, it must . . . be both regulated and without regulation: it must conserve the law and also destroy it or suspend it enough to have to reinvent it in each case" (p. 23).

But here the apparent contradiction—that the decision is both regulated and not regulated—is easily removed. The decision is regulated in the sense that it takes serious account of the law, but it is not regulated in the sense that it is not mechanically determined by the law. Judges take account of what the law says, but no general rule

[6] Jacques Derrida, "Force of Law: The 'Mystical Foundation of Authority' ", in D. Cornell, M. Rosenfeld, and D. G. Carlson (eds), *Deconstruction and the Possibility of Justice* (Cambridge, MA: Harvard University Press, 1992), References will be given in the text.

alone can determine its own interpretation and application, and the judges have to use their own sense of justice to make a final decision. As to Derrida's other formulation, that the decision must both "conserve the law and also destroy it", it is true that the decision conserves the law, but it is rhetorical excess to say decision destroys the law. A law would be destroyed in its application only if the application contradicted either the letter or the spirit of the law. This is hardly a feature of any application as such.

In the cases of both the gift and justice, Derrida's deconstructions fail to establish the impossibility of the concepts deconstructed. He describes some important contingent features of giving and judging, but his claims of inconsistency are not established. Some may respond that my criticism makes the mistake of trying to judge Derrida by standards that are not appropriate to his enterprise. But it is Derrida himself, as we have seen, who claims that deconstruction reveals that which is unthinkable in the sense of conceptual impossibility; and his arguments for conceptual impossibility explicitly take the form of deriving a contradiction from the concept. I agree that much of what Derrida is trying to achieve does not depend on arguments of this sort. But for deconstruction in his own sense of showing conceptual impossibility, such arguments must be his standard.

Similarly, although Derrida's deconstructive readings are rightly praised for their detail and subtlety, they often lack the rigor required to sustain their claims to have shown the incoherence or "undecidability" of a text. This is apparent, for example, from our discussion in Chapter 5 of his reading (in *Spurs*) of Nietzsche on woman and truth. The upshot of Derrida's analysis is that Nietzsche's view of woman is "undecidable" because it makes three mutually irreconcilable assertions. The first two occur within the framework of the traditional notion of truth (as representation of present realities). Here woman is said to be, on the one hand, a deceiving seductress and, on the other hand, a symbol of the distant ideal of truth. The third assertion, made from the standpoint of Nietzsche's critique of traditional truth, is that woman is the "affirmative power" (a Dionysiac artist) that sees through the pretensions of traditional truth. Derrida admits that there may be ways of reading these three claims as consistent, but then ignores this possibility and simply asserts that Nietzsche effects no such reconciliation. This is particularly odd, since his own distinction between the traditional notion of truth and Nietzsche's critique of this notion points to a straightforward reconciliation: if woman is in fact an undermining of the traditional notion, she is, in the context of that notion, the contradiction of truth (as traditionally understood). At the same time, Nietzsche's rejection of traditional truth (and his sense of irony) would lead him to say that, of course, woman is the ideal that fulfills the meaning of truth—by effecting the overthrow of the incoherent traditional notion. As such, woman possesses the affirmative power of the Dionysiac artist. At a minimum, Derrida has not reflected sufficiently on possible ways of finding a coherent reading of Nietzsche's text to warrant concluding that there is no such reading.

Even more glaring is Derrida's move from this alleged undecidability in Nietzsche's discussion of woman and truth, first, to the conclusion that "there is no such thing as the truth of Nietzsche, or of Nietzsche's text" and, then, to the even wider generalization that "there is no such thing as truth in itself". Derrida gives no indication of how an undecidability in one aspect of Nietzche's work would establish the undecidability of his work as a whole and even the undecidability of all texts. Admirers of Derrida often speak of the "rigor" of his analyses, thinking, no doubt, of the extraordinary closeness and complexity of his readings. But, unless a reading exhibits the logical connection between the perceptive details it marshals and the general conclusions drawn, there is no rigor in the logical sense.

Derrida and Marion on thinking the impossible

It might seem that literally thinking the impossible is flat out impossible on the grounds that asserting anything about something is to put it under a concept and so to assume that it is not inconceivable. But there is another way of thinking about inconceivability. A conceptualization succeeds to the extent that it excludes some possibilities in favor of others. The sign that something is inconceivable may not be that *no* assertions can be made about it, but that *too many* can. Of course, this is also the sign of a contradiction, which allows, for some predicate P, assertions of both P and ~P, which is in one sense the maximum of inconceivability. Ordinarily, philosophy, as we noted at the outset, begins with (apparent) contradictions and aims to resolve them by finding concepts that apply without contradiction (for example, some way of understanding freedom and determinism so that they do not conflict). The standard formula for resolving a contradiction, P & ~P, is "P in one sense, ~P in another sense". For what is conceivable, we can arrive at such a formula by precisely specifying the two senses that resolve the contradiction. By contrast, we can establish a contradiction by showing that there is, for a given case (say a square circle), only one sense (the square circle both is and is not a square *in the same sense*).

But there are possibilities in between our definitely resolving and our definitely establishing the contradiction. We might, for example, seem to have resolved the contradiction P & ~P by distinguishing two sense of P, but learn on further reflection that one (or both) of these senses involves another apparent contradiction, and then find out that our apparent resolution of this new contradiction itself leads to another contradiction, and so on and so forth. This could reasonably be taken as a sign that we are dealing with something that is inconceivable but not contradictory. We have reason to think there is a resolution for any specific apparent contradiction but also reason to think that every such resolution will lead to some other apparent contradiction.

Derrida, I suggest, is typically concerned with the inconceivable in this sense. Certain realities require that we say apparently conflicting things about them, holding that all of these assertions are appropriate, even though we realize that no concepts can fit them together consistently. We must say many things about consciousness, truth, justice, and so on without seeing how they can all be reconciled. In this sense, philosophy is discourse about the inconceivable.

Developing this discourse requires complementary moments of creative play and deconstructive criticism. Play is the process of expanding conceptual possibilities by letting language "go on holiday", expanding our range of meanings through puns, entomologies, free associations, and so on. This is needed to uncover all the concepts that may shed light on what we are talking about. Derrida's play places him at a maximal distance from analytic philosophy. But the essential complement of play is the deconstruction of all particular conceptual formulations, which requires a series of analytically rigorous arguments, each in turn making explicit an implicit contradiction in a specific conceptualization. It amounts, therefore, to a multiplicity of arguments, like those that Derrida applies to the gift and to justice, for the impossibility of a series of conceptualizations. Here, however, as we saw in the case of the gift and of justice, Derrida's penchant for condensed arguments with quick transitions based on ambiguous terminology defeats his purpose.

Supposing, however, that there is a domain to which concepts are inadequate, there remains the question of developing a non-conceptual mode of thought that can somehow express what concepts cannot. Derrida's most famous and most extensive effort in this direction centers on his notorious talk of *différance*, developed as an alternative to traditional philosophical vocabularies based on sharp conceptual distinctions.

The question, however, is whether *différance* is, in any sense, something we can think, since everything Derrida says about it amounts to a rejection of thinking about it in any particular way. Any hint of a positive connotation is nullified by scarce quotes that disavow it. As Derrida himself points out, his talk of *différance* is the equivalent of negative theology, except for its lack of any pretension to a moment of genuine assertion. It is a negative theology that stubbornly refuses to go beyond its denials. But this means that talk of *différance* is nothing more than a generic retrospective label for all of Derrida's specific deconstructions. Every time he shows how a contradiction arises from a given concept, he can say: "Here's another example of *différance*." But this merely reasserts the failure of a concept; it does not express some further non-conceptual truth.

Moreover, even if Derrida could deploy *différance* (or related terms such as "trace", "*khora*", and so on) to express non-conceptual truths, there is a serious question as to whether such truths would have any importance. For a truth is important only to the extent that it answers some question that matters to us. But it seems that any question that matters to us is formulated in the conceptual terms that define our interests and concerns (How should I live? Am I free? Can I hope for happiness?). A truth beyond any such conceptions does not speak to us.

This question of the relevance of talk about the inconceivable is especially important in assessing Marion's and Levinas's religious appeals to the inconceivable. Levinas and Marion both suggest that they offer something like phenomenologies of the inconceivable (incomprehensible), but here a distinction is required. Levinas indeed speaks of the Other as "incomprehensible" because "comprehension" is a form of domination entirely inappropriate to the focus of our moral obligation. But Levinas can hardly mean that there are no concepts that apply to the Other. The concepts of having a face (in Levinas's sense of the term), of being vulnerable, and of enjoining "Don't kill me" all apply to the Other. Moreover, there are many Others, and all of these concepts apply to each of them. Levinas's point about incomprehensibility is that the domain of the Other is unique and cannot be described in terms of any of the standard concepts that I apply to objects of my experience, not that it is simply beyond conceptual characterization. By contrast, Levinas, like Marion, insists that God must be regarded as incomprehensible in this strong sense. Since we have not discussed Levinas's views on God's incomprehensibility, I will limit my remarks here to Marion's approach.

We must also distinguish Marion's view of the incomprehensibility of God from Derrida's view, which we have just been discussing, of the incomprehensibility of fundamental philosophical topics. Derrida's view allows for the conceptual characterization of, say, justice and the gift, while insisting that we will never be able to establish the consistency of our characterizations as a totality. Marion, however, in the tradition of mystical theology, denies that any concepts can be asserted of God. We are required to deny any such assertion. This is not what Derrida means when he talks of the inconceivability of justice and the gift. Nor do Derrida and Marion necessarily disagree on these issues. In the discussion we followed, Derrida seems to agree that for God incomprehensibility requires the denial of all concepts, and Marion offers conceptual characterizations of the gift. But Derrida and Marion do disagree on what can be said about our experience of the incomprehensible God. Derrida says we cannot go beyond the negative stage of mystical theology, and Marion says we can.

Our question, in effect, is: what standards are there for evaluating Marion's assertions about God? But here Marion will object. He agrees that the question of whether there could be an experience of God (the Incomprehensible) is philosophical, as is the question of whether we could describe such an experience in positive terms (the point of disagreement between him and Derrida). But Marion would deny that philosophy can have anything to say about whether an experience of the Incomprehensible has occurred or about whether a given description of such an experience is correct.

But once someone claims to have had an experience of the Incomprehensible (a revelation, in theological terms) and offers language purporting to describe it, there may well be philosophical questions that need to be asked. This is because revelations—at least ones that are likely to be of interest to most of us—typically claim to provide answers to important philosophical questions. For Marion, who affirms the Christian (specifically, Catholic) revelation, the question is whether he can reconcile the claim that God is incomprehensible with the traditional claims of the Christian religion.

Christianity does, admittedly, emphasize God's greatness beyond the categories of our understanding. But it also appeals to the hopes and desires of human beings as they exist prior to hearing and accepting the Word. In particular, our deepest religious need is to know that we are safe in the universe, that there is a power willing and able to protect us against the worst horrors we can conceive, whether they be eternal pain, eternal isolation, or eternal extinction. There would be no point in worshiping a God who did not respond to that need. There is even a hint of this nestled in the otherwise relentlessly negative list of citations Marion gives from Church Fathers and Doctors to show how they reject any naming of God "in terms of presence". Athanasius is quoted as saying: "God is good and the friend of men . . . By his nature he is invisible and incomprehensible" (p. 34). Yes, exactly. Let God be as incomprehensible as you like, provided he is "good and the friend of man".

Suppose I do encounter the supremely incomprehensible. Does "incomprehensible" mean that what I encounter cannot be characterized as "powerful" and "loving" in the sense required by my need to be safe in the universe, that he cannot be said to be "good and the friend of man" in the sense in which I understand those words? Why, then, should I have any religious interest in such a being? Marion may respond that the incomprehensible God exceeds what I mean by "powerful" and "loving". Excellent, provided this excess is something that will guarantee my safety. So is it at least true that God will keep me safe *in my sense of that term*? Presumably, the answer is no. But, it will be said, I will be "safe" in some higher, excessive sense. Yes, but does that mean that I will not, for example, suffer eternal pain or loneliness or extinction? If so, then I do have some understanding of what it means to say that God is powerful and loving—"good and the friend of man". If not, what does this God matter to me?

The point is that the voice of revelation, if it is to have any force for human beings, has to speak to some fundamental desires that we have prior to encountering the voice. If the only message of the voice is that I shall be so utterly transformed that nothing will matter that mattered before, then why should I heed it? But, if the message speaks to what mattered to me before it spoke, then, to that extent, I can understand it. If Christian revelation is an experience of the Incomprehensible, then an account of it cannot assert any of the exciting and consoling things that most believers and non-believers have thought it was asserting.

Deleuze and the concept of repetition

As an example of conceptual innovation, I take Deleuze's introduction of a new concept of repetition at the beginning of his book *Difference and Repetition.*[7] I begin with a thought experiment: imagine that the opening chapter ("Introduction: Repetition and Difference") of Deleuze's *Difference and Repetition* has been submitted anonymously to, say, *The Philosophical Review* and, by some perverse misdirection, was refereed by an analytic metaphysician, quite innocent of the ways of French philosophy. I reproduce below the resulting report to the editor.

[7] Gilles Deleuze, *Difference and Repetition*, tr. Paul Patton (New York: Columbia University Press, 1994).

Report on "Repetition and Difference"

The author begins with a firmly asserted thesis: "Repetition is not generality". He explains the thesis by distinguishing "two major orders" of generality: "the qualitative order of resemblances and the quantitative order of equivalences" (all my citations will be from p. 1 of the ms), thus making clear that resemblance is one sort of generality. The author goes on to make explicit what he means by "generality", which he says "expresses a point of view according to which one term may be exchanged or substituted for another". Given these clarifications, his initial thesis says that repetition cannot be understood as a matter of (qualitative) resemblance or of (quantitative) equivalence, which allow us to exchange or substitute two things for one another. "By contrast," he says, "repetition as a conduct and as a point of view concerns non-exchangeable and non-substitutable singularities". In support of this claim, he cites the cases of "reflections, echoes, doubles and souls", which "do not belong to the domain of resemblance or equivalence" but which (presumably) are cases of repetition. Expanding on the example of doubles and souls, he says that "it is no more possible to exchange one's soul than it is to substitute real twins for one another".

Here things have clearly begun to go wrong. The examples of twins (doubles) and souls seem to support the thesis that repetition cannot be understood in terms of mere generality, since repetition requires recurrence of the very same (i.e., identical) thing, in contrast to replacement by a different but similar or equivalent thing. But, then, by the same token, the author's other examples become problematic. A reflection or an echo is not the very same thing as the face or sound it "repeats". Literal identity is surely at least one form of repetition, but admitting these further examples requires that we also allow for non-identical repetitions. But then is it not obvious that we should regard non-identical repetitions as matters of mere resemblance?

The author goes on to discuss what he calls "the apparent paradox of festivals", which, he says, "repeat an 'unrepeatable' ", in the sense that "they do not add a second or a third time to the first, but carry the first to the '*n*th' power" [???]. An example is said to be Bastille Day (which the French apparently call "Federation Day"), but this leads to some very muddy waters indeed.

A sympathetic reader can make a certain amount of sense of this example as illustrating the author's claim that there can be repetition without resemblance. As a past event, the original fall of the famous Parisian prison cannot be literally repeated; nonetheless, an annual festival commemorating the fall of the Bastille might be said to repeat the event in the sense of making it real to us once more (and more vividly and deeply than mere memory). At the same time, a commemoration of this event need not resemble it (although a commemoration might take the form of a reenactment, this is not necessary or even typical). So we might think of the festival as a repetition without resemblance.

But, for reasons I find hard to fathom, the author takes his example in a quite different direction, saying that this example of repetition "echoes . . . a more profound, internal repetition within the singular". First of all, how can the notion of repetition even make sense if it is understood as existing simply "within" the thing that is being repeated? Surely, the very idea of repetition requires that what repeats be in some sense outside of what is repeated? For example, even when we speak of repetition in terms of the literally identical thing, we inevitably refer to the same thing at a different time or in a different place (and of course the same thing need not always have the same properties).

A particularly puzzling feature of this "internal repetition" emerges when the author says that, because it is interior, it "reverses itself", so that "it is not Federation Day which commemorates or represents the fall of the Bastille, but the fall of the Bastille which celebrates and repeats in advance all the Federation Days [!???] (p. 1)". This claim contradicts the obvious truth that what repeats must always precede what is repeated. We might conceive of an event that somehow contains within itself ("internally") the force that leads to its repetition in future events. But why say that such an event is itself a repetition rather than what is repeated?

So much confusion, so many obvious mistakes, and on just the first page! Without irritating you with the details, I can assure you that the rest of the essay shows no improvement. At best there is a certain "progress" from blatant falsehood to almost total obfuscation as the author takes up the interpretation of such (scarcely philosophical) thinkers as Kierkegaard, Nietzsche, and Freud. My guess is that the author (no doubt an overly ambitious undergraduate) has a good amount of raw intellectual ability, but has not had anything approaching an acceptable training in philosophical thinking. Your rejection letter might discretely suggest the value of his considering one of the many excellent MA programs recommended in the Leiter Report.

A more sympathetic reader of Deleuze might point out that the report's objections obtusely assume that the ordinary meaning of repetition is relevant to Deleuze's discussion. On the contrary, it might be suggested, Deleuze is using the term "repetition" in a special technical sense (as, for example, Plato uses "form" or Husserl "intention") that need not conform to how we use the ordinary term. But in fact Deleuze is not using an ordinary term in an entirely new sense but, rather, rejecting the ordinary understanding of the concept *repetition* in favor of what he regards as a more adequate (philosophical) understanding. Admittedly, this means that the referee's appeals to ordinary usage are not decisive counterexamples to Deleuze's claims, as they would be if his project were the analysis of how we use the term "repetition". But, at the same time, we cannot just give Deleuze a free pass when he says things that contradict our ordinary understanding of repetition. The mere fact of such contradictions does not mean that he is wrong, but he needs to make a case for why and precisely how we should revise our conventional understanding of repetition.

To this, however, it will be rightly responded that Deleuze is not interested in refining or developing the ordinary concept of repetition. His project is to explode it into a radically new conception that will derive from the ordinary concept only in that it will be its successor in a fundamentally new way of thinking about basic metaphysical questions. Given this project, intuitions about repetition in the ordinary sense have little authority in Deleuze's discussion.

But, although our ordinary ways of thinking would, in principle, have little weight in evaluating the concepts proposed to replace them, they could—and should—play a vital role in helping us understand what the new proposals are. It is possible to present novel concepts in a fairly accessible way, starting from familiar notions and introducing new ones gradually by comparison and contrast with what we already know. It is not surprising that the inventors of new ways of thought, who have lived long amid their creations, are sufficiently at home to think directly in their terms and so are prone to plunge right into their new discourse. Even if they make occasional concessions to the reader, they typically fall back into talk that can only puzzle even the attentive and persistent. The result, for most of us, is an experience not far from trying to read a text in a foreign language of which we have only a marginal knowledge.

This explains what I suspect many know but few acknowledge: that, for almost all of us (even those who spend a good amount of time on recent French philosophy), books such as Deleuze's *Difference and Repetition* cannot be understood through a close, line-by-line reading. This is so, even if we are reasonably familiar with the topics and authors the book is discussing. We simply keep coming up against unexplained terminology and logical connections that make no sense. (It is precisely this that leads to reactions such as those of my fictional referee to the first page of *Difference and Repetition*.) After a certain amount of frustration, we may consult some of the profusion of introductions, guides, and companions that enterprising publishers shower upon us. Interestingly, however, these often useful texts do very little to tell us exactly what a given perplexing sentence or paragraph means. We get at best a summary that suggests a general gist but does not enlighten us about crucial details or, much worse, an almost literal paraphrase that is nearly as difficult to make out as the original.

The impossibility of a close reading does not mean that the book cannot be read. But the task calls for fairly desperate measures. There are two main possibilities (which may be combined in various ways), corresponding to different ways of learning a foreign language. The first is immersion. You just plunge in and keep reading even when you go for long stretches without understanding much of anything. Then you go back and read it again and again. Even on the first reading, occasional passages—oases in the desert—will seem relatively intelligible. (Concrete examples—usually rare in such books—are special delights.) You hoard these and eventually find that you can use them to begin understanding other passages. Still other passages start to snap into focus simply from repeated going over. It can help to jump around from place to place in the book and to juxtapose difficult passages that seem to have a similar thrust. Used alone, this is an immensely time-consuming and even dangerous method. The danger is that you will not really have come to understand the text but will have merely become facile at reproducing its particular sort of obscurity in your own thought. You may then go on to write the sort of books I mentioned that offer paraphrases that make no more sense than the original.

The second method is quicker and more agreeable, but it also has its risks. Here the strategy is to read the book, looking especially for intelligible passages, but not to expect to come anywhere near to understanding every passage. Instead, the idea is to construct in a more familiar language hypotheses about what the overall meaning of the text (or some portion of it) might be. One good way to do this, provided you have a fairly good knowledge of relevant philosophical issues, is to construct an account of the topic being treated that seems reasonably interesting and plausible and that connects to some extent with what you have been reading. Given this "interpretation", you go back to the text and see what specific details would have to mean if this were a roughly correct reading. Fitting in various details will likely suggest modifications of the interpretation, which you can then apply to further puzzling details. Eventually, with some luck, you may arrive at a restatement of the text in much more tractable language that has a plausible claim to be something like what the author had in mind. It is unlikely that your tractable interpretation will make sense of all the details of the text—you will have had to ignore some particularly gristly passages—but you will have a set of understandable, interesting, and not too implausible ideas that likely have some connection with the thought of the master thinker. If you are good at this sort of thing (and persistent), you may well write what I have suggested are the better sort of books about such thinkers. People will say, "Well, that seems to make sense! Why didn't Deleuze [or whoever] put it that way?".

As an example of this "better sort" of commentary, consider the following recasting of the main ideas in the opening pages of *Difference and Repetition*:

In ordinary usage, "repetition" typically connotes the opposite of novelty. What is repeated resembles what has happened before. Sometimes the resemblance is total: "It's hot today." "What did you say?" "It's hot today." But even when there are major differences—"Go to hell!" "What did you say?" "Leave me alone"—we judge that there was a repetition because the basic meaning or reality is very similar if not the same.

But Deleuze puts forward another way of thinking about repetition. Suppose we regard it not as a matter of something's conforming to (resembling) a previous state—of itself or of something else—but rather of something's effecting a new expression of its reality. On this view, to repeat is not to duplicate what I have been but to become something new that is, nonetheless, still me. Repetition no longer would be a matter of qualitative resemblance or quantitative equivalence; not, that is, a matter of replacing something with something else that is equivalent to it. Rather, it would be a matter of something that is irreducibly singular producing a novel version of itself.

Take the example of Bastille Day as a commemoration of the original event in the French Revolution. On the standard use, such a commemoration can at best express again what the revolutionaries did over two centuries ago. But we can instead take the commemoration as an expression of the continuing, always self-transforming reality of the French Republic. Indeed, since the "original" event contains implicitly what it has become over the years, we might say that (in the ordinary sense of the term) it had already "repeated" its subsequent representations. Similarly, to cite another of Deleuze's examples, we might say that Monet's first water-lily painting implicitly repeated from the beginning all the subsequent paintings in the series. That is, included in the "difference" that is the first painting's reality is the aesthetic force or power present in the works that followed.

Of course, to think of repetition in this way requires thinking differently about what a thing is to begin with. If we are prepared to think of the caterpillar, say, as repeating the butterfly, then we must think of the caterpillar itself as somehow also being from the beginning a butterfly. Thinking this requires a radical realignment of our metaphysical ideas. In particular, we must stop thinking of the being of things (what they are) as fixed identities and instead think of them as dynamic differences, as, that is, including all the conflicting novelties that they can explode into over time. In this way, repetition becomes not a principle of preservation of the same but of creation of the new. As a result, what is repeated is not, as the ordinary view has it, a different thing that falls under the same concept or generalization but rather a singular reality, falling under no fixed concept, that makes explicit a novelty that had previously been only implicit in it.

Indeed, the point of this new account of repetition is precisely to endorse the new metaphysical view that follows from it: the view, anticipated by Bergson's metaphysics of duration, that creative difference rather than enduring identity is metaphysically ultimate.

This is an example of what I call an "analytic" reading. Of course, it makes only a beginning of an interpretation that would need considerable further development to reveal Deleuze's metaphysics as a richly original achievement with important connections to the process-tradition of Bergson and Whitehead (and to the subsequent work of Badiou).[8] Such a reading should, moreover, be combined with some "going-native" reading to guard against completely reducing the text to a familiar meaning that it was obviously trying to go beyond. (It is also a good idea to play several analytic readings off one another to avoid oversimplifications.) But a significant connection to the familiar is essential if the novel concepts are to be intelligible. We are simply not capable of producing or absorbing concepts that have no serious connections to ways that we have been thinking. Further, even if we could spin novel concepts out of thin air, there would be no way that they could respond to questions or problems that concern us. Accordingly, if we cannot develop substantive and hermeneutically defensible analytic interpretations of philosophers like Deleuze, we have no way of properly understanding or assessing their thought.

A fundamental deficiency in Deleuze's writing is its failure to supply the needed connections to the familiar. Of course, we should be grateful for what we are given, and it may well be that some writers could not have combined their originality with greater accessibility. This, however, is not a merit, and when philosophers such as Deleuze fall short in intelligibility, we should recognize the essential philosophical role played by the commentators who supply it. Just as there is a tradition of modernist literature that *requires*, as literature, secondary explication, so too the work of some philosophers cannot be separated *as a philosophical achievement* from the labors of their analytic interpreters. Difficult texts may over time become more accessible, as their ideas become more familiar. On the other hand, even initially very accessible texts are likely to become more difficult with age, so overall analytic commentaries remain an essential part of the philosophical tradition.

My point here goes beyond the common complaint that Deleuze's writing is "unclear". The claim that a philosophical text is unclear can cover a multitude of sins—of either the author or the reader. I may find a text unclear because I have not read it with sufficient attention, because I am unfamiliar with some standard terminology employed, or because I have not read the authors the text is commenting on. Also, there are some authorial faults that a sympathetic reader can without much difficulty overcome: I may take the time to sort out unnecessarily complex syntax, look up esoteric words and references, distinguish topics that the author should have put in

[8] Major Deleuze interpreters such as Keith Ansell Pearson, Peter Hallward, Todd May, and Daniel Smith provide diverse and impressive examples of such developments. They are the source of the ideas in the "better sort of commentary" I sketched above.

separate paragraphs. There is also the very real possibility that the lack of clarity is neither the author's nor my fault. It may just be that the subject matter (the nature of consciousness, the source of moral obligation) is itself so difficult that, even with best efforts on both our parts, the topic will remain intractable.

My concern, however, is about the obscurity that arises because authors do not make a sufficient effort to connect their novel concepts to more familiar (even if technical) concepts that would allow an informed and conscientious reader to make an assessment of their claims. The result is writing that is *hermetic* in the sense that it effectively cuts itself off from the very issues of common concern that it is trying to address. Such writing requires the kind of sustained interpretative effort discussed above. But we have to make in each case a judgment as to whether the text merits the effort to understand it, and there is every reason to encourage authors to write in a more responsible way, rather than, as often happens, rewarding their failure to communicate with accolades of profundity. The problem is that just getting to know what such authors are actually saying is enough to occupy a good chunk of a philosophical career, and simply having seen the exegetical task through suggests a basically favorable attitude toward the work. Someone who would conclude after thorough study that Deleuze's *Difference and Repetition* is a lot of pretentious nonsense is likely to have thrown the book into the trash before getting anywhere near the end. As a result, the inventor of a short sharp analytic argument for a precise conclusion will often receive more informed critical discussion than the creator of an apparently profound but intractable system.

This is why, in contrast to the world of analytic philosophy, there has been so little profitable, progressive debate about the views of the major French philosophers. In a country with so many teachers and students of philosophy, there should be a strong tradition of lively philosophical discussion in articles and colloquia. Instead, the primary medium of expression has been a series of forbidding *magna opera*, so difficult as to be almost untouchable by detailed criticism. Foucault's conversational swipe at Derrida's "obscurantist terrorism" (which, as Foucault explained to John Searle, can reply to any criticism by claiming that the "idiot" reader did not understand the text) is much more widely applicable.[9]

To ask that new conceptual systems be tied to familiar concepts does not mean that the new concepts are reducible to the old familiar ones, only that their novelty be understandable in relation to what we already know. Nor does it mean that familiar ("obvious" in the sense of analytic philosophy) truths must be the evidence by which we evaluate the new claims. In many cases such supposed "truths" will be overturned by the new way of thinking. Deleuze, for example, proposes quite counter-intuitive views about identity and difference. Such views will typically be supported by the process that I call persuasive elaboration: developing, refining, extending, defending the new claims in ways that will exhibit their ability to illuminate questions that are of

[9] "Reality Principles: An Interview with John R. Searle", Reason.com, Feb. 2000, www.reason.com/news/show/27599.html.

interest to philosophers. I may, for example, come to see that Deleuze's views on identity offer attractive new options for discussion of the identity of indiscernibles. No such single instance can make a decisive case for a metaphysical system, but a variety of such successes can at least make an effective case for taking the system very seriously. But, if the new approach is to shed light on old problems, it has to be properly connected to concepts in which those problems have been formulated—even if its ultimate contribution is to argue for a radical revision of how we think about the problem. To cite another example, Deleuze introduces a way of thinking about truth that is very different from standard philosophical theories of truth. But, unless he can show how his concept relates to familiar concepts of truth such as correspondence, coherence, and pragmatic value, there is no way that we can appreciate it as a rival to these concepts.

Although my examples in this chapter have come from Deleuze, Derrida, and Marion, readers should have no problem recognizing similar problems with the writings of Levinas, Foucault, and Badiou that we have discussed. Levinas's development of an important approach to the problem of ethical skepticism is, as we saw, obscured by misleading rhetoric about murder and infinite responsibility. The later formulation of his ethics in *Otherwise than Being*, written partly in response to Derrida's critique in "Violence and Metaphysics", is drawn into the sort of impotent obscurity that we saw in Derrida's discourse on *différance*. More generally, Levinas's insistence on characterizing the ethical Other in the language of extreme paradox creates an unnecessary distance from the mundane categories of everyday ethical thinking that has to be filled in by the less dramatic but more rigorous work of commentators such as Diane Perpich.

Badiou, despite his claims to demystify metaphysics, writes in *Being and Event* page after page of prose that requires heroic interventions from sympathetic explicators to save it from unintelligibility. The vagaries of his discussion are highlighted all the more by the superior clarity available from his set-theoretic formulations, although there is not sufficient detailed connection of the mathematical formalism to the non-formal prose to remove the latter's many obscurities. As a result, as we saw, there are obvious major objections—for example, the tension between subjectivity and objective truth, the difficulty of distinguishing genuine events from their simulacra, the slide of his ethics toward mundane humanism—to which Badiou does not provide the careful responses the objections call for.

Despite his sympathies with Deleuze's metaphysics, Michel Foucault for the most part avoids the kind of fundamental unclarity we so often find in Deleuze (which is not to deny that Foucault's prose style, particularly before the 1970s, is often needlessly obscure). His own project is not the creation of new metaphysical concepts but the "excavation" (as an intellectual archaeologist) of the now alien concepts of past cultures, concepts at least as alien as those of Deleuze and Badiou ("the stark impossibility of thinking *that*").[10] Foucault's writing has its own difficulties, but they are more

[10] Michel Foucault, *The Order of Things*, tr. A. Sheridan (New York: Random House, 1970), p. xv.

stylistic than conceptual (with important exceptions such as the more philosophical passages of *The Order of Things* and his early literary essays). The systems of concepts (epistemes in the language of *The Order of Things*) he works with are not directly accessible to us; we cannot see the world through Renaissance eyes or translate seventeenth-century statements into our language. But the point of Foucault's histories is to compare prior conceptualizations to our own (for the sake of showing that our understandings are not inevitable), so there is, at least in principle, a premium on connecting the alien concepts to familiar. As a result, he tends to avoid some of the worst defects of recent French philosophical writing—not surprising since, as we have seen, Foucault deliberately eschews philosophy for history. He does, however, have a penchant for sweeping historical pronouncements that require far more detailed support than he deigns to provide.[11]

Conclusion

There is much to admire in the work of recent French philosophers. It maintains a fruitful contact with the history of philosophy and with wider intellectual and artistic developments. It has produced exciting conceptual innovations, and has developed them into powerful bodies of systematic thought. It has kept an admirable connection to the richness of personal, social, and political realities. Most importantly, it has faced up to questions about the limitations of conceptual thought. In all these ways, it remains superior to the bulk of work in analytic philosophy.

But recent French philosophers show significant weaknesses, particularly in logical rigor, clarity, and relevance. All of these are connected with what I have called their disdain for the obvious: their failure to give proper attention to the mundane concepts and truths of everyday life that are essential as premises of effective arguments, as comparison points for explanations of novel ideas, and as the locus of the pre-philosophical concerns that connect philosophy to our lives. This disdain has undermined much of what we might have hoped for from the French effort to think the impossible.

Nonetheless, French philosophy since the 1960s is an important resource for those who, often rightly, see analytic philosophy as lacking in a certain sort of intellectual imagination and too constrained by deference to the banalities of obvious truths. As the preceding chapters have shown, it suggests potentially fruitful lines of thought about, for example, the limits of conceptualization, the uniqueness of ethical obligation, the nature of religious discourse, the possibility of radical metaphysical innovation, and counter-conventional readings of the history of philosophy. But the riches of recent French thought typically require patient excavation, refinement, and development

[11] See, e.g., my discussion of Foucault's *History of Madness*, in my *The Cambridge Companion to Foucault* (2nd edn, Cambridge: Cambridge University Press, 2005).

before they will meet the (legitimate) standards of analytic philosophizing. They adumbrate achievements of thought that the humdrum analytic mind is not likely to envisage on its own. But, without the analytic insistence on doggedly thinking through the mundane details, these achievements will unnecessarily remain in—to use Derridian language—a state of the perpetually-to-come.

Bibliography

Agamben, Giorgio, *Potentialities: Collected Essays in Philosophy*, tr. Daniel Heller-Roazen (Stanford, CA: Stanford University Press, 2000).

Badiou, Alain, "The Adventure of French Philosophy", *New Left Review*, 35 (Sept.–Oct., 2005), 67–77.

—— *Being and Event*, tr. Oliver Feltham (London: Continuum, 2006).

—— *Ethics: An Essay on the Understanding of Evil* tr. Peter Hallward (London: Verso, 2001).

—— *Logic of Worlds (Being and Event 2)*, tr. Alberto Toscano (London: Continuum, 2009).

—— *The Meaning of Sarkozy* tr. David Fernbach (London: Verso, 2009).

—— *Saint Paul: The Foundation of Universalism*, tr. Ray Brassier (Stanford, CA: Stanford University Press, 2003).

Baugh, Bruce, *French Hegel* (London: Routledge, 2003).

Behler, Ernest, *Confrontations: Derrida/Heidegger, Nietzsche*, tr. Steven Taubeneck (Stanford, CA: Stanford University Press, 1991).

Bruns, Gerald, "Foucault's Modernism", in Gary Gutting (ed.), *The Cambridge Companion to Foucault* (2nd edn, New York: Cambridge University Press, 2005), 348–78.

Caputo, John (ed.), *Deconstruction in a Nutshell: A Conversation with Jacques Derrida* (New York: Fordham University Press, 1997).

Caputo, John D., and Michael J. Scanlon (eds), *God, the Gift, and Postmodernism* (Bloomington, IN: Indiana University Press, 1999).

Chaplin, Tamara, *Turning on the Mind: French Philosophers on Television* (Chicago: University of Chicago Press, 2007).

Deleuze, Gilles, *Bergsonism,* tr. Hugh Tomlinson and Barbara Habberjam (New York: Zone Books, 1988).

—— *Desert Islands and Other Texts, 1953–1974* tr. M. Taormina (Los Angeles: Semiotext(e), 2004).

—— *Difference and Repetition*, tr. Paul Patton (New York: Columbia University Press, 1994).

—— *Foucault*, tr. Seán Hand (Minneapolis, MN: University of Minnesota Press, 1988).

—— *The Logic of Sense*, tr. M. Lester and C. Stivale (New York: Columbia University Press, 1990).

—— *Negotiations: 1972–1990*, tr. Martin Joughin (New York: Zone Books, 1995).

—— *Nietzsche and Philosophy*, tr. Hugh Tomlinson (New York: Columbia University Press, 1983).

—— "Review of Jean Hyppolite, *Logique et existence*", appendix to Jean Hyppolite, *Logic and Existence*, tr. Leonard Lawlor and Amit Sen (Albany, NY: SUNY Press, 1997).

—— and Félix Guattari, *What Is Philosophy?*, tr. J. Tomlinson and G. Burchell III (New York: Columbia University Press, 1996).

Derrida, Jacques, "Il courait mort: salut, salut", *Les Temps modernes*, 51 (1996), 7–54.

—— "Force of Law: The 'Mystical Foundation of Authority'", in D. Cornell, M. Rosenfeld, and D. G. Carlson (eds), *Deconstruction and the Possibility of Justice* (Cambridge, MA: Harvard University Press, 1992).

—— *Given Time I: Counterfeit Money*, tr. Peggy Kamuf (Chicago: University of Chicago Press, 1992).

—— *Limited Inc* (Evanston, IL: Northwestern University Press, 1988).

—— *Margins of Philosophy*, tr. Alan Bass (Chicago: University of Chicago Press, 1982).

—— *Points . . . : Interviews, 1974–1994* (Palo Alto, CA: Stanford University Press, 1995).

—— *Positions*, tr. Alan Bass (Chicago: University of Chicago Press, 1981).

—— *Speech and Phenomena and Other Essays on Husserl's Theory of Signs*, tr. David Allison (Evanston, IL: Northwestern University Press, 1973).

—— *Of Grammatology*, tr. G. C. Spivak (Baltimore: Johns Hopkins University Press, 1976).

—— *Spurs: Nietzsche's Styles* (French–English edition, English translation by Barbara Harlow; Chicago: University of Chicago Press, 1979).

—— *Writing and Difference* tr. Alan Bass (Chicago: University of Chicago Press, 1978).

—— and Geoffrey Bennington, *Jacques Derrida*, tr. Geoffrey Bennington (Chicago: University of Chicago Press, 1993).

Descombes, Vincent, *Modern French Philosophy*, tr. L. Scott-Fox and J. M. Harding (Cambridge: Cambridge University Press, 1980).

Deutscher, Penelope, *How to Read Derrida* (London: Granta Books, 2005).

Dosse, François, *Deleuze/Guattari: Biographie croisée* (Paris: La Découverte, 2007).

Dreyfus, Hubert L., "Being and Power Revisited", in Alan Milchman and Alan Rosenberg (eds), *Foucault and Heidegger: Critical Encounters* (Minneapolis, MN: University of Minnesota Press, 1993).

Eribon, Didier, *Michel Foucault*, tr. Betsy Wing (Cambridge, MA: Harvard University Press, 1991).

Ferry, Luc, and Alain Renaut, *French Philosophy of the Sixties: An Essay on Antihumanism*, tr. Mary H. S. Cattani (Amherst, MA: University of Massachusetts Press, 1990).

Flynn, Thomas, "Sartre at One Hundred: A Man of the Nineteenth Century Addressing the Twenty-First? (Jean-Paul Sartre and Michel Foucault)", *Sartre Studies International*, 11 (2005), 1–14.

Foucault, Michel, "The Discourse on Language", in *The Archaeology of Knowledge*, tr. Alan Sheridan (New York: Pantheon, 1972).

—— *Dits et écrits* (4 vols; Paris: Gallimard, 1994).

—— *Essential Works of Foucault 1954–1984*, ed. Paul Rabinow (3 vols; New York: New Press, 1997, 1998, 2000).

—— "Foucault répond à Sartre", interview with J.-P. Elkabbach in *Quinzaine littéraire* (Mar. 1968), 20–2; repr. in Michel Foucault, *Dits et écrits*, i (Paris: Gallimard, 1994).

—— "Jean Hyppolite (1907–1968)", *Revue de métaphysique et de morale*, 74 (1969), 131–6.

—— "The Return of Morality", interview (1984) with G. Bardette and A. Scala, in Lawrence Kritzman (ed.), *Politics, Philosophy, Culture: Interviews and Other Writings, 1977–1984* (New York: Routledge, 1988),

—— *Language, Counter-Memory, Practice: Selected Essays and Interviews*, ed. Donald F. Bouchard (Ithaca, NY: Cornell University Press, 2008).

—— *The Order of Things*, tr. A. Sheridan (New York: Random House, 1970).

—— *Politics, Philosophy, Culture: Interviews and Other Writings, 1977–1984*, ed. Lawrence Kritzman (New York: Routledge, 1988).

—— *The Use of Pleasure*, tr. Robert Hurley (New York: Vintage, 1990).

Gutting, Gary (ed.), *The Cambridge Companion to Foucault* (2nd edn, Cambridge: Cambridge University Press, 2005).

—— *Foucault: A Very Short Introduction* (Oxford: Oxford University Press, 2005).

—— "Foucault's Philosophy of Experience", *boundary 2*, 29 (2002), 69–85.

—— *What Philosophers Know: Case Studies in Recent Analytic Philosophy* (Cambridge: Cambridge University Press, 2009).

Hallward, Peter, *Badiou: A Subject to Truth* (Minneapolis, MN: University of Minnesota Press, 2003).

—— *Out of this World: Deleuze and the Philosophy of Creation* (London: Verso, 2006).

Han, Béatrice, *Foucault's Critical Project: Between the Transcendental and the Historical*, tr. Edward Pile (Stanford, CA: Stanford University Press, 2002).

Hegel, G. F. W., *Hegel's Philosophy of Mind: Being Part Three of the Encyclopedia of Philosophical Sciences* (1830), tr. William Wallace (Oxford: Oxford University Press, 1971).

Hegel, G. W. F., *Phenomenology of Spirit*, tr. A. V. Miller (Oxford: Oxford University Press, 1977).

Heidegger, Martin, "Letter on Humanism", in *Martin Heidegger: Basic Writings*, ed. David Farrell Krell (rev. and expanded edn, New York: Harper Collins, 1993).

—— "Only a God Can Save Us: *Der Spiegel*'s Interview with Martin Heidegger", tr. M. P. Alter and J. D. Caputo, *Philosophy Today*, 20 (1976), 267–84.

Howells, Christina, "Conclusion: Sartre and the Deconstruction of the Subject", in Christina Howells (ed.), *The Cambridge Companion to Sartre* (Cambridge: Cambridge University Press, 1992), 318–52.

—— *Derrida: Deconstruction from Phenomenology to Ethics* (Cambridge: Polity Press, 1999).

Hyppolite, Jean, *Figures de la pensée philosophique* (2 vols; Paris: Presses Universitaires de France, 1971).

—— *Genesis and Structure of Hegel's* Phenomenology of Spirit, tr. Samuel Cherniak and John Heckman (Evanston, IL: Northwestern University Press, 1974).

—— *Logic and Existence*, tr. Leonard Lawlor and Amit Sen (Albany, NY: SUNY Press, 1997).

Janicaud, Dominique, *Heidegger en France* (2 vols; Paris: Albin Michel, 2001).

Kearney, Richard (ed.), *Dialogues with Contemporary Continental Thinkers* (Manchester: Manchester University Press, 1984).

Kojève, Alexandre, *Introduction to the Reading of Hegel*, tr. James Nichols Jr (New York: Basic Books, 1969).

Lawler, Leonard, *Thinking through French Philosophy: The Being of the Question* (Bloomington, IN: Indiana University Press, 2003).

Levinas, Emmanuel, *Totality and Infinity: An Essay on Exteriority*, tr. Alphonso Linguis (Pittsburgh, PA: Duquesne University Press, 1969).

Lévi-Strauss, Claude, *The Savage Mind* (Chicago: University of Chicago Press, 1966).

Merleau-Ponty, Maurice, *Signs*, tr. Richard McCleary (Evanston, IL: Northwestern University Press, 1964), 123.

Mouffe, Chantal (ed.), *Deconstruction and Pragmatism* (London: Routledge, 1996).

Norris, Christopher, *Badiou's* Being and Event (London: Continuum, 2009).

Paar, Adrian (ed.), *The Deleuze Dictionary* (New York: Columbia University Press, 2005).
Pautrat, Bernard, *Versions de soleil: Figures et système de Nietzsche* (Paris: Seuil, 1971).
Perpich, Diane, *The Ethics of Emmanuel Levinas* (Stanford, CA: Stanford University Press, 2008).
Poster, Mark, *Existential Marxism in Postwar France* (Princeton: Princeton University Press, 1975).
Rabinow, Paul (ed.), *The Foucault Reader* (New York: Pantheon, 1985).
Renaut, Alain, *Sartre: Le Dernier Philosophe* (Paris: Grasset, 1993).
Rockmore, Tom, *Heidegger and French Philosophy: Humanism, Antihumanism, and Being* (London: Routledge, 1995).
Rorty, Richard, "Deconstructionist Theory", in *The Cambridge History of Literary Criticism*, viii. *From Formalism to Poststructuralism* (Cambridge: Cambridge University Press, 1995).
Roth, Michael S., *Knowing and History: Appropriations of Hegel in Twentieth-Century France* (Ithaca, NY: Cornell University Press, 1988).
Sartre, Jean-Paul, *Being and Nothingness*, tr. Hazel Barnes (New York: Pocket Books, 1966).
—— *Beyond Existentialism and Marxism*, tr. John Mathews (New York: Pantheon Books, 1983).
—— *Critique of Dialectical Reason*, tr. Alan Sheridan-Smith (London: New Left Books, 1976).
—— "Existentialism Is a Humanism", trans. P. Mairet, in Walter Kaufmann (ed.), *Existentialism from Dostoyevsky to Sartre* (New York: Meridian, 1975).
—— "Intentionality: A Fundamental Idea of Husserl's Philosophy", tr. Joseph Fell, *Journal of the British Society for Phenomenology*, 1 (1970), 4–5.
—— "Jean-Paul Sartre répond" (interview), *L'Arc*, 40 (1966), 89.
—— *Life/Situations* (New York: Pantheon, 1977).
—— *Sartre by Himself*, tr. Richard Seaver (New York: Urizen Books, 1980).
—— *The Search for a Method*, tr. Hazel Barnes (New York: Knopf, 1963).
—— *The War Diaries: November 1939–March 1940* (New York: Pantheon, 1984).
—— *The Words*, tr. Bernard Frechtman (New York: George Braziller, 1981).
Schrift, Alan, "The Effects of the *Agrégation de Philosophie* on Twentieth-Century French Philosophy", *Journal of the History of Philosophy*, 46 (2008), 449–74.
Silverman, Hugh J. (ed.), *Derrida and Deconstruction* (London: Routledge, 1989).
Wahl, Jean, *Le Malheur de la conscience dans la philosophie de Hegel* (2nd edn, Paris: Presses Universitaires de France, 1951).
Worms, Fréderic, *La Philosophie en France au xxe siècle: Moments* (Paris: Gallimard, 2009).

Suggested Readings

Some suggestions for readers looking for accessible overviews of the six thinkers featured in this book.

Derrida

Caputo, John (ed.), *Deconstruction in a Nutshell: A Conversation with Jacques Derrida* (New York: Fordham University Press, 1997).

Derrida, Jacques, *Positions*, tr. Alan Bass (Chicago: University of Chicago Press, 1981).

Deutscher, Penelope, *How to Read Derrida* (London: Granta Books, 2005).

Howells, Christina, *Derrida: Deconstruction from Phenomenology to Ethics* (Cambridge: Polity Press, 1999).

Foucault

Gutting, Gary, *Foucault: A Very Short Introduction* (Oxford: Oxford University Press, 2005).

McNay, Lois, *Foucault: A Critical Introduction* (New York: Continuum, 1994).

May, Todd, *Between Genealogy and Epistemology: Psychology, Politics, and Knowledge in the Thought of Michel Foucault* (University Park, PA: Penn State Press, 1993).

Paras, Eric, *Foucault 2.0* (New York: Other Press, 2006).

Deleuze

Deleuze, Gilles, *Negotiations 1972–1990*, tr. Martin Joughin (New York: Zone Books, 1995).

Dosse, François, *Gilles Deleuze and Félix Guattari: Intersecting Lives*, tr. Deborah Glassman (New York: Columbia University Press, 2010).

Hallward, Peter, *Out of this World: Deleuze and the Philosophy of Creation* (London: Verso, 2006).

May, Todd, *Gilles Deleuze: An Introduction* (Cambridge: Cambridge University Press, 2005).

Levinas

Davis, Colin, *Levinas: An Introduction* (Notre Dame IN: University of Notre Dame Press, 1996).

Levinas, Emmanuel, *Is It Righteous to Be? Interviews with Emmanuel Levinas*, ed. Jill Robbins (Palo Alto, CA: Stanford University Press, 2001).

Morgan, Michael L., *Discovering Levinas* (Cambridge: Cambridge University Press, 2007).

Perpich, Diane, *The Ethics of Emmanuel Levinas* (Stanford, CA: Stanford University Press, 2008).

Marion

Caputo, John D., and Michael J. Scanlon (eds.), *God, the Gift, and Postmodernism* (Bloomington, IN: Indiana University Press, 1999).

Gschwandtner, Christina M., *Reading Jean-Luc Marion: Exceeding Metaphysics* (Bloomington, IN: Indiana University Press, 2007).

Marion, Jean-Luc, *The Visible and the Revealed*, tr. Christian M. Gschwandtner et al. (New York: Fordham University Press, 2008).

Badiou

Badiou, Alain, *Ethics: An Essay on the Understanding of Evil*, tr. Peter Hallward (London: Verso, 2001).

Hallward, Peter, *Badiou: A Subject to Truth* (Minneapolis, MN: University of Minnesota Press, 2003).

Norris, Christopher, *Badiou's* Being and Event (London: Continuum, 2009).

Index